Dynamic Alignment Through Imagery

Eric Franklin

Human Kinetics

To my mother and father, Joan and Jules Franklin, for their generous support throughout the years.

Library of Congress Cataloging-in-Publication Data

Franklin, Eric N.
    Dynamic alignment through imagery / Eric Franklin.
        p.   cm.
    Includes bibliographical references and index.
    ISBN 0-87322-475-2
    1. Dance--Physiological aspects.   2. Posture.   3. Body image.
4. Mind and body.   I. Title.
    RC1220.D35F73   1996
    615.8'2--dc20

                                        95-47857
                                        CIP

ISBN: 0-87322-475-2

Acquisitions Editor: Judy Patterson Wright; **Developmental Editor:** Julie Rhoda; **Assistant Editors:** Susan Moore and Sandra Merz Bott; **Editorial Assistants:** Jennifer J. Hemphill and Andrew T. Starr; **Copyeditor:** Barbara Field; **Proof-reader:** Kathy Bennett; **Indexer:** Craig Brown; **Typesetter and Layout Artist:** Julie Overholt; **Text Designer:** Stuart Cartwright; **Photo Editor:** Boyd LaFoon; **Cover Designer:** Jack Davis; **Photographer (cover):** Howard Schatz; **Photographers (interior):** Eric Franklin, Steven Speliotis, Mark Spolsky, and David Fullard; **Illustrators:** Eric Franklin, Katharina Hartmann, and Sonja Burger; **Printer:** United Graphics

Printed in the United States of America   10 9 8 7

Human Kinetics
Web site: www.HumanKinetics.com

United States: Human Kinetics, P.O. Box 5076, Champaign, IL 61825-5076
800-747-4457
e-mail: humank@hkusa.com

Canada: Human Kinetics, 475 Devonshire Road, Unit 100, Windsor, ON N8Y 2L5
800-465-7301 (in Canada only)
e-mail: orders@hkcanada.com

Europe: Human Kinetics, 107 Bradford Road, Stanningley
Leeds LS28 6AT, United Kingdom
+44 (0) 113 255 5665
e-mail: hk@hkeurope.com

Australia: Human Kinetics, 57A Price Avenue, Lower Mitcham, South Australia 5062
08 8277 1555
e-mail: liahka@senet.com.au

New Zealand: Human Kinetics, P.O. Box 105-231, Auckland Central
09-523-3462
e-mail: hkp@ihug.co.nz

Contents

Foreword

*I*t seems like only yesterday that I was a student at the American Dance Festival (ADF), getting my first in-depth exposure to the use of imagery in dance. That was in 1981, following on the heels of taking Lucy Venable's Movement Fundamentals class at The Ohio State University, in which I had first encountered Dr. Lulu Sweigard's work and her book *Human Movement Potential: Its Ideokinetic Facilitation*.

The use of imagery in dance intrigued me enough that I pursued a special project encompassing Sweigard's book and the writings of her protégé Irene Dowd. Dowd spent several years at The Juilliard School working with Dr. Sweigard, and after Sweigard's death she became the primary catalyst for the continuation and expansion of her work. At ADF in 1981 I took Irene Dowd's Anatomy for Dancers class and was fortunate to be asked to return the next year as Irene's assistant in the class. My work with her was eye-opening in many respects—imagery being one of them. The power of imagery both to change inappropriate habitual movement patterns and to teach dancers was an inspiration to me. I returned home to the small college dance program that I directed in Florida, informed and inspired to develop a new approach to the education of dancers.

Each summer until 1991 I returned to the American Dance Festival, initially as associate dean and later as coordinator for the Workshops for Professionals. During those years my knowledge and understanding of the scientific aspects of dance, including imagery, continued to expand and grow as I worked with such teachers as Martha Myers (now dean of ADF), Glenna Batson (herself a protégé of Irene Dowd), and Betty Jones. Betty, in particular, was instrumental in deepening my knowledge, particularly as it applied to the teaching of dance. She had worked for 15 years as Sweigard's assistant at The Juilliard School prior to Dowd, and as a great master teacher she has been responsible for integrating much of Sweigard's imagery work into dance technique throughout the world.

It was at ADF in 1991 that I first met Eric Franklin, who had been invited to come from Zurich to teach a class called "Achieving Peak Performance in Dance." Eric's breadth of knowledge and his creativity in imparting this knowledge to the students impressed me immediately. The evolution and culmination of his work, as expressed in this volume, *Dynamic Alignment Through Imagery*, has impressed me even further. Eric's genius lies in his ability to synthesize a wealth of information from the diverse fields of anatomy, biomechanics, physiology, physics, the somatic realm (Feldenkrais, Alexander, Body-Mind Centering®, etc.) and the artistic realm. So much is presented here that one reading will not be sufficient; it is a book one will return to over and over, either in whole or in part, to relearn and reinforce the information provided. The text is written in clear, concise language, easily understandable even without a scientific background. The illustrations are illuminating, provocative, and humorous; above all they clearly convey the ideas.

My own work bridges the dance and medical environments. As a dance educator working with students and professionals in both the rehabilitation and conditioning arenas, I use imagery frequently to reinforce and integrate concepts. The dozens of examples in this book will be a valuable resource for me to draw upon. For instance, I now can discuss concepts of overall body alignment using two of Eric's images: the head floating up with the body dangling easily from it (see figure 2.2a) and the head as a balloon with the body as a string hanging down from it (see figure 15.4). These images are useful for standing, walking, sitting, sitting down, or getting up.

Many of the images in the anatomical sections of this book are especially valuable for working with patients undergoing rehabilitation. For example, patellar alignment problems are common in both dancers and nondancers. Eric suggests these images to help patients achieve a more symmetrical use of the vastus muscles and correct patellar alignment: (1) the kneecap gliding easily in its well-lubricated groove, like a wet bar of soap slipping in a smooth groove; (2) descending in a plié—the kneecap as a small balloon floating upward effortlessly; (3) sand pouring out of the knees as you plié, with each leg's hip socket and knee in the same plane as the second toe and the sand falling downward along this plane; and (4) reins attached to both sides of the patella and reaching upward along the femur, pulling equally.

The use of imagery in all areas of human movement has grown and attained a new level of sophistication in the last decade. This book and its companion, *Dance Imagery for Technique and Performance*, are powerful tools for movement specialists to use in their work. Eric Franklin has given us a tremendous resource to inform and enrich whatever endeavors we are pursuing in the movement arena. I applaud his efforts and contributions and encourage readers to make full use of this valuable resource.

Jan Dunn, MS

Acknowledgments

I am most grateful to June Balish, whose intelligent and well-informed advice significantly contributed to both the form and content of this book. I would like to thank Margrit and Ruedi Loosli who relieved me of administrative tasks so I could write. A special thank you goes to Zvi Gotheiner, Martha Myers, Amos Pinhasi, and Cathy Ward for their feedback and input over the last three years.

I would like to thank my editors at Human Kinetics, Julie Rhoda and Judy Patterson Wright, for their excellent work on this book. They were always responsive to my questions and generously offered their expert advice and guidance.

I would like to thank the following choreographers, dance and body therapy teachers, and institutions: Glenna Batson, Andre Bernard, Bonnie Cohen, Irene Dowd, Stephanie Skura, Mark Taylor, the Institute for Movement Imagery Education, Charles and Stephanie Reinhart and the American Dance Festival.

The book's copious illustrations would not have come into being without the help of the gifted artists Sonja Burger and Katharina Hartmann, with whom I was able to create many of the drawings. I am also grateful to photographers Howard Schatz, Mark Skolsky, and Steven Speliotis, and to photographic models June Balish, Felicia Norton, and Mark Taylor.

Introduction: How I Came to Use Imagery

*A*t the *Gymnasium Freudenberg* (Mountain of Joy), the Swiss Latin preparatory school in Zurich that I attended for six and a half years, I learned many valuable things. My back, however, acquired the skill of stooping over Latin verse for hours on end. The school's rigorous class schedule, which started at 7:10 A.M., was hardly what you might expect in a gymnasium, a place where physical activity takes place. At the *Gymnasium Freudenberg,* little emphasis was placed on sports: There was no football team, no track team—or any team for that matter. But I loved to dance, and in the evenings I danced and exercised in the cellar at home, alone or with my brother. When I graduated from school, therefore, my posture was not as bad as it might have been, although it took years to reverse the "Latin-verse effect."

When the school put on its first theatrical production, to my surprise I was selected to play the lead. I knew nothing about auditioning, but I had apparently struck the right note. I remember being told that I didn't have to do much to be funny. I wasn't sure what the director meant by this statement until I rolled onto the stage for the first time. We were producing Molière's *Le Bourgeois Gentilhomme,* and I played this rather simple-minded, rich bourgeois trying to learn to dance. As I bounced about the stage with great enthusiasm during rehearsal, the fellow playing the dance teacher was very perturbed. His dancing was, of course, supposed to look totally superior to mine. Finally, I learned to look clumsy. I believe my trick to achieve this awkwardness was to imagine my legs wiggling like rubber and my neck stiff as an oak. (You are welcome to try it.)

When I first attended a ballet class, the teacher told me that my back was crooked as a banana. This correction was given in the strict Swiss manner of teaching: First teachers told you how sorry you looked and then they yanked you into the right shape. The remark was delivered with an undertone of "How dare you show up in class with that kind of back." I can still see the outraged look on the teacher's face, which naturally made me feel sad and self-conscious. I wondered how to straighten my back. I was taught the pulling-up method, which seemed to be the standard procedure. My belly button was supposed to stick to my lumbar spine, my buttocks needed to "tuck under" somehow, and my chin had to recede. The question was how anyone could enjoy dancing in this position. Breathing seemed out of the question. My back didn't actually *feel* like a banana, so I kept trying to imagine what the teacher was seeing. I tried to imagine my back in a position that would justify such a cry of indignation. But this didn't bring me closer to solving the problem.

REINFORCING WHAT YOU WANT

I now know that I was actually reinforcing the opposite of what I wanted. If you don't want your back to look crooked, you shouldn't focus on it *not* being "crooked as a banana." Instead you need to replace the image of a banana with that of something straight—a waterspout, for example. Put simply, your mind is a large screen filled with the images you have absorbed throughout the day. It is instructed by these images and the thoughts that accompany them. The problem is that most of your 50,000 or so thoughts, flashing images, notions, and so on, are similar to those of the previous day. As the images and thoughts repeat, they slowly but steadily effect a change in the direction the images suggest. According to Indian Ayurvedic medicine, if you want to know what thoughts you have had in your life so far, you should look at your body (Chopra 1990). To help clarify the connection between thought process and posture, try the following experiment.

Sit on a chair in a slumped position and think: "I feel great, fantastic . . . never better. I am having the time of my life." Notice the discrepancy between your posture and your thoughts. Now reposition yourself in a vibrant, upright sitting posture and think: "I feel awful, sad, dejected." Again, your thoughts do not match your posture. In a good posture, it is more difficult, albeit not impossible, to have depressing thoughts. Posture reflects thoughts; thoughts mold the physical being.

If posture and thought process are intimately connected, then, in a sense, your thoughts are constantly sculpting your posture, changing your alignment. The reverse holds true as well: Your posture influences your thinking. Your thoughts are part of a powerful matrix that influences your posture. The flood of words and images around you affects the way you sit, stand, and walk. Notice how comforting, encouraging words of praise from a parent or trusted teacher can immediately improve your posture: "Good! Well done! Perfect! Beautiful! Excellent job!" Conversely, observe the tension stifling all movement in a class being told it's "not good enough."

Both the pictures and the words in our minds influence the feelings in our bodies, which in turn feed our thoughts and mental pictures. To create powerful and dynamic alignment, we can use this roundabout cycle to our technical advantage if we fertilize with constructive information and weed out destructive thoughts.

PURPOSE AND WILL

To accomplish something, you must first have a clear purpose and the will to fulfill it. In dancing, for example, purpose can be reflected in a mental plan for executing a new and difficult dance step with specific imagery to help solve technical problems. To do this intelligently, you need to increase your ability to observe what is going on inside your body. Increasing inner awareness while dancing is also an important step in becoming your own teacher.

After graduating from the *Gymnasium* in Zurich, I went to New York because I was convinced it was the place to learn how to dance properly. I enrolled at New York University's Tisch School of the Arts where, ingrained with the Swiss work ethic, I pushed myself very hard. This resulted in a great deal of emotional pressure, so I was not the most relaxed person. I remember lying in bed and tensing my muscles, just to see how much strength I might have gained; obviously my sleep wasn't very restful.

I found the first part of my anatomy class with Andre Bernard very interesting. We learned about bones and posture, and I eagerly took notes. The second part of class was a bit unusual, though. We would lie on our backs and imagine our anatomical parts or a symbolic representation of our bodies changing in various ways. It was nice to lie down in any case, just to get some rest. The class was at the end of the day, and it was difficult to stay awake after an intense schedule of dance. However, if I could stay alert and concentrate on the images, I seemed to be more rested and my body less achy than if I simply dozed off for a half hour.

We were instructed to practice daily because it would take time for the images to change posture and movement habits. My habits were obviously lacking because I had a recurring backache and knee problems. I had seen several doctors, but none of them could figure out what was wrong. (I now know that my problems were due to bad leg and back alignment.) At one point I was even told that I had only two or three months of dancing left in my knees. Swimming gave me some relief and brought my muscles back to normal for a while. However, if I didn't swim for a week, the pain would recur.

One day as I practiced imagining my legs hanging over a clothes hanger and watching my back spread on the floor (see figure Ia and b), I suddenly experienced an incredible release of muscle tension. It was a tremendous relief and brought tears to my eyes. From then on, I practiced imaging with increased motivation, and my back tension and knee problems receded. It had taken a year to effect this release, but the experience taught me several valuable lessons in the use of imagery.

I had no way of knowing that using imagery would release my back tension in such a marvelous way. Nevertheless, I practiced purely on faith that it could work as nothing else had. The result was better than I had anticipated. I learned to trust the image, and that there was no limit to what can be accomplished with imaging. I discovered that a postural change initiated as an image creates and reflects a psychological change. Being centered is not just a biomechanical event.

Improving my posture eliminated my emotional pressure, reducing my mental stress. Some people unconsciously shy away from using imagery precisely because of its power. Their fear of the emotional release associated with a physical release is simply too great. Through years of teaching I have found that some people are tremendously attached to their physical and mental tension; it has become so familiar that it seems essential to their identities. Those who profess their willingness to improve their alignment are often not ready to do so on an emotional level.

Changing alignment in a dynamic way, not just altering your external shape, changes your relationship with the whole world and the people in it. A static change is just a momentary forcing of your body into a more upright position. It

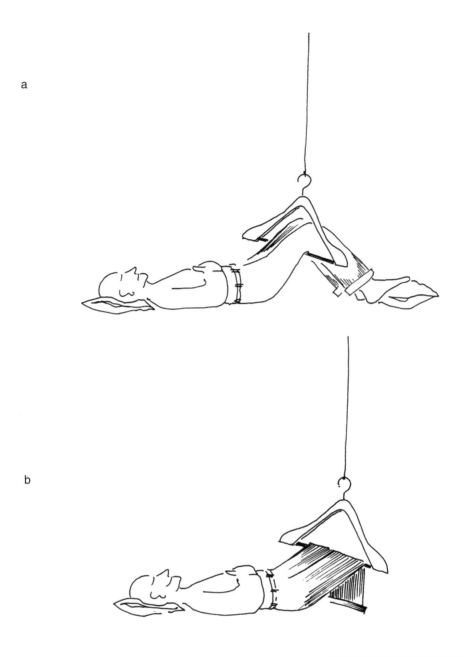

Figure I   Pants legs collapsing over clothes hanger.
Adapted, by permission, from L.E. Sweigard, 1974, *Human Movement Potential* (New York: Harper and Row).

lasts about as long as you pay attention to it. As soon as you continue your activities, you "collapse" into your previous posture. A dynamic change includes your whole being, your entire identity. To improve your alignment, you must be willing to embrace all the consequences to your personality, a transformation that may be overwhelming. I cannot emphasize this point enough: Since we are integrated beings, we need to change the whole as we change a part, or improved alignment is merely a cosmetic adjustment that crumbles under the slightest test in the real world (i.e., a dance performance). I have often watched dancers who have good posture while doing an exercise reveal their true (slouched) identity as soon as the teacher explains the next exercise.

Dynamic alignment needs to withstand the influence of our surroundings. This is not easy because much of what is socially nurtured in postural imagery, particularly in advertisements, is highly static, tense, and slouched.

My pelvis had been habitually misaligned and tilted forward (as is obvious in photos I have from this period). The resultant lumbar lordosis (forward curvature of the lumbar spine) was excessive, shortening the back muscles in this area and putting strain on my ligaments and joints. Seeing my back spread out on the floor helped my lumbar spine to drop down (aided by gravity) toward the floor, lengthening the lumbar curve (although by no means do you want to straighten out the curve!). Letting my legs hang over the clothes hanger released the excessive (rocklike) tension in my legs, allowing my pelvis to balance easily on top of my legs, finding its perfect, nonrigid alignment.

But why did it take so long for anything to happen? Well, first of all, my scientific background made the whole idea of imagery seem a bit suspect, even esoteric. I believed that only hard work with plenty of sweat dripping from your brow could improve your movement skills. It is difficult to grasp that such purely mental training will greatly improve your progress because it usually takes a while to build up enough mental power to have a noticeable effect on the body. In a society looking for immediate results, this lag time is one of the main reasons that many people give up early on imaging.

Learning imaging is akin to learning a language. Who would complain about not being able to read a French newspaper after only two weeks of French lessons? It can take up to a year of consistent practice to learn a language well enough to read a newspaper, just as it took me a year of practice at imaging to effect a release of tension in my back. I learned to stick with an image, even if it did not produce results initially.

As I became more and more aware of the impact that thinking has on the body, I began to study with every teacher I could find who used imagery and to read every book I could find on the topic. To my great joy, my dancing skills improved rapidly, and five years after being called "banana back" I was dancing in a New York company.

Using imagery is not very effective without personal desire and intention, and even with clear intention, imagery is a subtle process that requires patience. However, if used systematically, imagery can work long-term miracles, attacking the roots of your alignment problems. Forcing changes in your body may yield short-term gains but greatly increases the chance of injury. So don't give up on imagery; in time you will discover its amazing potential.

USING IMAGERY FOR ALIGNMENT

This book is divided into four parts. Part I discusses the origins and uses of imagery (which we have already touched on in the introduction) and provides a first taste of dynamic imagery in practice. Part II lays the biomechanical and anatomical foundation for understanding complex imagery based on physics and kinesiology. Part III provides anatomical imagery to help fine tune your alignment and increase your awareness of your body. Part IV further discusses posture and alignment and provides a wealth of exercises. In a related book entitled *Dance Imagery for Technique and Performance,* I discuss improvisational imagery (also useful in improving alignment), imagery in dance technique, choreography, and performance.

I have chosen to illustrate some of the images. I am aware that an illustration is always done from a specific point of view, and that the same image could look differently if drawn by someone else. Most of these illustrations have gone through numerous stages and changes and are, in a sense, momentary pictures of an unfolding process. Therefore, they should serve as concrete and, I hope, inspirational starting points for your own exploration.

Although the book is intended to benefit dancers and students of all styles, I chose to describe the movements using ballet terminology because I feel it is the most universally recognized and consistent dance vocabulary. At some points, I have also used somewhat technical anatomical terminology so as to be more specific. However, I usually define the terms in context (and illustrate the more complex concepts).

This book can be used as a general reference or as a guide for systematic study. Most likely, teachers who use this text will reorganize the material to suit their preferred mode of presentation. For those practicing without a teacher, the following are a few suggestions to help you in exploring imagery.

First, read through the introductory material in parts 1 and 2 and practice the exercises. Continue practicing as you proceed to the anatomical section, even if you do not fully understand all of the material. Your understanding will grow with your imaging experience.

The material presented in part 3, anatomical imagery, can be approached in two ways. In a class situation, with teacher supervision, it may be preferable to proceed in the sequence presented in the book. If you are practicing on your own, select some material from each of chapters 12 through 17 for daily study as well as holistic imagery from chapter 1 and chapter 18. Select imagery that appeals to you, and stick with your selection until you feel you are ready for something new. This could mean working on the same image for a day, or for several weeks or even months. For example, you may use choose to use a different image for the pelvis every day while sticking with the same holistic image for a longer period.

At least once a day, practice in the supine position. Throughout the day, take every opportunity to practice in the sitting and standing positions. Stop your desk work for a moment and focus on a sitting exercise. Work on standing and walking images when you go shopping (but continue to pay attention to traffic lights). Do not limit your practice to the time you spend in class. Although class time is conducive to intensive concentration on alignment, limiting your effort in this way will create the notion that improving your alignment is something that is done only in class. It is equally important to practice during your daily chores, when you normally would not be thinking about your alignment. This is an essential part of integration and will speed your progress immeasurably.

I have frequently observed dancers entering class in their "this is me" (body image) alignment and, as class begins, adjusting their bodies into their "dance class" alignment. "Class alignment," always sprinkled with tension, looks unnatural. Because it does not conform to your body image, it cannot be effortless, making it difficult to achieve your highest level of technique. There is a constant battle going on in your nervous system between your body image alignment and your dance class alignment. Also, your dance class alignment is less reliable than your body image alignment because it requires more effort to reestablish.

You should also use constructive rest (described in chapter 12) several times a day to stay in touch with your imagery and reduce the amount of old alignment information that pours into your nervous system. Remember, even after you have decided to improve your alignment, you are still mainly reinforcing your old alignment; your old habits are still 99 percent (or more) effective. The goal is to reduce this percentage as quickly as possible, to integrate new information rapidly. Your most important allies in this effort are practicing in the supine position and using imagery during everyday activities.

PART

I

Posture and Dynamic Alignment

*A*t the risk of sounding like an advertisement, I can truly tell you that the benefits of creating dynamic alignment are many. Better alignment improves the efficiency of your body, reducing strain on both a physical and a psychological level because physical strain and exhaustion tend to dampen your mood and general outlook on life. Problems that may seem insurmountable in the depleted state become manageable when you are physically prepared.

The energized body exudes confidence. Improved coordination and observation skills enable you to progress faster in sports or dance. Your mind is trained to grasp three-dimensional movement sequences and perform them more accurately. You feel new connections and relationships within your body that continuously help you find improved solutions to your movement problems.

Better biomechanical transfer of forces through the joints and body systems reduces the likelihood of injury. Even nutrition is enhanced, as the increased flexibility and reduced strain improve circulation of body fluids such as lymph, blood, and sinovial fluids. Finally, it is an excellent method of resting and regenerating your body after physical activity. Best of all, you do not need a suitcase to improve your dynamic alignment on the road; your mind is capable of training you any time, any place.

In the following sections, I use the term posture to denote the overall picture presented by your body when you are standing, sitting, or lying down. Alignment emphasizes the aspect of posture that is concerned with the geometric relationship of the parts of the body, usually in the standing position.

CHAPTER 1

The Roots of Imagery for Alignment

*A*pproximately 35,000 years ago, there appears to have been a sudden expansion in the creation of body ornamentation and the use of visual imagery. This flowering of the visual sense did not coincide with an expansion in brain mass, which had been stable in Homo sapiens for at least 90,000 years (White 1989). Visual thinking was a truly revolutionary development that pervaded all areas of human cultural evolution. It became the basis of rituals, as humans imagistically transformed into other animals and elements for various purposes such as healing or hunting. The healing and performing arts both grew out of the rituals engendered by imaging.

According to Jeanne Achterberg (1985), imagery as a healing tool has its roots in the 20,000-year-old tradition of shamanism. She writes, "The shaman's work is conducted in the realm of the imagination and their expertise in using that terrain for the benefit of the community has been recognized throughout recorded history" (p. 11). Magician and curer, the shaman is also both dramatist and performer. Julius E. Lips, PhD (1956) contends that modern drama developed from cultic-religious performances and mimic dances, in which actors initially impersonated gods and eventually took on the roles of jesters, clowns, and storytellers.

The very good time enjoyed in the "theater" by peoples even of the most primitive cultures shows that the deepest roots of theatrical effect have nothing to do with complicated stage mechanisms, individual stardom, or fashionable playwrights. Imagination is the magic cue. (p. 181)

Our perspective on the origins of alignment as it relates to the human body cannot be complete without a glance at the civilization of ancient Egypt more than 4,000 years ago.

Posture was of paramount importance, as can be surmised from the depiction of the pharaohs: They were the image of perfect alignment (although a teenage pharaoh probably slouched as much as his not so kingly counterparts). Why then these serene and magnificently aligned pharaohs? Why were the Egyptian people presented with this kind of an image and not a naturalistic one (which the highly skilled artists of the time could have easily produced)?

In the Egyptian culture, alignment seems to have been a basic necessity of life. Once a year, the landscape turned into a black, muddy quagmire, thanks to the Nile, whose profuse swelling obliterated all boundaries. An Egyptian farmer, on discovering that his parcel of land had shrunk due to poor alignment of the ropes used by the alignment corps (or whatever they were called), would have complained. For the Egyptians, this loss of land had to be avoided at all cost (there wasn't much time to grow crops). Order, and with it perfect alignment, was truth. Therefore, the pharaohs were (or should have been) the image of perfect alignment. To depict the pharaoh in any other position, such as gnawing on a chicken bone while sprawled out on a couch, was scandalous (there was such a "revolutionary" period, but it only lasted 20 years out of 3,000). Sitting or standing, the pharaohs had to be models of good posture—strong, yet calm and in control, ready to create order out of chaos.

The pyramids, too, were aligned with uncanny perfection, quite a feat without modern measuring tools. The following is a wonderful image from my lecture notes: Only twice a year, at the temple of Abu-Simbel, formerly on the banks of the Nile, a streak of sunlight passes precisely over the eyes of four figures (situated 60 meters within the mountainside!). To create such stunning architecture, you *must* have great imagination and visualization skills (from a lecture by Robert Thomas, March 13, 1995).

Thus, we investigate the power of the imagination, which seems so inextricably linked with the performing arts. For a more extensive history of the use of imagery in healing, I recommend reading *Imagery in Healing* by Jeanne Achterberg and *Seeing With the Mind's Eye* by Mike Samuels, MD, and Nancy Samuels (1975). Although as dancers we often need to heal ourselves and others (such concerns are addressed in later chapters), here we focus on the origins of imagery as a tool to improve artistic ability.

The following provides more background on the evolution of the science linking imagery and movement, a sort of "Who's Who" in ideokinesiology (imagery as related to movement).

HEINRICH KOSNICK AND MABEL TODD

At the turn of the century, Heinrich Kosnick, a pianist in Munich, developed a system of mental imagery to enhance the skill of his students. Calling his method "psycho-physiological," Kosnick recommended imaging while in a supine yoga position. He found the images he created to be so effective that he wrote two books, *Lebensteigerung* (*Life-Enhancement*, 1927) and *Busoni: Gestaltung durch Gestalt* (*Shaping Through Form*, 1971). Busoni was a respected pianist and teacher who was trying to establish a scientific foundation for his work. Writing elegantly and concisely, Kosnick (1971) suggested in-depth knowledge of anatomy as a prerequisite to experiencing the correct functioning of the body and stated that the directed will leads to the movement goal. A pupil of Kosnick's, Margrit Bäumlein-Schurter, wrote a book of exercises called *Übungen zur Konzentration* (*Exercises to Enhance Concentration*, 1966).

Around the same time that Kosnick was developing his ideas, American Mabel Todd, author of *The Thinking Body* (1972), used her great skill and insight into the functioning of the human body to create astonishing changes both in herself and in her students. If her poetic and profound writing is any reflection of her teaching, it must have been a transforming experience to witness her work, which she referred to as "structural hygiene." Her books, which also include *Early Writings:1920-1934* (1977) and *The Hidden You* (1953), emphasize the elegant construction of the body and its ability to change in response to will. Todd, who taught at Columbia University Teachers College, had movement difficulties caused by a serious accident. Although it seems the doctors of her day were unable to help her much, by using imagery, she was able to fully regain her ability to move. She is credited with proposing "hook lying," or the constructive rest position, as a training position for mental imagery (see Constructive Rest, chapter 6).

LULU SWEIGARD AND IDEOKINESIS

Working with dancers, Lulu Sweigard (1978) researched and developed Todd's ideas, defining ideokinesis as "repeated ideation of a movement without volitional physical effort" (187). In 1929, she initiated a study on the effects of imagery on alignment to "determine whether ideokinesis . . . could recoordinate muscle action enough to produce measurable changes in skeletal alignment" (p. 187). In meeting with students for weekly 30-minute sessions over 15 weeks, Sweigard (1978) discovered nine lines of movement along which most postural change took place.

The Nine Lines of Movement

The following descriptions of the lines of movement and their effects are accompanied by occasional references to imagery in this book that relates directly or indirectly to each line of movement.

1. Line of movement to lengthen the spine downward (part III, figures 13.11 and 13.16) releases tightness of the back muscles, especially in the lumbar region.

2. Line of movement to shorten the distance between the midfront of the pelvis and the twelfth thoracic vertebra activates the deep and superficial pelvic muscles in front of the pelvis that counterbalance the erector spinae group. Activating this line releases tension in the erector spinae.

3. Line of movement from the top of the sternum to the top of the spine can either lengthen or shorten, depending on alignment needs. It improves the alignment of the upper spine in relation to the pelvis, allowing the head to balance on an axis in a manner that releases tension in the neck and shoulder muscles.

4. Line of movement to narrow the ribcage improves the flexibility of the ribcage, thereby improving spinal alignment and diaphragmatic action.

5. Line of movement to widen the back of the pelvis releases tension across the back of the pelvis, allowing the femur heads to center in their sockets. Weight transfer from the legs to the pelvis, and vice versa, is greatly improved by this line (part III, figure 13.21).

6. Line of movement to narrow the front of the pelvis balances the widening across the back of the pelvis. It increases the stability of the front pelvic arch and activates the muscles in the front of the pelvis. Figure 1.1 shows the Sweigardian zipper.

7. Line of movement from the center of the knee to the center of the femoral joint brings the whole leg into alignment, greatly benefiting the knee. This movement balances the muscular action around the femur and allows greater control of the leg (part II, figure 9.5, the resultant force).

8. Line of movement from the big toe to the heel centers the weight thrust through the ankle joint by allowing the longitudinal arch of the foot to be "resurrected."

9. Line of movement to lengthen the central axis of the trunk upward. The summation of all the other lines, this movement allows you to attain your ideal height and release superficial muscle tension (figure 2.4a).

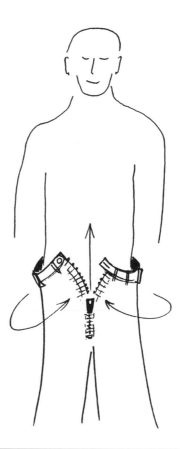

Figure I An imagined zipper closing up the front of the pelvis.

For more information on the nine lines, I recommend Sweigard's *Human Movement Potential: Its Ideokinetic Facilitation* or Irene Dowd's article, "Ideokinesis: The 9 Lines of Movement," in her book *Taking Root to Fly*. Dowd studied with and assisted Sweigard at The Juilliard School from 1968 through 1974. In her book, Dowd enriched and expanded the ideokinetic work developed by Todd and Sweigard. Dowd, an expert in the art of touch, has a keen eye for detecting alignment and movement problems. Her illustrations convey a sense of flow and interconnectedness within the human body and the space surrounding the body. Dowd has taught at many major institutions such as Teachers College, Columbia University, Wesleyan University, and the American Dance Festival. Currently, she maintains a private practice in New York, is a regular guest faculty at the National Ballet School of Canada, and is a member of the dance faculty at The Juilliard School.

Sweigard's Goal

Using a direct, one-to-one approach, Sweigard hoped to raise the standard of what was considered normal movement ability. She called her method an education rather than a cure. To Sweigard, ideokinesis was not a relaxation technique but a way to balance muscle action around the joints.

It is important to understand that relaxation and tension are related. Although balancing muscle action requires the release of tension in certain muscle groups, it also entails an increase in tension in other muscle groups. In many instances, people with shoulder tension do not just need to relax their shoulders. They also need to increase the tone in the central supporting muscles and organs of their bodies as a foundation for permanently reducing shoulder tension. Muscles often become tense to compensate for inefficiency in another area of the body. Although some images seem geared to either increasing or reducing tension, the result of visualizing an image is usually a complex redistribution of muscular tension, edging toward the desired balance around the joints. Sweigard (1978) writes:

> The all-important voluntary contribution from the central nervous system is the idea of the movement. Concentration on the image of the movement will let the central nervous system choose the most efficient neuromuscular coordination for its performance, namely innate reflexes and feedback mechanisms. (p. 6)

Ideokinesis Versus Kosnick/Bäumlein-Schurter

According to Bäumlein-Schurter (1966), the process of realignment begins with releasing work, which is followed by the creation of "life-carrying tone." This notion differs from Sweigard's, at least in theory. From the very beginning, the ideokinetic method sets out to activate flaccid muscles and release tense muscles simultaneously. The aim is to move toward balanced muscle action from the outset of the training. In practice, most beginners can better apply releasing imagery (the shoulders melt like ice cream, the back spreads out on the floor) than activating imagery (the central axis lengthens upward). For the experienced imager, however, releasing and activating imagery are opposite sides of the same coin: The effect of a releasing image is also experienced through the concomitant activation of flaccid musculature; the effect of an activating image is also experienced through the concomitant release of tense musculature. Therefore, there is more similarity in the practical application of ideokinesis and the work of Kosnick/Bäumlein-Schurter than is apparent from the underlying theories.

BARBARA CLARK

Barbara Clark, first a client, then a student of Todd's, wrote three manuals entitled: *Let's Enjoy Sitting-Standing-Walking* (1963), *How to Live in Your Axis—Your Vertical Line* (1968), and *Body Proportion Needs Depth—Front to Back* (1975). Several of Clark's students, among them Andre Bernard, participated in the creation of *Let's Enjoy Sitting-Standing-Walking.* Most recently, Pamela Matt of the dance faculty at Arizona State University wrote *A Kinesthetic Legacy: The Life and Works of Barbara Clark,* a fine in-depth look at Clark's great contribution to this field. Clark created some very valuable exercises to increase awareness of the central axis, paramount to any improvement in alignment (see below).

Clark's student, Andre Bernard, began teaching at the Dance Department of NYU School of the Arts in 1965. Bernard, whom I first encountered at NYU in 1979, is very skilled at using his hands to help in visualizing anatomy, a process called tactile aid. The images seem to pour out of his hands. His deep, resonant voice, especially valuable during constructive rest sessions, contributes to the overall impression of an image. Bernard once described Clark as "a primitive abstractionist, using basic, earthy thinking; her imagery is like a Picasso painting" (lecture notes, 1982). Both Clark and Bernard gave sessions to dancers and actors, among them Marilyn Monroe, who was supportive of Clark's writing effort (Matt 1993).

Many other excellent teachers were trained by Barbara Clark, including John Rolland who wrote *Inside Motion: An Ideokinetic Basis for Movement Education* (1984). Rolland taught alignment at the Vermont Movement Workshop and in 1981 was invited to teach in the Modern Dance Department of the State Theater school in Amsterdam (now called the School for New Dance Development).

CIRCLING YOUR AXIS

(This exercise is adapted and expanded from Barbara Clark and Andre Bernard.) Stand in a comfortable position with your arms hanging at your sides and imagine a vertical line or force beam originating on the floor between your feet and moving up through the center of your body. This line must be recreated at every moment; you cannot take it for granted; you need to infuse power into it continuously. Your body seeks to orient itself around this line, which is your central axis. (It is as if the individual cells of your body find this axis a convenient line of orientation.)

Lift your feet off the ground alternately by flexing easily in your hip sockets. Feel your central axis between your shifting legs. Begin to rotate around this axis. The axis does not move through space. Like a merry-go-round, your body revolves slowly about its central post. Once you have completed a 360-degree circle, try turning to the other side. Notice the difference between turning to the left and turning to the right.

Find a reference point just in front of your toes, perhaps a division between two tiles or a scratch on the floor. It should be something that you cannot feel with your toes (or you could cheat). Rotate again to the first side, maintaining your focus on the horizon. After you have finished your revolution, check your reference point to see if you have moved forward, sideways, or to the back. Repeat to the other side and check your reference point.

Now do the exercise with your eyes closed. When you believe you have completed a 360-degree revolution, open your eyes and check your position. Repeat the exercise to the other side.

By now you should have discovered which is your easier turning side (usually the side where you deviate less from your central axis).

The point of this exercise is to discover the precise difference in sensation between turning to one side and turning to the other. What small chunk of sensation is missing on one side that the other side possesses? How exactly does the axis change from one side to the other? Does the axis look different, have a different quality, when you turn to one side versus the other? Can you interchange sensation or quality between the sides to balance them?

Now you are ready to circle your axis by doing small quarter-turn hops. After every quarter-turn hop, do one hop in place. The sequence is: Quarter-turn hop, hop in place, quarter-turn hop, hop in place, quarter-turn hop, hop in place, quarter-turn hop, hop in place; repeat the exercise one more time to the same side.

Again, practice to both sides. Then try the same exercise with half turns and finally whole turns (even double turns, if you are an experienced dancer or gymnast).

I practiced the above sequence frequently with the Swiss national gymnastics team. It showed clearly that jumping power alone (of which they had plenty) will not create successful double turns in the air. A clear concept of your axis will use less "random" power and improve your turns.

JOAN SKINNER

During her dance training, Joan Skinner, who performed with the Martha Graham Dance Company, the Cunningham Dance Company, and many others, discovered that many of the things she was taught created a forced style of movement, causing tension and pain. Working on her own for several years, studying the Alexander technique, she discovered a new method of training based on the body's own knowledge. In a radical departure from traditional dance training, Skinner's classes might involve lying on the floor immersed in an image or improvising to a haikulike totality image. (Haiku are short Japanese poems that evoke a certain mood; see chapter 7.) Skinner's method, which she called Releasing, uses poetic imagery and provides a profound base for effortless movement and control. According to Stephanie Skura, choreographer and teacher of the technique:

Letting go is a crucial preparation for allowing an image to truly move you. Releasing does not have to do with moving softly; it has to do with a constant flux without grabbing onto anything. You get your orientation not by holding onto some center, but by letting the energy flow within you, through you, and around you. This is not an industrial age, mechanistic view of energy; it is not something finite that you can manufacture, store, and use up. You feel yourself as part of a greater energy. (personal interview, July 1993)

The concepts inherent in Skinner Releasing remind me of Heracleitus, Greek philosopher of Ephesus (around 500B.C.), who maintained that all things were in a state of flux. He said that unity persists through constant change and used the analogy of the river to explain: "Upon those who step into the same rivers different and ever different waters flow down" (*Encyclopædia Brittanica*, 1966 ed., "Heracleitus", 386). Not all things need to be changing at all times. Rocks and mountains can be temporarily stable, but they will eventually change as well.

The concept of flow is crucial to creating dynamic alignment. Just as we have said that your mind can *sculpt* your body into a certain posture, your mind can also help your body *flow* into better alignment. And here is the good news: A flow cannot be held because it then ceases to be a flow; therefore, alignment based on this notion cannot become rigid. If you begin to realize that your alignment is flowing, constantly changing, even if on a cellular or molecular level, you are able to take charge of this flow. Using imagery, you can constantly guide your alignment toward increased efficiency without ever holding onto it. If you were to stop the flow, even in what appears to be a biomechanically well-aligned position, tension would ensue. The building blocks of our body, the cells, are both filled and surrounded by fluids. Therefore fluid motion is inherent in our very structure.

SOMATIC DISCIPLINES

Dancers have found various somatic disciplines that are not specifically oriented toward dance to be very useful in improving their skills. Ancient disciplines such as yoga are so central to many forms of dance that I would be remiss not to credit them adequately, although it is beyond the scope of this book to delve deeply into them. Not necessarily based on the use of imagery such as ideokinesis and Skinner Releasing, the following beneficial techniques apply imagery (usually nonmetaphorical) in certain contexts.

Alexander Technique

Donald Weed (1990), a teacher of the Alexander technique, writes that all of the work can be distilled down to two discoveries:

(1) In every movement you make, there is a change in the relationship of your head with your body that precedes and accompanies that movement, and which either helps you or gets in your way. (2) The conscious mind has the capacity to override every system, including the natural ones. (p. 26)

The Alexander instructions, which allow the head to go up and forward and the back to widen, seem to harmonize well with the imagery used by Todd and Sweigard. The Alexander concept of inhibition, of "saying no" to the habitual mental and physical reactions, is very relevant to imagery work as well.

To use an image effectively, you first need to clear your mind. You cannot be in a nervous state, your mind filled with a jumble of thoughts, and then pile some images on top of all that. It simply does not work. You must be open and receptive to new possibilities in your body. Nor should it be necessary to act on every impulse that comes to mind or muscle. (A muscle impulse is one that you feel in your body before you realize in your mind what you want to do.) In fact, you need to learn how to react as little as possible to any irrational urge to *do* something. In this way, you can become selective about how you perform a movement, choosing the most efficient of the many movement patterns available. The proper pattern can only be found in a peaceful state—a state in which impulsive movement patterns can be ignored, overridden, or "inhibited."

Autogenic Training

The purpose of Autogenic Training (AT), a technique developed by the German Dr. I.H. Schultz (1982), is to release tension, lower your heart rate, and change other physiological conditions of your body. The imagery used here relaxes and calms the body and mind, suggesting heavy limbs, a cool forehead, and a quiet heart. AT also uses self-talk in the form of positive affirmations. It is interesting to compare images used by Schultz, Kosnick, and Sweigard to reduce overall body tension: Schultz (AT) directs his students to experience the limbs becoming heavy; Sweigard suggests the body as a suit of clothes collapsing front to back; and Kosnick (as related by his student Bäumlein-Schurter) has the body sink downward into the ground.

Funktionelle Entspannung (Functional Relaxation, or FR)

Functional Relaxation is a somatic movement therapy developed in Germany by Marianne Fuchs, who was trained in the German Mensendieck method. The goals of FR are to experience weight, inner rhythm, and movement in the expirational phase of breathing to promote an economical use of the body. Fuchs uses imagery in a variety of ways. For example, a series of exercises in FR "remembers" the 15 inner spaces by clearly visualizing them. These inner spaces, together with skeletal awareness, are very important to the upright posture. Fuchs (1984) also points out that faulty movement and postural patterns created by negative emotions can only be remedied through the use of positive feelings and images .

Moshe Feldenkrais

With Feldenkrais technique there is no right or wrong posture. The technique asks questions such as: What is your structure? Where are you? What are you doing? What is your intention? Feldenkrais uses movement exercises, some of them deceptively simple, to create astonishing changes in flexibility and movement patterns. It sometimes requests the student to perform a movement on one side of the body and only visualize it on the other side, or to imagine a movement several times before actually doing it. Author Layna Verin (1980) states that Feldenkrais accomplishes its results by

enabling you to become more sensitive to differences. By devising a configuration of movements that cannot be performed without this refinement. By making you aware of the minute interval between the time your body mobilizes for movement and you actually do that movement—the minute interval that allows you to exercise that capacity for differentiation and to change. (p. 84)

Body-Mind Centering®

Founded by Bonnie Cohen and associates in 1973, the School for Body-Mind Centering® (BMC) teaches movement through anatomical, physiological, and developmental principles. Cohen, whose original background is in the fine arts, dance, and the theater, was licensed as an occupational therapist and a neurodevelopmental therapist by the Bobaths in England. She also studied Neuromuscular Reeducation (another name for Todd's imagery work) with Andre Bernard and Zero Balancing, a bodywork method developed by Fritz Smith and Katsugen Endo ("the art of training the nervous system") with Haruchi Noguchi in Japan.

Imagery is intrinsic to BMC and is applied to the musculoskeletal, respiratory, digestive, circulatory, nervous, and hormonal systems. Child development is explored in detail; early movements such as creeping, crawling, and rolling are related to the evolutionary stages of the animal kingdom. Bonnie Cohen recently published *Sensing, Feeling, and Action: The Experiential Anatomy of Body-Mind Centering*, a collection of articles that had formerly appeared in the *Contact Quarterly*.

FROM CRAWLING TO STANDING

Get onto all fours and prowl around the floor like a child who is pretending to be a tiger in the jungle. Occasionally the tiger decides to become playful and rolls onto its side and back, or may even do a complete roll. Next the tiger practices crawling backward, as if retreating from a threat, only to recoil off its powerful hind legs and increase the speed of its forward motion.

Begin to crawl forward at an ever-faster pace, and finally, change as harmoniously as possible to an upright walk. As you continue to walk, imagine that you are still crawling. (It is particularly important just to think the image, not to do it.) Notice how this affects your alignment. Now begin to run, and imagine that you are a tiger bounding across the grasslands with a flexible spine and soft paws.

All of the above-mentioned methods are strikingly original and creative. They are linked by their use of imagery—in some form or another—as a catalyst for change. In the following chapter we will explore how a variety of postural models can contribute to our understanding of dynamic alignment.

CHAPTER 2

Postural Models and Dynamic Alignment

*T*he purpose of this chapter is not to create a limited definition of posture and alignment but to broaden our sense of posture and open up many possible routes to improving our alignment. There are numerous approaches to aligning our bodies, and we can gain insight from each of them, rather like putting on different colored glasses. One moment we perceive the body as a stack of cubes, the next moment as a pendant mobile.

Dynamic alignment is neither a static nor a finite state; you are not working toward the day when you finally attain perfect alignment. Even if your alignment is already good, there is always room for improvement. You are constantly moving to a deeper level of experience, an even subtler adjustment, a new perception.

WHAT OUR POSTURE REVEALS

Posture reveals our genetic and social heritage as well as the sum of our accumulated mental and physical habits. There are as many types of posture as there are human beings. Your posture is constantly and imperceptibly changing, reflecting your psychological state. If you took full-length photos of yourself from the front and side every morning and looked at them in sequence, you would see that your posture is in constant flux. Your posture for the day depends on what you did the previous day, your psychological state and body tone when you went to bed, the position you slept in, and changes in your body image, among other factors. In a photo taken in the evening, you would likely be shorter and your body would have rearranged itself in the direction suggested by your movement habits and tasks of that day.

A skilled dancer can detect daily postural changes and factor them into his or her alignment in both dynamic (moving) and static (still) states. Larry Rhodes, who was the department chair of NYU when I was a student there, once noted the following: One of the first things that needs to be done in a dancing day is feeling the subtle adjustments that need to be made to gain full functionality.

Daily changes accumulate so that postural habits become more visible with age. Many people "shrink" with the passing of time, partly because the body contains less and less water as it ages. Also, the body must resist gravity, the tendency to be pulled toward the earth's center. Todd's term *postural pattern* implies that the outward manifestation of body shape is the result of an inner network of forces. Postural controls depend on the functioning of the central nervous system, the visual system, the vestibular system, and the various receptors located in the musculoskeletal system. According to Todd (1972): "The postural pattern is that of many small parts moving definite distances in space, in a scheme perfectly timed, and with the exact amount of effort necessary to support the individual weights, and to cover the time-space-movement" (p. 22). Sweigard (1978) defines the upright posture in relation to a physical parameter:

> The consistent and persistent alignment of the parts of the skeletal structure in relation to the line of gravity when the subject assumes an easy standing position with the weight evenly distributed—according to his or her own judgment—on the feet, with the ankles in the sagittal plane of the femoral joints and with the arms hanging freely at the side. (p. 173)

Every human has a certain upright posture that yields the most efficient use of his or her body. In dance, aesthetics influence posture, sometimes interfering with efficiency.

POSTURAL HABITS

Partly developed in utero, our movement habits are reflected in how we manage each of our daily tasks. After birth, we go through a complex set of developmental stages at a rate determined by genetic, social, and other cultural forces (Piaget 1993). Once a baby is able to sit, we marvel at its ability to balance its head perfectly over its torso. Despite having a considerably larger head relative to the rest of its body than an adult, a baby will sit in good alignment according to the rules of efficient mechanics, even if the parents and older siblings slouch at the dinner table. If the parents continue to be bad examples of alignment, however, the child will most likely model this behavior and allow its efficient posture to deteriorate.

Of course, myriad other factors influence the development of our movement habits—the games we play, our immediate environment, the climate, our innate interests and talents, the way in which we explore our environment, and how we imitate our playmates. I remember meeting the father of one of the young gymnasts I was coaching in Zurich in 1989 and recognizing him as soon as he walked into the gym by the way he carried his shoulder blades—his posture was very similar to the patterns I knew so well in his son.

Cultures with lifestyles that foster good alignment usually entail varied movement tasks in everyday life: sitting on floors, carrying baskets on the head, and running (even adults) to greet visitors to the village. Such cultures lack comfortable furniture that promotes flaccid "hanging out." The Xhosa women of the Transkeian Territories of eastern South Africa rarely walk but *dance* home from their work in the fields. I haven't seen many people dancing home from their office work, although they probably need the exercise more than the Xhosa.

It is difficult to carry something on your head while slouched. The deep pelvic and leg muscles maintain power, and the hip joints remain flexible in a deep-knee crouch position, the working posture in many eastern countries. This seems to be a universal position in childhood, as it is used by young children across all cultures (figure 2.1). On the other hand, it is easy to get accustomed to lying (you can hardly call it sitting) on soft living-room furniture. This kind of posture reduces body tone needed for good alignment. The hip joints lose their flexibility because they are not exercised over their full range, which in turn increases the strain on other body structures in an effort to compensate for this lack of flexibility.

Figure 2.1   A child using a deep-knee crouched position during play.

IN SEARCH OF IDEAL POSTURE

The purpose of the following section is to explore some of the varied approaches to improving posture and defining ideal alignment. It is not about finding the one and only right method of gaining ideal posture, but discovering how a multitude of ideas can inform our sense of alignment. The richer the sources we can draw from the more dynamic the resulting alignment.

The Somatic Approach to Ideal Posture

Much insight into ideal alignment can be gained by looking at the diverse notions of the following representatives of the somatic field and their uses of imagery:

1. Moshe Feldenkrais (1972), founder of the Feldenkrais bodywork technique:

. . . a tree that has grown upright, will bend its top in whatever direction the wind is blowing. In the same way, good upright posture is that from which a minimum muscular effort will move the body with equal ease in any desired direction. This means that in the upright position there must be no muscular effort deriving from voluntary control, regardless of whether this effort is known and deliberate or concealed from the consciousness by habit. (p. 76)

2. Joan Skinner (1990), founder of the Skinner Releasing technique:

When we're dealing with alignment in these classes, we're dealing with multidirectional balancing—not holding the balance in any part of the body, but relating to multigravitational fields. When this alignment is harmonious with the larger energy systems, it releases the individual. Distortions of alignment constrict the individual. These distortions are constrictive because they are warps of the energy patterns which flow through us and around us and out of us and into us. A Releasing alignment is not a fixed alignment; it's always in flux. Everything is relative to everything else. So I see it as harmonious or not harmonious. When it's harmonious, then something is unleashed, then power and energy are released and that becomes Releasing dance. (p. 13)

3. Ida Rolf, PhD (1989), founder of the Rolfing bodywork method:

In human bodies, symmetry along all three major axes is the only ultimate answer, not merely alignment in a vertical dimension. Achievement of this three-dimensional symmetry requires a deep awareness of the sum total of body elements. It calls also for recognition of the mechanics of individual underlying units. Each segment is characterized by its own elements of outstanding structural significance. (p. 34)

4. Charlotte Selver and Charles Brooks (1981), proponents of Sensory Awareness:

In easy and balanced standing we mobilize precisely the energy needed to counterbalance the pull of the earth and permit full sensing of the total organism. Work on balancing is begun only after a considerable degree of inner "awareness" is reached. We have to be able to give up using the eyes to orient ourselves and begin to rely entirely on sensing. We begin to notice that the finest changes in weight distribution often make a world of difference in sensations of effort or ease in muscle tissues and breathing. With the gradual approach to equilibrium comes a feeling of lightness, freedom and peace incomparable with any other experience. One begins to discover that one is in constant flux; nothing is static. (pp. 121-122)

5. Lulu Sweigard (1961):

The unattainable "perfect posture" shows the skeletal framework in perfect alignment, in strict agreement with all principles of mechanical balance.

Approaching the ideal promotes those attributes so important to the performing artist: (1) a slenderized figure; (2) optimum flexibility of all joints; and (3) minimum expenditure of energy, both in the maintenance of the body in the upright position and in the performance of movement. (p. 1)

Metaphors of Bodily Efficiency

There are many theories on how to maximize the efficiency of the body to keep it healthy and injury free. One approach suggests that the body is a machine that can be perfected by improving its mechanical functioning. In this scenario, we are dealing with an intricate combination of pumps, pipelines, pulleys, levers, and power stations controlled by a grand computer. If we oil, trim, and adjust this machine so that everything is in place, mechanical force transfers efficiently through the entire system.

A somewhat different approach comes from the East: The body is thought to be an interconnected field of energy. The flow of energy through designated pathways determines the body's state of health. Freeing and/or balancing these pathways, as is done in Chinese acupuncture and acupressure, for example, allows for optimal functioning.

Since ancient times, mental balance has been recognized cross-culturally as the basis of the well-functioning body. As the ancient Romans stated: *"Mens sana in corpore sano,"* "A healthy mind will be found in a healthy body." Many ancient and some very recent healing traditions try to create a state of mind that optimizes bodily function. French psychotherapist Émile Coué (1857–1926) contributed substantially to the reemergence in the West of the notion that the mind holds great power over the body. Famous for his formula, "Every day in every way, I am feeling better and better," he based his method on the power of the imagination.

Metaphors Aren't Ageless

We seem unable to envision an outside object that does not exist within us in some form. Architecture, arches, domes, walls, canals, chemical factories, and computers can all be found within us. Even if a discovery seems like a revelation, entirely new, sooner or later the sciences come up with something similar in the body. Plato even states in the *Phaedo* that everything we can conceive of preexists as a so-called form or idea. We take this one step further by saying that everything we can conceive of preexists in our human form.

Each society takes its metaphors for bodily function from its most prevalent machines. In ancient Rome, for example, the heart was an oven because an oven was a standard household item. The notion of the heart as a pump didn't arise until the industrial age made pumps commonplace (Miller 1982). Later, a more refined knowledge of body chemistry revealed that the heart is also a gland. Once the cell was discovered as the basic building block of tissue, science began to divide and subdivide the body into ever smaller units.

Postural Models

A model is an image that attempts to clarify dominant structural and functional aspects. Close to the scientific norm, or apparently completely removed from it, a model may be the first glimpse of a new insight, a fresh look at things that should not be immediately discarded if they are off the beaten track. The history of science is full of correct ideas that were initially rejected. For example, Watson and Crick's model of the DNA structure, the double helix, wasn't an exact representation, but rather a first look at a structure presented in such a way that the human mind could readily visualize it. Some models share notions, while others seem to be completely at odds with each other. Sometimes parts of one model can be added to another one, creating a mixed model.

Is there a comprehensive metaphorical model that embodies the complete structural and functional nature of erect human posture? If defined, will it help us find our "ideal" alignment? The following exercise describes three models offered to focus attention on particular aspects of posture, thereby forming the basis of better understanding that can lead to a deeper experience of posture. I have found that spontaneously varying the models creates a more dynamic sense of alignment.

SWITCHING AMONG MODELS

Let's practice switching from one model to another. By doing this, we can approach the same issues from a number of angles. Finally, we will "mix" the models. The following models emphasize the relationship between the head and the rest of the body:

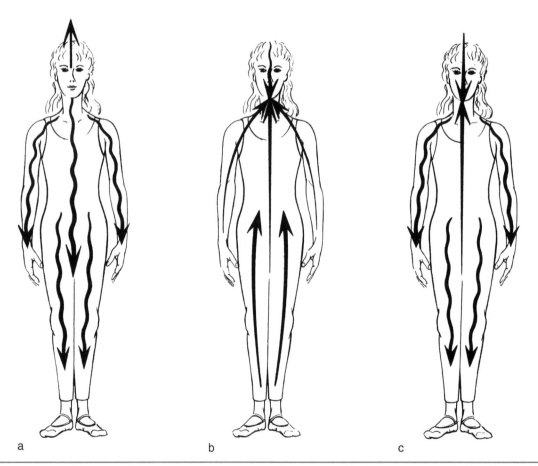

a   b   c

Figure 2.2 (a) Your head floats up and your body dangles easily from your head. (b) Think of the body providing support for the head. (c) "Mixed" postural model.

Your head floats up and your body dangles easily from your head (figure 2.2a). If you prefer to use a metaphor, you can think of your head as a balloon and your body as the string hanging down from it (see also figure 15.4). Practice this image while standing, walking, sitting down, and getting up.

Think of the body providing support for the head. The head balances easily on top of the spine (figure 2.2b). Metaphorically, you could think of the body as an upward surging energy that culminates at the top of the spine. The head floats on this energy. Another metaphor for this model would be that of a waterspout (the body) buoying the head on top. Practice this image while standing, walking, sitting down, and getting up. (See figure 18.5.)

After you have familiarized yourself with both models individually, try switching from one to the other in your mind's eye. Which of the models appeals to you? Is the experience you derive from the models the same or different?

Now let's create a "mixed" model as in figure 2.2c. We will transfer the dangling aspect from model A to the arms and legs only. We will use the upward energy from model B, but limit it to the core of the body and the spine. We will also use the concept of the head sitting on the top of the spine from model B). Practice this mixed image while standing, walking, sitting down, and getting up. Feel free to create other "mixtures."

The following paragraphs describe some of the basic postural models that will be of use to us in creating dynamic alignment.

ATOMARY AND PLANETARY

Coined by the Greek physical philosopher Democritus, the word *atomon* means "indivisible." According to his theory, the only things that exist are the atoms and the void. Everything we know of consists of different configurations of these atoms. Between the atoms is emptiness. After death, we disintegrate into these small, indivisible particles, a reassuring notion for the ancient Greeks to whom life after death was not necessarily an enticing prospect.

In the atomary or planetary postural model, the human body is seen as a miniature solar system, with all the parts oriented to and arranged around a common center, maintaining specific relationships within the whole (figure 2.3). Orientation toward a common center is, of course, an important image in dance. The parts may be seen to circle, loop, draw an ellipse, or spiral around the center. In the ideal arrangement, the relationship of the parts to the center creates the most efficient posture and movement. Function is impeded if the parts are too bunched or too spread apart. Depending on the individual, this may mean moving the parts lower, higher, nearer, or farther in relation to the center. Ultimately, "center" can be a point in space, a line, or even a plane.

As can be surmised from his famous drawing of a man in a circle, Leonardo da Vinci believed man's center to be at his navel. Da Vinci most likely got this idea from reading *De architectura* by the Roman builder Vitruv (33-14 B.C.), who writes:

The natural center of the human body is the navel. If a human being outstretches his hands and feet and one puts a compass on the navel as center, both the tips of the fingers and the tips of the toes are touched by the resulting circle. If the circle is connected to the human shape, so is the square. If one measures from the soles of the feet to the top of the head and compares the result with the distance between the outstretched arms one finds the same size in width as in height. (translated from *Tages Anzeiger Magazin* 1993, 39)

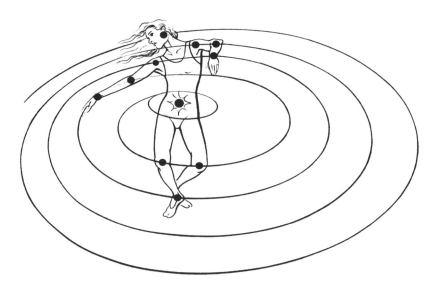

Figure 2.3   Human body as a miniature solar system.

BUILDING BLOCKS/CENTERS OF GRAVITY

Used by Mabel Todd and Ida Rolf, PhD, among others, this model visualizes the main units of the body, such as the head, torso, and pelvis, as building blocks. Todd (1972, 59) writes: "If the median line of the structure passes directly through the center of the weight of each block, gravity will exercise an equal pull on all alike, and the structure will stand." More units can be added to differentiate between the head, neck and shoulders, abdomen and pelvis, thighs, knees and feet. The parts can be pictured as square blocks, cylindrical spools, or spheres. They may consist of wood, stone, or bales of hay; they can be hollow or dense. In correct alignment, the line connecting centers of weight is perpendicular to the ground (see figure 2.4a). If centers are not aligned, muscular imbalance, strain, and inefficiency result (see figure 2.4b). As Rolf points out above, the three axes passing through each of the blocks—the vertical, sagittal, and transverse—need to be aligned with each other. Suzanne Klein-Vogelbach (1990), a German movement therapist, compares the body systems in motion to a chain but substitutes the picture of a block pyramid or cone for static analysis. If the lower block is larger than the one immediately above it, the connecting structures are subject to the least strain, as exemplified by the spine.

Looking down on a seated 12-month-old from above, one can clearly see the alignment of the "main blocks," head over pelvis (figure 2.5). A child playing with blocks intuitively applies these principles, sometimes with astonishing dexterity. When my three-year-old daughter and I build high towers of blocks, she can casually plunk another block on top of a tower without disturbing the fragile structure. These childhood experiences of structural balance can be called on to help fine tune the sense of alignment.

Figure 2.4   (a) In correct alignment, the line connecting centers of weight is perpendicular to the ground. (b) If centers are not aligned, muscular imbalance, strain, and inefficiency result.

Figure 2.5   Looking down on a sitting 12-month-old from above.

BUILDING BLOCKS

Focus on your spine and imagine it composed of wooden building blocks arranged in a somewhat imperfect fashion atop each other as viewed from the front. Allow a magic force (or magic fingers) to move these blocks into excellent alignment with each other. Think of this force as coming equally from both sides (figure 2.6).

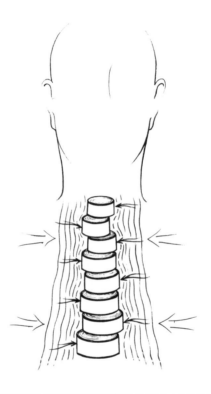

Figure 2.6   A magic force aligns the spine.

TENSILE COMPRESSION

A refinement of the building-block model, a tensile-compression model, holds the structure upright by creating a balance between elements that resist being compressed and those that resist being elongated. Figure 2.7 shows a "playground tree," as they are called in Switzerland. Vaguely reminiscent of the human form, it features all the elements of a tensile-compression model. Its central compression member, a wooden pole, can be likened to the spine. Arranged circularly around this axis are the tensile parts, the hanging ropes and girders. The top loop corresponds to the shoulder girdle hanging from the apex of the spine, the middle loop to the ribcage hanging from the thoracic spine, and the final loop, rather low and small, to the pelvis. Unlike the "tensegrity" model described below, this structure depends very much on the central pole for its integrity. To turn the playground tree into a tensegrity model, you could attach the ropes firmly on the top and bottom and take the slack out of them so that the structure would be maintained even if the tree were uprooted.

Figure 2.7   A "playground tree," in Switzerland, an example of a tensile-compression structure.

**TO BE
A TREE**

Imagine yourself to be a tree. Your arms are the branches and your upper body and legs are the trunk. Be aware of the upward force of the trunk and of the downward pull of the hanging branches. Now imagine being covered with snow. Watch the snow slide off the branches.

CIRCULAR CHAIN

Mabel Todd (1972) further differentiated the tensile-compression model, writing about three primary planes in the body that determine balanced alignment. A tensile plane created by the axes of the legs extends upward through the thigh joints. A compression plane created by the axis of the spine extends sideways and downward "through the lower border of the sacrum." The third plane is "produced by the laterally extended line of gravity." She found that the best balanced upright position is that in which these three planes are parallel to each other and "their forces in balanced action."

The balancing power between the compression members in the back and the tensile members in front is like the bicycle chain. Should something happen to make either portion of the chain relax or contract more than the other, it could not be moved forward, around, back, and up over the little wheel, and forward again smoothly. . . . Power, in the form of compression force, comes down the back and turns forward through the pelvis, and as tensile force it travels upward again from the pelvis to the top of the chain, through sternum, hyoid, mandible, to the base of the skull, and down the spine again. (p. 215)

The expression "up the front and down the back" originates from this model.

CHAIN OF ACTION

Go for a stroll and imagine that your walking movement powers a bicycle chain that moves up the front of the body and down the back (as described above). You can also use the image of an energy flow or a conveyor belt. Now try imagining yourself running to power the bicycle chain. Keep the chain moving smoothly up the front and down the back.

WATER-FILLED BALLOON/CELLULAR

Bones and muscles alone are not responsible for posture. The connective tissue and the organs are also involved. The organs are not just passive weights that need to be carried around by the bony framework and muscles; they can contract and even move around a bit. Muscles depend on the organs for their "fuel." Humans consists mostly of water contained in and between the cells and in the connective tissue, rather like water-filled balloons stacked on top of each other and bound together with large rubber bands (the connective tissue) to create a balloon tower. Deane Juhan (1987), instructor at the Trager Institute and author of *Job's Body*, describes a model of the human body as a water-filled balloon tightened by circular cords and shaped into a cylinder. He writes:

At this point, our cylinder does not really need an internal skeleton in order to remain upright; in fact, a skeleton could even be suspended inside the cylinder from the top, without its toes touching the bottom, supported solely by the tension of the pressurized walls of the bag. (p. 81)

This view is similar to the Noguchi exercise system described in *Zen Imagery Exercises*, by Shizuto Masunaga (1991), in which the body is viewed as organs and bones suspended in an aqueous solution, contained in a large bag of skin. If you cradle a baby in your arms, it feels like a little balloon filled with warm water, not like a structure that is primarily maintained by bony girders.

You can, of course, carry out the image ad infinitum: If the organs are water-filled balloons in their own right, then the "master" balloon would contain smaller balloons, which again would contain even smaller ones, the cells. In reality, the cells are not impermeable, as are latex balloons, but allow fluids to pass through their membranes by osmosis, permitting two adjoining compartments to balance their concentration of salts.

Whether corded or stacked, the balloon structure is capable of bearing weight yet is flexible and resilient enough to adapt to many situations. The same alignment principles as with the building-block model apply here. The importance of this model lies in the fact that it appreciates the supportive function of each individual cell, the connective tissue, the fluids, and organs of the body. It allows us to feel fluid inside the body while maintaining a clearly delineated structure outside. The bones can be seen as spacers that help maintain the overall shape. The ideal water-filled balloon model can bear and move weight without losing elasticity. Weight bearing actually helps distribute the nutrients within the balloon. Figure 2.8a shows a balloon-type model with spacers, and figure 2.8b a compression-type model.

Figure 2.8   (a) The bones can be seen as spacers that aid in maintaining the overall shape of the balloons. (b) In the compression model, weights rest on each other like building blocks.

TENSEGRITY

The tensegrity model, created by Buckminster Fuller, consists of beams and wires. The beams represent bones, and the wires are the muscles and connective tissue such as tendons, ligaments, and fascia. The great tensile strength of the wires absorb the force created by weight and thereby prevent the beams from being compressed. The building-block model requires heavier materials because the compression elements carry all the weight. The tensegrity model can carry larger loads than a building-block model of equal weight and remain resilient. If you compress a tensegrity model, it will rebound immediately (figure 2.9a & b). Alexandra and Roger Pierce (1989) contend that the body is more like a "tensegrity mast" than a single spherical structure. "A tensegrity mast is a vertical interweaving of individual tensegrity cells. The spine, with its tapestry of soft tissues built up around the outthrusting bony processes of each vertebra, bears a striking resemblance" (p. 39).

a   b

Figure 2.9   (a) If you compress a tensegrity model, (b) it will rebound immediately.

RUBBER-BAND TENSEGRITY

Seat yourself in an upright position without leaning against the back of your chair. Think of your spine as a tensegrity mast. Imagine the connections between the individual vertebra (spacers) to be numerous small rubber bands. These rubber bands maintain the upright integrity of the spine by keeping the vertebrae aligned on top of each other. Allow your spine to bend in any direction, stretching some of the rubber bands. As they contract, the rubber bands restore the spine to its original alignment. The spine is not rigid, but bobs back and forth for a while until coming back to its full upright resting position. Repeat the exercise in another direction, maintaining awareness of the reboundlike quality of the return to center.

TUBULAR

Stanley Keleman (1985), bodyworker and author of *Emotional Anatomy,* refers to the body as an organization of tubes and pouches. "Uprightness is the ability to structure and coordinate tubes, layers and pouches in the field of gravity" (p. 18). He describes three basic layers of the body. Digestion and breathing take place in the innermost layer; the middle layer provides support and movement; the outer layer, the skin, separates us from the outside world. The layering aspect of the tubular model is very valuable in creating a three-dimensional feeling of movement and alignment. Using the planes and axes to improve your alignment may limit your perspective to the notion of two-dimensionality. Tubes add depth.

LAYERS

1. **Three discrete layers:** Visualize the three basic layers of the body. The innermost is organ (or the marrow of a bone on a limb), the middle layer is muscles, and the outer layer is skin. Imagine initiating movement from the different layers. What is it like to initiate movement from the innermost layer? From the middle layer? From the outermost layer? Once you have gained a sense of the different layers, try to switch your awareness rapidly from one layer to another. Notice how this affects your movement.

2. **Interconnected layers:** So far you have been focusing on the depth of the three separate layers: deep to superficial, superficial to deep. Now focus on the concept of one layer interconnected throughout the body. Begin with the skin. Become aware of how it covers the whole body. Notice how stretchable and strong it is. Notice that it is constantly interfacing with the environment. Once you are attuned to your skin layer, move down to the muscle envelope and feel that layer throughout the body. Notice the inherent strength of the muscle, its potential for movement, its elasticity, its power. Now move to the next-deepest level, organ and bone. Concentrate on that layer throughout the body. Notice the stability of the bone and the plump, resilient volume of the organs. Finally, go to a even deeper layer—focusing your awareness inside the marrow of the bone and the core of the organs. Now head back up to the surface of the body. Guide your awareness back through the consecutive layers like a submarine coming up from a deep dive.

Each model discussed in this chapter brings us closer to the concept of dynamic alignment—the clear-cut shapes of the building block, the bounciness of the balloon, the depth of the tubular layer, the self-contained resilience of the tensegrity model, the loops and circles of the atomic model. Shape and motion are intertwined; motion creates shape, and the shape contains the motion that created it.

CHAPTER 3

Body-Mind Interactions

*I*n a sense, we are surrounded by a sea of information, impressions, and events, and we are constantly choosing to react or not to react to this environment. We also have an inner sea of thoughts, images, and emotions that influence our actions. This chapter investigates several theories on how imagery affects the body, but before considering them, let's try to better understand the concept of body-mind interaction by comparing the body to a ship at sea (figure 3.1).

The captain (the brain) looks out for danger and makes sure that the ship is on course. If danger arises, the captain needs to evaluate the situation and decide how to act. Fortunately, the ship's systems can function independently of the captain's conscious awareness, or he would not be free to steer the ship. He is assisted by information from his radar mate and lookouts (eyes, ears, nose) and his navigational charts (memory). The ship has a gyroscope (vestibular system, reflexes) that automatically keeps it upright. Experienced at sea, the captain has mastered many difficult skills (developmental memory, sensory memory). Once he makes a decision about what action to take, he does not need to run down to the machine room (muscles, organs) himself to change the speed and the direction of the ship. Instead he sends his command through an intercom (nervous system) that connects to the machine room. If the machine room operators (lower brain functions) have received clear orders, they perform all the necessary tasks independently of the captain. They make sure that the angle of the rudder and the rotations of the propeller (bones as levers) conform to the captain's orders. Occasionally, they will need to inform the captain of a problem with the machinery (uneasiness, pain). The captain may choose to go to a harbor (doctor, therapist) for repairs, or to ignore the problem for the moment if there is imminent danger.

Figure 3.1   The ship at sea is a metaphor for body-mind interactions.

The ship, of course, will only maneuver as well as the skill of the captain permits. To improve his skills, the captain might choose to take some additional training (body therapies, imagery training). It is said that a good captain identifies with and becomes one with his ship (physicality, sensory awareness, embodiment). He might find ways to become more aware of the special behavior of his ship at sea. He might also ask the mechanics to inform him about inherent problems with the rudder and motor (sensory acuity). The more he knows about his ship and its behavior in all kinds of weather, the better he will master difficult situations.

Obviously, we need to train our captain-brain to guide our ship-body with greater skill. Perhaps less obviously, the reverse holds true as well—our body teaches our brain. Once trained to be fully conscious, the sensory abilities inherent in our anatomy are a source of tremendous information. We must train ourselves to process and react to that information as soon as it is sensed.

Everyday thinking is not sufficient training for complex changes in our mind-body organization. Like muscles, our brains get stronger at whatever they do regularly. If we practice visualization techniques and use imagery, our brains get better at doing that. Conversely, if our minds regularly wander off into a jumble of random thought, they get better at that. To understand how best to train our thought process, we need to know more about the nature of consciousness.

THE BRAIN AND CONSCIOUSNESS

The basic question as put forth by Owen Flanagan (1991) in *The Science of Mind* is: "How can a physical device give rise to conscious experience?" Or stated in reverse: How can a purely mental experience, an image, give rise to a material change? Sweigard (1978), quoting Mabel Todd from a privately published book and from *The Thinking Body* (1972), explained that the image changes the patterning of the nervous system:

Change is possible only through the enormous task of recoordinating the neuromuscular pathways responsible for the habitual balance and movement patterns. It can be accomplished only if the method of teaching informs, stimulates, and challenges the student. . . . The idea of the movement alone suffices to start all movement along its most suitable path. This concept as a method of teaching was first proposed by Todd. Her basic premise was that "concentration upon a picture involving movement results in responses in the neuromusculature as necessary to carry out specific movements with the least effort." She derived this theory empirically, through extensive experimentation. (p. 6)

The above statements are based on the premise that the mind and the brain are identical. Having a thought or holding a picture in the mind sends a message through the nervous system because thoughts and the nervous system are connected.

Recent scientific studies and advances in physics have spawned fierce controversy over this premise of the inseparability of mind and body. The machinists explain consciousness as a pure function of the brain, which is a supercomputer whose functions they cannot explain. The mysterians, who contend that there is an aspect to mind that we just do not understand, counter that there is no way to scientifically evaluate an individual's way of experiencing.

A. Damasio, a neurologist at the University of Iowa, was interviewed in the October 10, 1991 issue of the *New York Times*. "When I ask you to think of a Styrofoam cup," he said, "you do not go into a filing cabinet in your brain and come up with a ready-made picture of a cup. Instead you compose an internal image of the cup drawn from its features. The cup is part of a cone, white, crushable, three inches high and can be manipulated."

Children cannot use imagery or conceive of a new object until they have experienced its various components in the terms mentioned above. The accumulation of sensory perceptions of an object lead to the ability to image it: "I feel heavy like a sack of sand." With children, you first have to establish these concepts by playing with a sack filled with sand—or a tin soldier, which is heavy and metallic, or a cloth doll, which is light and malleable. The process begins with the baby taking objects into its mouth. Using this sensory method, the baby soon learns to distinguish the feel of wood from the feel of cloth and the round shape of a teething ring from the square shape of a building block. Later, a doughnut can be appreciated as something that is round as well as soft; still later, one can also recognize the letter O in the doughnut. This is why an important part of imagery training is sensory stimulation.

BENDING YOUR ARM

Imagery affects the body. Experience in the use of imagery reveals that certain ways of thinking are more effective than others.

Ask a friend to extend one arm straight to the side and tell him or her that you are going to try to bend the arm. Notice how much your friend can resist your effort. Then tell your friend to think of a river of energy flowing through the arm and out into space. He or she should keep the image of energy flow alive as you again try to bend the arm. You will notice that the arm is harder to bend, even though your friend has not suddenly become stronger. Certain ways of thinking increase the body's force without altering the structure. (Adapted from Robert Fritz, author of *The Path of Least Resistance*, 1984.)

THE NERVOUS SYSTEM

Let's take a closer look at the intercom—the brain-body network called the nervous system. The sensory part of this network reminds of me of an enormous market. Like a messenger sent out from the brain to get specific information, for example, about the position of a limb, the nerve cell, or neuron, can be thought of as the brain's personal shopper. Amid the jumble of voices touting oranges, apples, broccoli, and turnips (information about limb positions), it needs to find lettuce only.

Neurons consist of a cell body with a nucleus, dendrites, and an axon. There are three types of neurons: sensory, motor, and interneurons. Interneurons allow communication between sensory and motor neurons, among other higher tasks. Sensory neurons gather information and provide stimuli for reflex activity, then bring the information to the attention of the central processing unit, the brain. Motor neurons carry commands to their attached muscles. If enough motor neurons are "firing," the muscle will contract.

There is, in fact, a strong similarity between firing a gun and stimulating a muscle. Instead of gunpowder, electrochemical activity is shot down the axon, the neuron's lengthy arm (Miller 1982). Because a single muscle fiber always releases the same amount of work at the same time, the motor neurons need to fire many shots at many fibers to activate an entire muscle.

The metaphor fails, however, to incorporate the whole class of operations in the nervous system that are not excitations but inhibitions. Is it possible to fire a shot that inhibits? Instead of stimulating a process, an inhibitory signal restrains or stops a process. Compare this concept to how a dam regulates the flow of water through a river. The amount of water arriving at the dam cannot be regulated, but what can be regulated is how much water is retained and how much is allowed to continue its flow down the river basin.

The body's dam is made of certain chemicals called amino acids (Gottlieb 1988). They are activated by command of the higher brain or cortex. The cortex "exercises all of its effect on the rest of the brain through inhibition" and ensures that the flood of messages from the lower brain is properly regulated (p. 40). Muscles receive excitatory and inhibitory messages all the time. If excitation dominates, the dam is not functioning and the river banks of the structure are overwhelmed. The result is loss of coordination and spasticity. As in the case of the ancient Nile, the whole country, or anything resembling conscious movement, may be lost. Good alignment, like water control, is a balance between sufficient stimulation of muscle activity to create an upright stance and sufficient restraint of muscular activity for this stance to be as effortless as possible.

The nervous system is divided into the central nervous system and the peripheral nervous system. The central nervous system consists of the brain and the spinal cord. The cord transfers information to and from the brain and is encased within the spine and the dura, an extra-strong connective tissue covering. The peripheral nervous system can be subdivided into the somatic and the autonomic systems. The somatic nervous system maintains contact with the outside world and sends impulses to the striated muscles used in gross and subtle movement. The autonomic nervous system controls the internal organs, which generally are not consciously controlled (although, with practice, such control can be exercised to a limited degree).

THE BRAIN

The human brain consists of some 100 billion neurons, which is roughly equivalent to the number of stars in the Milky Way (Flanagan 1991). The main portion of the brain, the cerebrum (Latin for brain), is divided into lobes that relate to the overlying cranial bones. The frontal lobes are said to control movement and produce speech; the parietal lobes receive and process data from the senses; the temporal lobes hear and interpret music and language; the occipital lobes specialize in vision.

The cerebellum, located just below the cerebrum, is responsible for skilled movement. The cerebellum retains the coordination of the dance movement sequences we have learned, storing them in the brain to be recalled when necessary. For example, when I was a student at NYU, my fellow students and I asked Larry Rhodes to demonstrate multiple pirouettes. Although he hadn't pirouetted in a long time, he astounded us with an astronomical (so it seemed to us) six or seven perfect turns. He explained that once the correct feeling for a movement has been firmly established, you only need to recall the sensation and the body will automatically (with the help of the cerebellum) reproduce even complex movement sequences.

Other brain structures include: the amygdala, which generates emotions from perceptions and thoughts; the hippocampus, which establishes long-term memory for facts and events; the thalamus, which relays sensory information to the cortex; and the brain stem, which controls automatic body functions such as breathing. The cerebral cortex, which is only a few millimeters thick, covers the four lobes that make up the left and right hemispheres of the brain.

Left Brain and Right Brain

Generally, the left hemisphere of the brain is considered to be logical, rational, intellectual, and deductive and the right to be metaphorical, intuitive, imaginative, and timeless. Recent studies, however, have proven such neat compartmentalizing of brain functions to be false. Some people seem to have language areas on the left and right sides of the brain. Patterns or organizations of language ability have been found to be as unique as fingerprints. Knowledge of words and concepts is found to be spread widely throughout the brain. A third-party mediator, the convergence zone, is needed to join the knowledge.

Much is being discovered about the hemispheric functions through people who have experienced partial damage to the brain. For example, people with damage to an area on the right side of the brain where sensory signals are processed exhibit unusual behavior. They are paralyzed on the left sides of their body, but, as the medical section of the December 6, 1994 *New York Times* reported, "when asked if they can tie their shoes or wave their left arm, they say 'of course I can.' Ask them to do it and they say, 'O.K., happy to oblige.' When they fail to move and the researcher asks why, they say, 'Give me time. I'll do it!' Eventually they may say that they don't feel like it now and will do it later."

According to Achterberg (1985), the left hemisphere controls the actions we tell ourselves to take: When we think "extend left leg," our bodies obey according to an established pattern of neuromuscular coordination. She writes: "The image system of the right hemisphere can also exert this control by sending thought pictures to the appropriate muscles; for example by imaging a hand opening like a flower" (124). Ernest Rossi (1986) states that the right hemisphere plays the primary role in the production of "raw" imagery, but that the images can be "cooked" in a secondary process by the left hemisphere. This can be seen in people's eye movements when they are being tested for imagery and spatial relations (p. 32).

Jacobson (1929) demonstrated that thinking intensely about a certain movement activates the appropriate neurons that control the muscles involved in that movement. Consistent with these findings, Sweigard (1978) showed that consistent practice of certain images results in an overall change in postural alignment. The ability to effect changes in the body through visualization seems to be quite "natural." As Achterberg (1985, 126-27) points out, "the wide dispersion of brain areas involved in imagery, especially visual imagery, indicates the importance of imagery to the survival of the species," and it seems that "the body/mind responds as a unit. No thought, no emotion, is without biochemical, electrochemical activity; and the activity leaves no cell untouched."

Body-Mind Pathways

Larry Dossey, MD, a physician of internal medicine with the Dallas Diagnostic Association and a former chief of staff of Medical City Dallas Hospital, states: "the mind can penetrate to the cellular level of the body and modify 'mindless' bodily processes. No longer in the category of mere folk wisdom or superstition, the body-mind connection is now a matter that has been demonstrated by careful scientific inquiry" (p. 24). Rossi (1986) proposes that the limbic-hypothalamic system of the brain is the prime candidate for the role of connecting mind and body. The hypothalamus is the major regulator of the body's basic systems, such as hunger, thirst, temperature, heart rate, and blood pressure. Recent research reported in the *New York Times* on August 31, 1993, shows that:

The brain uses virtually identical pathways for seeing objects and for imagining them—only it uses these pathways in reverse. In the process of human vision, a stimulus in the outside world is passed from the retina to the primary visual cortex and then to higher centers until an object or event is recognized. In mental imaging, a stimulus originates in a higher center and is passed down to the primary visual cortex, where it is recognized.

Mind Versus Body

Although we may have pathways from mind to body and from body to mind, questions remain. How did the mind get into the body? Is the body the only outlet for the activities of the mind? In attempting to solve these problems, are we trying to make bread without dough? There are several schools of thought.

The mysterians believe that there is an incomprehensible component to mind that is nonmaterial. Physicists Bohr, Heisenberg, and Margenau agree that "consciousness cannot be fully accounted for by the physical sciences as they are currently understood" (Dossey 1985, 163). Experiments in quantum optics show that events can influence each other faster than any signal can travel between them (Chiao et al. 1993). Perhaps images are not bound exclusively to the nervous pathways. "In quantum mechanics, the irrational has indeed come to pass: Interactions between the nonmaterial and material are commonplace" (Dossey 1985, 163). There is mounting evidence that the mind's influence can be found outside the body. If you divide a colony of worms with identical genetic material into two groups and give them to two separate groups of experimenters the following occurs: If the experimenters are told that the worms are especially intelligent, they will do better than the other group, whose "trainers" are told that the worms are especially "stupid." Since you cannot coax a worm with sweet talk or caresses, perhaps the attitude of the trainers influences the worms' ability to learn. Does this imply that the mind has effects outside of the brain? Thomas Nagel (Gelman et al. 1992), professor of philosophy at Rutgers University, explains as follows:

Imagine you come across a wiggly, crawly creature. You put it in a box and leave it awhile. When you open the box, a butterfly flies out, and you say, "Gee, that's got to be the wiggly, crawly creature." Nothing else went in, it has to be the same; but you can't imagine how it could be. That's the problem with consciousness, the butterfly that emerges almost magically from the brain. (p. 46)

Can the thinking mind affect things and people directly? Could it be that the mind of the teacher influences the student directly, not just through the use of words or touch? I have known teachers of dance with the attitude: "Very few people were made to dance, and certainly not most of the people here." Watching the students in such a class, I see tension, sullenness, self-distrust, and a failure to achieve. I am sure we have all experienced the benefits of receiving encouragement, or what is often referred to as positive "vibrations." It seems that the more deeply an image is held in the teacher's mind, the better she or he can convey it, and the more likely the student will react to it. Sometimes the presence of a certain teacher makes a student perform better. Perhaps the student's ability reflects the teacher's attitude. Perhaps the student feels more confident or simply wants to do better. Mabel Todd (1972) writes:

> When doing exercises under instruction we are apt to think that we move or direct the moving of the muscles. What actually happens is that we get a picture from the teacher's words or his movements, and the appropriate action takes place within our own bodies to reproduce this picture. The result is successful in proportion to our power of interpretation and amount of experience, but most of all perhaps to the *desire to do* [sic]. (p. 33)

And this desire to do will certainly be reinforced by a teacher who believes that you have the ability to succeed.

THE BODY'S NAVIGATORS: THE SENSES

> The capacities to think ahead, to recognize novel situations as harbingers of good or ill, and to speedily and imaginatively solve problems are among our most valuable capacities. They were almost key to our survival and proliferation of our species. . . . Overall, our brain is the most powerful anticipation machine ever built. (Flanagan 1991, 319)

When we consciously decide to move, we need information. To gather this information, we have six senses (including the sense of proprioception, which tells us our body positioning). We even have seven senses if you include right brain intuition or the sudden hunches we have all experienced. Even though the sensory information we receive seems complete, it is only relatively so. A shark's eyes, for example, according to the December 10, 1992 Zurich Edition of the *International Herald Tribune*, are equipped with lenses seven times as powerful as ours. Sharks can sense a drop of fish extract in quarter-acre lagoon six and a half feet deep. They even have a sense that enables them to detect bioelectric fields radiated by other sea creatures guiding them to the heartbeat of a flatfish buried in the sand.

Imagine you are in a dark room with a flashlight in your hand. If you shine the light in one direction, you can see a chair leg; if you shine it in another direction, you see a vase and a telephone. Although you only see parts of these objects, you still recognize them. If the flashlight emitted a ray of light as thin as a laser beam, this would be a good representation of how limited our senses are.

The brain purposely gives us a sense of completeness to make us feel safer. The senses send the brain information about our environment, registering what changes and what doesn't. The nervous system does not supply us with all the information it gathers with its sensors throughout the body. If it did, we would be flooded with information. The brain completes the picture, makes sense of it, gives it meaning (Schwarz 1988). An image localized in only one part of the body can powerfully influence the entire body. The image may be just one aspect of what is needed to change the whole. Trying to process all the information needed to make a change may be overwhelming, but give the brain just one hint and it can absorb the other changes below the level of consciousness.

The more you can develop the richness of your senses, the greater the impact of your images. Like a painter who needs to create the subtlest changes in hue, we need to hone the precision of our sensory images.

> ## SOME SENSORY IMAGES
>
> 1. **Sensory richness:** Imagine a waterfall in front of you. See the sunlight reflected in it, making it glitter like a fluid diamond; feel the pressure created by the water's force; hear the high and the low pitches of a crescendo; taste the water droplets on your lips; smell the pungent, enriched air.
>
> 2. **Sensory stimulation:** Carry a sack of rice on your head for a moment. When you remove it, you can readily experience your head floating upward. Walk on all fours with the same sack on your back, moving your back up and down. When you remove the sack, you will find that your back is more flexible and snakelike.
>
> 3. **Projection of a sensory experience:** Knead a piece of clay and experience its malleability. Then focus on a spot in your body that needs to be more malleable and project your experience into that area. Hold a piece of wood in one hand and a piece of cotton in the other. Notice the difference in texture and quality. Shift your concentration from the hardness of the wood to the softness of the cotton. Project this experience onto a point in your body that needs to transform from hardness to softness.

THE DEVELOPING MIND: THE ROLE OF IMAGERY

The baby's capacity to "image" may begin very early. The baby understands that an object exists, even if part of it is hidden, as early as five months of age. At this age, the baby realizes that the toy has a life of its own; it doesn't just exist when the baby looks at it. At about 12 months, the baby can purposely imitate other people by using a memory or an image of something it has seen. At about two years of age, the child can think ahead and solve simple logistical problems by imagining their outcomes. Before building a tower of blocks, the child can decide that it wants the tower to be very high and realize that it will need to collect blocks from all over the playroom to achieve this. The child is using its visual memory to plan ahead. It can imagine stories it has been told and can begin to play roles and imitate the contents of these stories. In the next stage, the child begins to practice social skills such as imaginary cooking and shopping, putting objects into new relationships with each other and endowing them with qualities (Kavner 1985). As a parent, you know not to pick up the Kleenex (they are bedcovers) and to leave the pencils in place (they are forks and spoons). The child can now also imagine new spaces—the bed is a boat, and beneath the covers is the wolves' den.

At age three, the imagination turns even more vivid. The child turns into a baby elephant munching on grass (straws), but can instantly change back to being itself if necessary (to drink something). It may go through a ritual of transformation, shaking and wiggling to convert to a crocodile, only to become a lion a minute later. Children love to imagine they are animals and to invent imaginary playmates.

Because children can constantly change themselves and the objects around them, many children's books and games are image based. A book I had when I was a child suggested: "A bird can fly. So can I, I can squirm like a worm, Swish, I'm a fish. A clam is what I am. Pitter pitter pat I can walk like a cat" (Krauss 1950). In another, I remember reading the following: "There was the school, so white in the morning sunshine it seemed to sparkle! Peter felt as if there were sparkles running around inside him, too. . . . Peter felt as lonely as a cloud going no-where" (Kingmann 1953). Both images contain interesting themes for dance improvisation, and it is certainly hard to slouch when you've got sparkles inside your body.

Fantasy rules at this stage of development. Children imbue inanimate objects such as dolls, fluffy animals, even spoons, with consciousness—a notion that lasts until about the age of eight. Hide and seek becomes very interesting. The child may still have difficulty imagining all the spaces to hide in the home, but once these places have been discovered, it can remember them and seek them out. Imagery is also tied to movement tasks at this age. Playing jump over the rope, my three-year-old requested the rope to go higher and said that she was going to jump up to the ceiling. She then jumped "higher than ever."

Magical thinking and fantasy become highly developed. At age four, children begin to use symbols, which also connect to their increased language skills. They can distinguish among a great variety of animals and even the individual characters of animals of the same kind. The four-year-old uses imagery in an increasingly adult fashion, relating it more to the adult reality of purpose and achievement. At this age, visualization is approaching the peak of its development (Kavner 1985, 69). The child can now place itself in unusual and inventive situations, see relationships among imagined situations, develop empathy, imagine what it is like to be mommy or daddy or a favorite character from a children's book, and envision all the things that this character has to deal with. Often the child has a favorite imaginary character that he or she likes to play. The child loves to invent stories around this character and will never tire of listening to a parent tell about the imaginary things happening in this character's life. At this age, improved motor control and balance enable more complicated movement sequences and the first signs of being able to learn gymnastic or dancing skills. A child will now begin to imitate even difficult movements that adults are practic-ing, such as a pirouette (spinning on one foot), and at times quite successfully. They are not concerned with failure or success, only with having fun.

Because children are natural imagers, even the smallest events are impor-tant sensory-image builders: carving a snowman, pouring hot applesauce, drawing with gooey finger paints, splashing through puddles, listening to the sounds at the zoo. The more our sensory memory is "filled" with tactile, visual, and kinesthetic information, the easier it will be to create imagery later in life (figure 3.2). Images based on childhood experiences are particu-larly powerful because everything is so new and fresh. The same image will evoke a different response from each person, because each sensory cupboard is filled with a personal mix of experiences. This holds true for all of the images contained in this book. The ones you respond to most are reinforced by your own sensory memory.

Figure 3.2   Images based on childhood experiences are particularly powerful.

THE PENDULUM

The following exercise is found in Kükelhaus's (1984) book *Urzahl und Gebärde* (*Primal Number and Gesture*, originally published in 1934). Hang a pendulum from your finger (if you don't have a pendulum, you can create one by hanging a key from a string). Now look away. Don't pay any attention to the pendulum, but think of it turning in a circle. Concentrate as much as you can on *circle*. Don't do anything else. Try not to consciously move your finger. You will find that the pendulum will begin to move in a circle. Try the same experiment using the image of a straight line or an ellipse. You will find that the pendulum's movement will reflect the image in your mind. Then stop the pendulum and try to recreate the same circle, line, or ellipsoid by intentionally moving your finger. You will find that it is much more difficult to create a delicate regular circle using conscious control. By using imagery, you can often achieve a more fine-tuned motion than with voluntary action.

You may have noticed that if you think about moving to the right and then actually move to the right, the movement will be smoother and easier. However, if you think about turning your head to the left and then turn it to the right, you will feel resistance; it will not be quite as easy. Your nervous system immediately starts creating the muscle setup that supports your imagined action. Many problems in dance can be avoided by recognizing and eliminating "contraindicated" imaging. For example, if you think "lean back" or "hold" while turning, it becomes difficult. Instead, support the action by thinking "turn" or "revolve" (see the chapter on pirouettes in *Dance Imagery for Technique and Performance*).

CHAPTER 4

Individual Patterns of Habitual Movement

*A*t birth, our movement repertoire is relatively small. As babies, we are equipped with only rudimentary survival movements, although recent research points to some astonishing capacities of babies (Schrader 1993). Inherent patterns guide the motor development of babies through a great variety of stages that finally lead to walking. Most likely, each stage of development needs to be processed to ensure motor coordination in adulthood.

Developmental therapies aim to help the patient reintegrate missing developmental stages. Infant reflexology therapist Vojta (1992) has demonstrated that by stimulating certain reflex points, a patient can rediscover important developmental movements. Vojta attributes some postural problems to the lack of certain movements during development.

Cohen (1993a) has found that the more developmental patterns we have experienced, the more avenues of expression are open to us:

> if the body is the instrument through which the mind is expressed, then one can just play more kinds of melodies, or different kinds of verse, timbre. (p. 100)

Four basic locomotor movement patterns can be observed in phylogenetic (evolution of the vertebrate animals) and ontogenetic (growth of the individual human being) development: spinal, homologous, homolateral, and contralateral, the first three of which are the more primitive motor patterns that underlie the future, more complex patterns (Cohen and Mills 1979).

The spinal movement pattern consists of bending the body forward, backward, and sideways, as in a forward or backward arch or a side bend in dance. In homologous movement, the upper and/or lower limbs move symmetrically at the same time, such as in a sauté (vertical leap) from first position.

The homolateral movement pattern is an alternation of motion between the sides of the body. The left arm and leg move together and the right arm and leg move together, as seen in the crawl of a lizard. Figure 4.1 shows a baby reaching for a toy in a homolateral pattern. In the contralateral pattern, the left arm and the right leg move together, or vice versa. This is the typical crawling pattern of infants before they begin to walk.

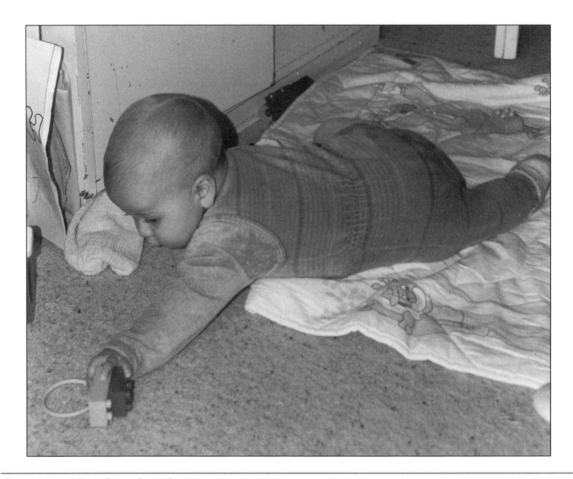

Figure 4.1   Homolateral reach.

WRONG HABITS THAT FEEL RIGHT

Personal style of movement is formed by genetic background, developmental patterns, and habits acquired continuously throughout life. Changing movement habits is not always easy because what you have been doing all along feels normal, and any change, even if it is to your advantage, feels abnormal. Unless you "evolve" into new movement habits very slowly, change sends an alarm through the body: "This is not the way you normally move, this is not your habitual posture, this is not your habitual alignment." There is a delightful description of the effects of change by Ellen Goodman of the *Boston Globe* in the August 26, 1993 Zurich edition of the *International Herald Tribune:*

A Catskill comedian used to tell a story about his first time away from home and home cooking. After a week in army boot camp his stomach started to feel funny. He was convinced that something was terribly wrong with his digestive system, and perhaps his entire body. Well, after much medical consultation, the problem was diagnosed. For the first time in his life he wasn't suffering from heartburn.

I remember working on the hand of a student who had been complaining about it feeling restricted. When I asked, "How does it feel now compared to your other hand?" he said that the hand I had worked on felt very smooth and flexible, whereas the other hand felt like a block of wood. He also said that the smooth and flexible hand did not feel right just yet; he needed to get used to this new sensation as part of himself.

When you begin to change something, you may go through a state of sensory "confusion" or disorientation. This may be a good sign, signaling that "rewiring" is taking place in your nervous system. Many of the familiar feelings related to how you move are becoming outdated, even though they still feel more comfortable and the new way of moving feels strange. You can probably see that you are doing better, but for a new movement habit to really take hold, it needs to feel natural. However, this does not mean that if you are not feeling confused you are not making progress.

CHANGING WITH THE HELP OF IMAGERY

There is no one specific reaction to progress and change. Some dancers learn consistently, others in spurts and starts, and still others seem to be making no progress until virtually overnight their ability moves to a higher level. At times, a certain pressure needs to build up before any great improvement can be made. Therefore, don't feel frustrated if you are doing your best and it doesn't seem to make much difference. Your body and mind may be preparing for a big leap forward.

When you do experience a breakthrough, there is a terrific new sensation of freedom and ease of motion. Often such "experiences" have been prepared by workings of the nervous system that are beneath our conscious awareness. At times, you may have such an experience and there will be no trace of it the next day, although usually you will regain it with time.

If you want to ensure that you will be able to recreate an experience more readily the next day, tie it to an image that symbolizes the experience. The image can be kinesthetic, visual, or tactile. The idea is to recall the experience by visualizing its symbol.

Perhaps after a training session your shoulders feel free of tension as never before. Create an image to go with the feeling. Don't be satisfied with simply thinking, "Gee, my shoulders feel looser." Think of an image that describes the looseness more precisely. Is the sensation like having a silken scarf draped around your neck? Is it like fluffy cotton balls falling on your shoulders? Or like a stream of warm water being poured over them?

Once you have chosen an image, you only need to think "fluffy cotton" or "silken scarf" to recall the sensation. By practicing calling forth the image regularly until the new sensation has established itself more firmly in your subconscious, you will speed up the process of creating better alignment and movement.

Once you have become more experienced, you can rely less on imagery from external sources and work with images that arise spontaneously out of the vast resources of your mind, out of your "movement intuition."

The development of imaging skills can be divided into three phases:

1. Learning the basic imagery concepts and skills—developing an understanding of the process.

2. Creating imagery from external sources and practicing calling it forth over and over.

3. Working with your own spontaneous imagery. Although in this phase you may still be using external imagery, you are sufficiently trained to know that an appropriate image will present itself when needed.

MOTIVATION AND CHANGE

In working with imagery, you must be highly motivated to create the focused imagery necessary for success. You can't be wondering "Am I there yet?" as you try to achieve a desired movement goal. You must focus on experiencing the process as fully as possible, because it is that heightened awareness that is going to make you succeed in reaching your goal.

Let's try a little experiment. Take a moment to raise your arm above your head. Did you actually do it? Or did you say to yourself, "I'll just imagine it; I don't really feel like lifting my arm." If you did raise your arm, did you do it with pleasure, or were you apathetic?

The higher the "motivational energy," the better the quality of movement. We've all had days when we didn't feel like working out or taking a class (rarely, of course). On such days it is more difficult to get moving (at least initially) than on a day when you're just raring to go. Injuries usually occur on days when you are less than perfectly motivated, providing further evidence of the impact mental state has on movement quality. When we are tired or uninvolved, we feel the effort of each movement. When we are energized or involved, movement is effortless and time flies. Our images are crystal clear, our senses are acute, every fiber of our being seems to be cooperating. The motivation seems to be coming from the cells themselves; our muscles seem to have an intelligence of their own. It is as if they hardly need to be told what to do, they are so involved in the task and ready to perform it.

THE BODY IMAGE IN ALIGNMENT

Achterberg (1985) writes about the neurological basis of the body image:

> . . . body image itself is generally lateralized in the right hemisphere. When damage occurs in the parietal lobe of the right hemisphere through a stroke or injury, the patient may fail to recognize part of his or her own body. (p. 122)

The term "body image" has gone through conceptual changes in this century. It can be thought of as the sum of our visual, tactile, gustatory, olfactory, and kinesthetic sensations, but it also includes awareness of posture, intentionality, aims, and inclinations. Heinz Werner (1965), editor of *The Body Percept,* points out another aspect of body image: "The spatiality of the body (unlike that of external objects) is not a spatiality of mere positions but a spatiality of situations" (p. 100). Werner describes an image used by Merlau-Ponty to clarify his point: "If I stand in front of my desk and lean on it with both hands, only my hands are stressed and the whole of my body trails behind them like a tail of a comet" (Merlau-Ponty 1962, 100).

Body image is a dynamic phenomenon, not just a sensory image. Every activity continuously modifies it. Body image includes our experience of the body's enclosing surface, the shape and volume contained within this surface, its weight and closely related tension state (Naville 1992). We can train ourselves to perceive these elements more clearly and distinctly through imagery exercises, thus modifying the overall body image. The detailed and simultaneous perception of many elements of the body image should be an important part of improving your alignment. In dance, the term *physicality* refers to a very complete, moment-to-moment experience of motion based on a highly differentiated body image. In this sense, physicality helps us become aware of our moment-to-moment changes in alignment.

As the child develops, so does its body image. The child must first learn to distinguish between itself and the environment, and only slowly does it become aware of its own body shape, of its individual body parts, and of their names and interrelationships.

Language is a prerequisite for detailed body orientation. Once we can imagine a body part and can see its form and place in space, we can begin to talk and finally write about it. Therefore, our choice of words when speaking about an image is related to the response the image will elicit. Also, the same words can cause a variety of responses based on the individual's body image and sensory memory. If you say: "Imagine your shoulders (the location, shape, surface, feeling of the shoulders are assessed) dropping downward" (strictly speaking, the shoulders keep their shape and surface contours as they move downward), you address a different mix of body image elements than when you say: "Imagine your shoulders melting downward" (the shape and the surface outline of the shoulders change as they move downward). Yet other responses may result from using words such as: "Imagine your shoulders hanging . . . falling down . . . sliding downward." Each individual's exact response will depend on his or her personal experience of the language that has been used. Often the only way to find out which choice of words is best (has evoked the greatest response) is by requesting feedback from the individual.

One of the few ways to gain direct insight into people's body image and specific alignment problems is by looking at drawings they create of themselves. A drawing can reveal a sense of the relative importance and awareness of one's body parts. Of course, the subjects must not be aware that their drawings are being used for this purpose or they may portray themselves as having well-aligned bodies even if they do not.

The drawing in figure 4.2a was done by a four-year-old child. The head is differentiated from the torso, but there is no neck. There are arms, legs, and a slight indication of feet. The drawing in figure 4.2b was done by the same child at age five. Note that several new components of the body image have arrived: hands with individual fingers, eyebrows, ears, and distinct feet.

a   b

Figures 4.2   (a) Drawing by a four-year-old. (b) Drawing by a five-year-old.

PERCEIVING YOUR BODY IMAGE

1. **Drawing your body image:** Once a week, make a drawing of yourself in standing position as viewed from the front and another as viewed from the side. Put the drawings in a book, date them, and do not look at them for at least three months (do not look at the last drawing you created when you put the newest one in the book). After three months, place them side by side in chronological order. Do you detect a pattern? A shift in your

alignment? This is especially interesting if you are working on your alignment during the documented period.

2. **Malleable clay:** Lie on the floor. Think of yourself as a piece of clay that is very malleable. Now think of the most elegant and skilled hands touching your body and beginning to shape it into the ideal, most functional form. Try imagining the hands of Michelangelo or Leonardo da Vinci creating a beautiful work of art out of your body, such as the sculpture of "David" in Florence, Italy.

3. **Imaginary sculptor:** You are made entirely of clay. Move your body into a variety of postures and let the imaginary artist create your ideal form. Watch as the artist's imaginary hands improve and perfect each pose you get into. Don't limit yourself to traditional shapes and forms; any position can be perfected by the imaginary sculptor. Do not worry about what perfect is; let the sculptor take care of that.

Every shape and position we take, especially if it is new, contributes to our personal body image. The relationship between body image, especially its visual and kinesthetic components, and what we actually look like is important in dance. Unlike the artist, we cannot step back from our drawing and compare our inner pictures with the outer reality. Looking at videotapes of ourselves is often a very surprising experience. We notice that the way we felt, or what we pictured ourselves doing, does not necessarily correspond to what we see on the screen.

Proprioception is an important part of our overall body image. The term is derived from the Latin *proprio* (self) and *capto* (to grasp). The proprioceptors, the sensing devices that tell us the exact position of our limbs, are located in our skin, muscles, and joints. The other major organs of balance and body position are tiny stones called otoliths, which are located in the vestibule of the inner ear. They hang on stalks called hair cells that are stimulated by the stones when we move our heads. Another type of hair cell floats in a fluid in the ear's semicircular canals. When the fluid moves as we change our head position, the hairs move. Of course, our eyes are the most obvious determinants of our position in space, but thanks to all the other assistants of our sensory apparatus, we can close our eyes and still determine where we are in space. All of this information is relayed to the brain, where the evidence of motion is interpreted and pieced together.

Dancers are specifically trained to perceive shapes, and usually reproduce them better than nondancers, but anyone can learn to improve their "shape memory." In many instances, it is useful to be fully aware of one's own position and simultaneously control an outside activity. While supporting a partner in a pas de deux, for example, a dancer maintains his or her partner's equilibrium as well as his or her own posture. Inferior alignment in this situation can cause injury. Images increase awareness of position and dynamics, "filling" the body with new sensory information and enriching the body image.

The richer the body image, the more pathways there are to improving your alignment. Concentrating on position provides valuable feedback for fine tuning the body image and, with it, your alignment. Many movement teachers are skilled at filling in "gaps" in a student's body image by pointing out parts of the body that seem to be "unfelt" or "unclear." A dance teacher might say: "See the whole shape of your back, feel the leg moving through space, see the line of your arabesque." Touch is a powerful way to influence body image because it is one of the first ways we experience the boundary of our body. The dancer's experience of body boundary may be radically different from that of the nondancer. A dancer's relationship to space can be compared to the painter's relationship to the canvas. You want to be able to paint with very fine strokes, not just broad ones. Many exercises to increase awareness of body boundary are featured in *Dance Imagery for Technique and Performance.*

The way a person experiences his or her surrounding space can actually influence alignment. If the space is experienced as threatening and constricting, the body may shrink away and become tense. If the space is experienced as welcoming and confidence-inspiring, the body will tend to open up and release tension. It is interesting to observe passengers leaving a cramped airplane after a long journey from a cold climate. As they emerge to what seems like infinite space and warmth, their alignment changes: Their bodies can finally take the space they need.

Relationship to space is pivotal in improving alignment. Many factors besides size influence how your body responds to a certain space: the people in it, past experiences you have had in the space, the colors, the odors, even the texture of the furniture.

TAPPING THE POSITION

Move into various positions and let your partner tap you lightly all over your body. The contact will help you sense the whole position as clearly as possible before you move into another position, where your partner begins tapping you again. Repeat the exercise several times until you can move from position to position and mentally scan your whole body to experience its total surface. As you gain experience, try to perceive the entire body surface at once.

INFLUENCING BODY IMAGE

Use specific images to influence your body image. If your arms are short, imagine them long. If your feet don't point, imagine perfect feet. Think of yourself as perfectly proportioned. If you feel your back is short and tight, create an ideal back for yourself. Think of yourself as having the power contained in Aladdin's lamp, of knowing that your wishes will be granted.

EXTERNAL SPACE AND ALIGNMENT

During the course of a day, observe how your body reacts to the various spaces you enter. Try to change the spaces you are in using your imagination. If you find a room constricting, imagine it to be the most spacious and luxurious room possible.

CHAPTER 5

Imagery Categorization

*I*magery can be categorized in several ways. These sometimes overlapping classifications illuminate the many applications of imagery.

SENSORY IMAGERY

When we hear the term imagery, we usually think of pictures in our mind's eye. But an image need not be visual, it can be located in any one of our senses. Often the most powerful imagery is composed of a variety of senses. If you imagine yourself standing under a waterfall you may have the sensory experiences of seeing and feeling the water pouring down your body, hearing it thundering all around you, smelling its fresh scent as well as tasting it in your mouth. By using many senses you begin to enrich the image, which makes it more effective. This is not always easy, because most of us prefer to image in one or two senses. Notice which type of sensory imagery feels least comfortable to you and gradually add these elements into your imaging practice.

Visual

Most people are familiar with this the type of imagery. When you see your fingers extending into space or your head floating up like a helium-filled balloon, you are using visual imagery.

Kinesthetic

Kinesthetic imagery involves the physical "feel" of a movement. For example, you may imagine how the body feels in the air in a split jeté before actually performing one, or imagine the space around you to be soft and cushiony. Noticing kinesthetic changes is a very important tool for realignment as well as for accomplishment of any movement.

KINESTHETIC IMAGING

Take a few minutes to move one of your feet in many different ways. Imagine it to be as malleable as a piece of clay. Wiggle it, shake it, circle it, tap it against the floor, pick up and release an imaginary towel with your toes. Then stand up and compare the feeling in your left and right foot and leg. You may notice that your legs feel as though they are aligned differently. One leg may seem to have more volume, or to be straighter than the other.

Tactile

Tactile imagery is closely related to kinesthetic imagery. In fact, the two are sometimes combined under the joint heading of "tactile-kinesthetic." I like to distinguish the two because purely kinesthetic imagery need not be elicited by touch, but it is a prerequisite for tactile imagery. If you can remember how a teacher adjusted your pelvis to correct its alignment, you can repeat the process in your mind's "tactile eye." In this way, you can reinforce the image until it becomes ingrained in your nervous system. Practicing imagery with a partner is aided by specific tactile imagery of where, how, and when you touch or are touched by your partner. You may also conjure imaginary massaging hands to release shoulder tension.

Proprioceptive

Proprioception, the sense of body position, is not usually considered in its own category. However, I do so because there is imagery that is proprioception-specific.

PROPRIOCEP-TIVE IMAGING

1. Stand with your weight equally distributed on both feet. Lift one foot off the floor and balance for a moment. Do the same with the other leg. Lift one leg again and imagine that a clone of that leg is still standing on the floor. Notice the difference between your ability to balance when using and not using this image.

2. Lift your arms overhead and bring them back down to the sides of your body. Repeat the movement. Now imagine that you have a pair of imaginary arms placed overhead. As you lift your real arms, lower your imaginary ones, and vice versa. How do lifting and lowering your arms feel different with or without this proprioceptive imagery?

Olfactory

The sense of smell, very important for animals, is less important for humans than the visual and auditory senses. Yet olfactory images can be powerful. A smell can instantly conjure the distinct ambiance of a place visited long ago. Smells attract and repel us like no other sensory stimulation. Try the olfactory image of moving through a space filled with the scent of a luscious perfume and notice how it affects your posture.

Auditory

Auditory (aural) imagery can be used by musicians to hear beforehand the sound they want their instruments to produce. Dancers can hear the music in their "mind's ear" while practicing certain dance sequences. Before doing a pirouette, it is helpful to have a sense of hearing your turning rhythm. Jaclyn Villamil, ballet teacher and Laban Movement analyst, once suggested the auditory image of hearing an ascending scale as you raise your leg into extension. In alignment practice, you can "hear" the strength of your central axis, imagining it to be a powerful geyser. You might also remember the pitch and timbre of a helpful correction you received in class and can store it in your auditory memory for future use.

Gustatory

Gustatory images govern the realm of taste. A good cook can imagine how a sauce will taste before mixing the ingredients, or how the taste of a soup will change depending on what spices are added. An actor might imagine the tastes his or her character encounters during a lunch scene. Clay Taliaferro, original member of the José Limon dance company who is famous for his role in Limon's choreography of *The Moors Pavane,* directed the dancers at a workshop in France to be involved in the movement as if tasting it, as if chewing on a sweet, succulent carrot.

DIRECT AND INDIRECT IMAGERY

Direct imagery is a nonverbal representation of an actual movement (Overby 1990). You are using direct imagery when you visualize your fingers extending into space. Indirect imagery is metaphorical; an external event or object is projected onto and used to clarify a process or movement. When you envision your scapula rotating as you elevate your arm, you are using direct imagery. When you picture your scapula as a wheel, you are using indirect imagery. Visualizing an arm cutting through space is direct imagery. Once the arm cuts through space as a sword, the imagery becomes indirect.

ABSTRACT AND CONCRETE IMAGERY

In her book *Moving from Within,* Alma Hawkins (1991), founding chair of the UCLA Dance Department, distinguishes between concrete and abstract images. Images such as stretching an elastic band are concrete, whereas the image of something unpleasant pushing you down is abstract. Abstract images readily allow you to develop their content. They are psychological in that they depend on what bubbles up from your inner reaches. Concrete images are fixed by general consensus. Everyone will agree on the basic look of a snake, even though snakes have different lengths and color patterns. When dancers are motivated by "a force" pulling them to the same spot on stage, they are using an abstract image.

INNER AND OUTER IMAGERY

Imagery can also be categorized by where it is located. Children can transform their outer reality by conjuring an imaginary forest or beach. In dance, you can place your image inside your body, on the surface of your body, in the near or intimate space surrounding you, in your slightly larger personal space, or on the whole stage, even the entire world.

Images are used extensively in sports psychology to paint a vivid picture of a goal you would like to achieve as if it has already been achieved. These images can have both internal and external components, such as the crowd cheering and how your body feels once you have succeeded.

Inside the Body

These are images that improve alignment, such as visualizing the central axis inside your body. Inner imagery may also be used to modify your movement quality, such as imagining that you are made of molasses. Many interesting images can be explored in this area, such as imagining a wind blowing inside you or imagining that you are filled with water. You will find many other examples in the section on improvisation in *Dance Imagery for Technique and Performance.*

I hope that you never fracture a bone or tear a muscle, but if you do, you may be able to use inner imagery to speed your recovery. Gerald M. Epstein, MD (1989), in his book *Healing Visualizations,* reports of mending a bone with imagery in three weeks instead of the expected three months. He had the patient visualize the ends of the bone knitting together for three minutes at three- to four-hour intervals. There is no scientific explanation for this dramatic increase in speed of recovery, although many similar cases have been reported.

Outside the Body

As previously mentioned, images that control the external environment can likewise change the body's alignment and energy. Because you can mentally transport yourself, you suddenly look, feel, and move differently.

VAST PLANE— SMALL ROOM

Imagine yourself on a vast plane at sunrise. See and feel the sun coming up over the horizon. Then imagine yourself stuck in a small room without any windows. Notice how the images affect your posture, your alignment, even your breathing.

Two of the first highly acclaimed athletes to apply mental rehearsal imagery were French Alpine skier Jean Claude Killi and high jumper Dick Fosbury (Dardik & Waitley 1984). Killi would picture himself skiing down the slope, seeing all the bumps and curves and planning precisely how he would pass through the poles. Fosbury visualized himself clearing the height he had selected. Employing a similar technique, a dancer might imagine going through a dance routine with perfect ease or finding the through-line of an entire dance by running through it mentally.

SPONTANEOUS IMAGERY

This book contains hundreds of images for you to practice and hone your imagery skills. Ultimately, you will be creating your own imagery, or, as I experience it, you will be discovering imagery. Many of the images that I use in a class setting or when training myself come to me "out of the blue." They suddenly and most appropriately appear on the screen of my mind's eye (or any of the other senses). Obviously, this is a highly intuitive function, but I believe that the years of training with "outside" imagery enabled the mind/body to "understand" my training and teaching needs and create an ongoing link between the task at hand and the image that will be most helpful in the specific situation.

Even when working with an image that you have not discovered yourself, the specific way in which you experience an image is highly individual. No two people experience the same image identically. Therefore, the descriptions of the images in this book, as well as the drawings, should not be considered absolute, but as a starting point for your individual explorations. In this sense you are always using your own imagery.

Sometimes imagery appears as a spontaneous flow, a free association of images. Sometimes these images seem very related, at other times they seem to be jumping from one topic to the other. Here is an example of spontaneous free association imagery that I experienced recently:

Shoulder blades bouncing, as if on a physio ball, . . . they are socks filled with sand that now pours out, . . . they are fluffy like feather-filled pillows, . . . the eyes are yawning, they seem crooked, . . . sending breath into the sockets, . . . the sockets gently cradle the eyes, like a cherry sitting in pudding, . . . pelvic floor expands as I inhale, sitz bones widen, parting like curtains in a draft of wind.

How does such a spontaneous chain begin? It seems that the mind/body "calls" you to the right spot, linking the areas that need attention, creating new imagery to keep the input into the mind/body system fresh and stimulating.

SELF-TEACHING IMAGERY

Certain types of imagery are helpful in providing feedback on the status of your alignment and body balance. Usually it takes a considerable amount of practice before one can use imagery in this fashion. Examples of this kind of image are:

- While in a supine position, imagine yourself to be floating on a magic carpet. As the carpet lands on the floor, do both sides of the carpet touch down at the same time? Does the right touch down before the left? Does the bottom part touch down before the top? The way the carpet lands can inform you of imbalances and preferences in the use of your body halves.

- While in a supine position, imagine the pelvis to be a burlap sack filled with rice. There is an open seam on either side of the sack. Let the sand pour out of the left and the right sides of the sack. Does it flow out of both sides equally or does it seem easier to visualize the flowing on one of the sides? If it is easier to image the flow on the right side as opposed to the left, this could indicate increased muscular tension on the left side of the pelvis.
- Imagine you can exhale through your sitz bones, as if they were straws. Does it feel like you can do this equally on both sides? If a sitz bone "does not want to exhale," this could indicate tension in the musculature surrounding the sitz bone and most likely the corresponding hip joint.

CHAPTER 6
General Guidelines Before Imaging

$\mathcal{A}$s with any other skill, the ability to image will benefit greatly from systematic practice. To obtain maximum benefit from such practice, it is important to approach it with the proper attitude.

CONCENTRATION

What is concentration? Mira Alfassa (1982a) writes: "It is to bring all the scattered threads of consciousness to a single point, a single idea. Those who can attain perfect attention succeed in everything they undertake; they will always make rapid progress" (p. 143).

Concentration is total focus on what you are doing. If your thoughts toss about randomly like tumbleweed, using imagery will be difficult, if not impossible. To test your ability to clear your mind, try thinking about nothing for just one minute. Why would you want to think about nothing? It creates an open space that can be filled at will with specific content. Clearing your mind, focusing on your breath or on a specific point or object, is also very calming. Many relaxation techniques are based on this ability. Because we take the thoughts flying around in our head for granted, it feels normal to be in a scattered state. Eminent performing artists and athletes, however, connect their peak physical performance experience to an elevated level of mental concentration.

Calming the mind allows us to experience the body as a whole. Shunryu Suzuki (1970), who helped popularize Zen meditation in the West with *Zen Mind, Beginner's Mind*, writes: "To stop your mind does not mean to stop the activities of mind. It means your mind pervades your whole body" (p. 41). Zen even uses images to explain concentration: The mind is as quiet as an undisturbed lake. Thoughts are like clouds passing by that want to reflect in the lake. Don't watch the clouds, let them go by. Once you can control what does and does not reflect in the lake, your imaging will become very effective. This is also true for the spontaneous production of imagery. The intellectual analytical mind needs to be calmed so that it becomes receptive to imagery. Cathy Ward, former soloist with the Erick Hawkins Dance Company, teaches: "You lose your concentration and your movement stops." June Balish recounts the teaching of Jennifer Muller, who put it even more simply: "Technique is 99 percent awareness" (author notes).

Total concentration, therefore, is a prerequisite to good dancing and alignment. Without it your dancing will be like riding on a road full of potholes as you drift in and out of full consciousness. You will be unable to connect movements and create movement flow; you will be unable to feel your whole body in space; you will be unable to clearly express the choreographer's intent. Dancers often miss out on the full benefits of dance class because they spend a good part of it just getting focused. Although for most of us, learning how to concentrate is a matter of practice, Larry Rhodes once said that he never had trouble concentrating because he was just so interested in dancing.

Concentration is essential in maintaining optimal alignment through a complicated movement sequence. In the time it takes the distracted mind to regain full concentration, an unsupervised body part can slip out of alignment and sabotage your technique. Because posture is maintained by innate reflexes, you won't fall over if you don't concentrate on your body, but in performing difficult movements, maintaining total concentration adds another dimension of control.

According to the May 28, 1993 Zurich edition of the *International Herald Tribune*, eminent conductor Kurt Masur was once more than a minute into leading the New York Philharmonic in a performance of Charles Ives's "The Unanswered Question" when he suddenly signaled the orchestra to stop playing. Turning to the surprised audience of 2,700 concertgoers in Avery Fisher Hall, he advised: "Just concentrating makes you healthy, so if you are listening with the same concentration to our music making, you would enjoy it and will forget to cough."

FOCUS

1. **Think about nothing:** Sit in a comfortable position and try to think about nothing for just one minute. When you first try this, you will find that your mind wanders and every little noise or itch may distract you. Just keep practicing several times a day. Taking one minute out of your schedule is certainly not a major sacrifice. If you find it impossible to think about nothing, select a point of focus or keep track of your breathing, counting each breathing cycle as one count. Focus on an object such as a stone, a shell, or a point on the curtain. Choose something to focus on that is plain rather than thought-provoking.

2. **Area of focus:** One method that I have found very helpful in discovering things about the body is to concentrate on a certain anatomical structure and see what ideas about the area emerge. I usually choose an area in

which I want to create more motion, flexibility, or awareness. Select an area of the body that you would like to concentrate on, such as the connections between the ribs and the spine. Move in any fashion you desire and keep your focus on that area. Notice the images that arise. If your mind wanders off to an irrelevant subject, gently bring it back to that area.

3. **Angle of observation:** Another important factor in visualizing body parts is your angle of approach. Watching the spine from the front is not the same as watching it from the back, or from above or below. Choose an area of the body such as the hip joint, and use your mind's eye to watch it from differing angles as you move. Watch it from in front, in back, below, and above. Certain angles will give you insights that others will not provide.

4. **Subdividing time:** Another very important aspect of concentration is the ability to "make more time." If you can concentrate intensely on a given action, time seems to lengthen, giving the nervous system an opportunity to learn more about the action and induce necessary corrections. Raise your arms above your head, then lower them. Perform this action again, paying as much attention to every moment of the action as possible. Note how the sensations you experience are totally different.

POSITIONS FOR ANATOMICAL IMAGERY WORK

Most of the images described in this book can be practised in a variety of situations: lying on the floor, sitting, walking, waiting for a bus, mowing the lawn, or dancing. When you start imaging, I recommend practicing 20 minutes a day in one of the supine positions described below. Some images are specific to standing or seated positions. Generally speaking, a balance among practice in the supine, sitting, standing, and moving positions is advisable. As Irene Dowd notes, the process

of imagining, or visualizing movement in the mind's eye can be done while you are not actually performing any movement whatsoever, or while you are performing a simple or complex movement pattern that is different from what you are visualizing, or while you are performing the same movement pattern that you are visualizing. (p. 7)

Yoga Resting Position

The yoga resting position, sometimes called the "corpse pose," is suitable for most imagery exercises. However, when the legs are outstretched, their weight tends to pull up the top of the pelvis, increasing the curvature of the spine, especially in the lumbar region. Viewed from the side, the spine is shaped like a double-S containing two convex and two concave curves. The concave curves, or hollows, of the back are called lordosis; the convex areas are called kyphosis. The Y ligament, the strongest in the body, connects the femur to the front of the pelvis and causes leverage action of the legs on the pelvis, tilting it forward. This

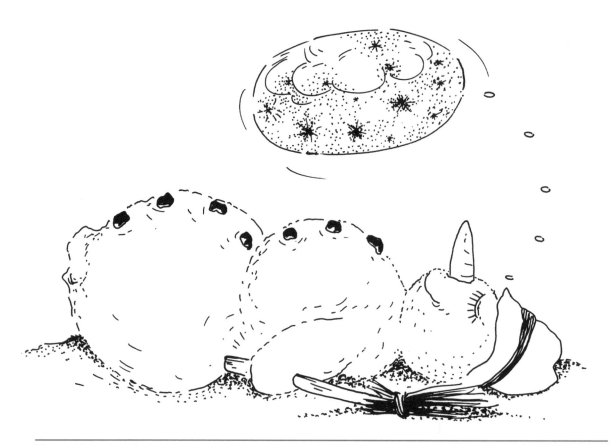

Figure 6.1   For obvious reasons, the snowman images snow.

in turn results in an increase in lumbar lordosis. If this position elicits pain or tightness, roll up a towel and place it under your knees. Elevating the knees should be sufficient to allow the lumbar spine to rest on the floor (figure 6.2). If the lordosis is very pronounced, place a soft towel under the small of your back as well, allowing the lumbar spine to rest on the towel; however, do not let this cushion push the lumbar spine into increased lordosis.

To align your head with your spine, it may be helpful to put a rolled-up towel under your neck and a cushion under your head. Your face should be horizontal to the floor, with your chin neither pointed up toward the ceiling nor pulled into your neck. In some instances, it is desirable to have your head slightly flexed, with your neck subtly lengthened to aid energy flow, but in no case should your neck be extended. Small homemade pillows filled with barley or millet make fine cushions for various padding purposes.

Finally, placing a small, lightweight pillow on your stomach may lend a feeling of weight and centeredness and increase your awareness of the breathing process. As we inhale, the abdominal wall rises a little, and the slight resistance afforded by the weight of the pillow increases the tone of the breathing musculature. As we exhale, the abdominals contract, move down, and aid in expelling air from the lungs. The added weight of the pillow slightly increases the expiratory force of the abdominals, making exhalation more complete. Finally, the pillow also reflects the give of the organs as they are slightly compressed on inhalation. After practicing a while with a pillow, you can use your sensory memory to place an imaginary pillow on your stomach for a similar effect.

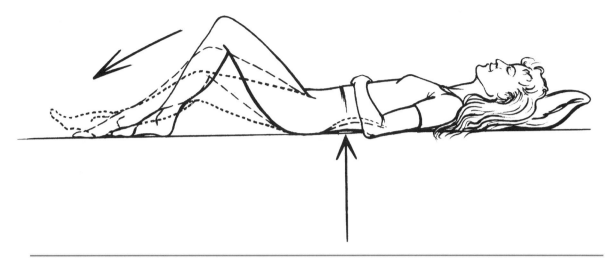

Figure 6.2   When the legs are outstretched, their weight tends to pull the pelvis forward, curving the spine and increasing lumbar lordosis.

Constructive Rest Position

Mabel Todd encouraged a supine position called hook lying to facilitate the imagery process. Lulu Sweigard called it the constructive rest position (CRP) because it is a means of resting that aims to create more efficient posture. Lying supine changes the orientation toward gravity by spreading the body in a horizontal alignment. Having the floor support the large surface area of the body helps release tension. Because no effort is required to maintain a position, as in standing and sitting, you can concentrate on the images without having to tense any part of the body. This is an important point because in the CRP, you are feeding your body pure imagery signals with the goal of creating improved alignment. While standing or sitting, there is always strong competition from the old patterns (figure 6.3).

Figure 6.3   In the constructive rest position (CRP, left), you are feeding your body pure imagery signals.

CONSTRUC-
TIVE REST
POSITION

Ideally, you should lie on a carpet or mat in a quiet area where the floor is not cold. Once on your back, bend your knees at a 90-degree angle, allowing your lumbar spine to rest easily on the floor. For most dancers, the dominant tone in the external rotators makes the legs fall to either side in this position. If this happens to you, fasten a scarf or a comfortable belt around your legs. Don't fasten it directly at your knees, as this might create a feeling of constriction. As an alternative, lean your legs against each other, knees touching. When tying a belt around your legs, make sure that your ankles, knees, and hip joints are in the same sagittal plane and that both of the leg axes are parallel to the median sagittal plane. It may be more comfortable to have a soft cushion under the balls of your feet, especially if you have high tone in the knee extensors. This will keep your legs from stretching too much. Proper head alignment is achieved in the same manner as described for the yoga resting position. A variation of the classic constructive rest position involves placing the legs on a bed or a chair, making sure that the lower legs are parallel to the floor. This variation helps prevent cramping in the heels (figure 6.4).

Photo by Arsène Saheurs.

Figure 6.4 A variation on the classic CRP involves placing the legs on a bed or a chair, making sure that the lower legs are parallel to the floor.

When to Use Constructive Rest

- Any time you feel the need to regenerate and revitalize yourself.
- Before going to bed, to release tension and engender a deeper, more refreshing sleep.
- In the morning, to enhance energy and coordination throughout the day.

- Before a performance; however, be sure to allow plenty of time after resting to do a regular warm-up. Constructive rest does not replace cardiovascular revving up and preparatory warming of musculature and connective tissue.

- After any strenuous activity, such as morning dance classes; whenever you feel the need to recharge your batteries during the day.

When Not to Use Constructive Rest

- Do not do constructive rest when you feel like being physically active.

- Doing constructive rest for longer than 40 minutes may actually increase tension.

Guidelines for Using Imagery

✓ The image must be in the present moment, visualized as vividly as possible, involving as many of your senses as possible. If you are imaging sparkling water bubbles moving up your central axis, hear them crackle and pop, let them tickle the front of your spine, taste the bubbles, smell their freshness.

✓ Although never static, the image must have precise location and direction inside the body. If you imagine your back spreading out like butter, visualize the process of melting, not the result, the molten butter.

✓ In the yoga resting or constructive rest positions, it is all right to move slightly to adjust your position, but otherwise no further movement should be used to support the image.

✓ Do not evaluate the process as it is happening. This additional mental activity only diffuses the process, decreasing its clarity and effectiveness. Imagery is primarily a right-brain function. Critical left-brain comments, even if well intended, will destroy an image that may hold great meaning and insight for you personally. An image cannot be judged superficially. Full understanding only comes from experience. It might take years before an image suddenly makes sense and starts to have meaning for you. In this way, an image is like a time capsule—you never know when its contents will be unearthed.

✓ Do not worry about feeling anything specific or be concerned about the correct way to feel while imaging. Trying too hard will prevent a new process from emerging. Open yourself to the image and let it do its work. Analyze the results when the imagery session is over.

✓ Look at every image as though you have never seen it before—with a fresh perspective. If you cannot let go of a previous experience, you will not be able to have a new one. Forcing a new image into your consciousness or holding onto an old image reverses the desired effect. An image that "worked" yesterday, for example, need not work today. By letting go of the need to make progress, you progress faster because the body begins to support the evolving experience physically rather than intellectually.

✓ You may verbalize your images in thought or, if the situation permits, aloud: "I see my central axis vibrating like the string of a guitar, sending ripples of sound into the surrounding space."

✔ Use music and sound to enhance the image. Play a soundtrack with wave sounds to accompany the visual image of waves during improvisation. Switch off the sound, but continue to improvise and hear the wave sound in your mind's ear. Listen to Mozart while using any image. An experiment at the University of California at Irvine suggests that listening to 10 minutes of Mozart piano music improves intelligence for a short period thereafter (*International Herald Tribune*, Zurich edition, October 15, 1993). Almost any type of music will have a beneficial effect. Listening to music will allow an image to unfold hidden treasures.

✔ It is helpful to begin an imagery session by focusing on your breathing. Your breathing patterns can tell you a lot about your alignment and muscle tone. Changes in your breathing patterns, a deepening and slowing of your breathing rhythm, for example, is often a sign that an image is working. Comparing your breathing patterns before and after an imagery session will help you discover the relationship between your alignment and your breathing.

Sitting and Standing

If you have difficulty concentrating or tend to doze off while supine, sitting may be an alternative, although it lacks some of the benefits of the supine position. To

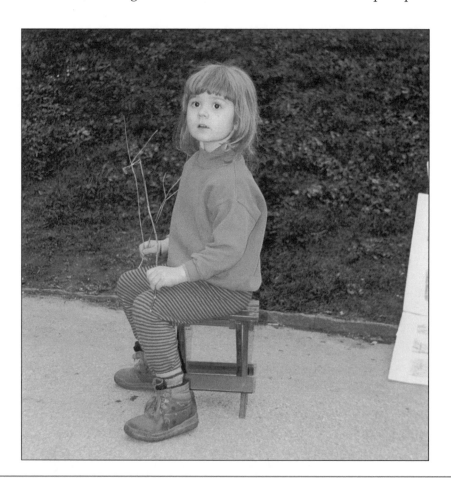

Figure 6.5   Ideally, a chair should have a level surface and be of such a height that your thighs can be approximately horizontal to the floor with both feet solidly on the ground.

practice imagery while seated, you need a good chair. Ideally, the seat should have a level surface and be of such a height that your thighs are approximately parallel to the floor with both feet solidly on the ground (figure 6.5). Detailed sitting exercises can be found in the section on the pelvis in chapter 11. As mentioned earlier, if you are only beginning to use imagery, avoid doing a lot of work in the standing position. While standing, we easily lapse into old movement patterns because the center of the body is much higher in relation to the supporting surface and therefore less stable.

USING IMAGERY WHEN IN MOTION

The value of being at rest when using imagery is that you do not reinforce habitual patterns of movement. However, much can be gained by using imagery when standing, walking, or doing other everyday movements. (Specific imagery exercises for walking and running can be found in *Dance Imagery for Technique and Performance*.) In this way, you can also make use of any unproductive time you might have—waiting for a bus, subway, or train, for example. Skillful use of imagery while moving can give instant feedback about your current alignment, why you have difficulty achieving a movement goal, and which specific image most helps you to correct a problem.

INHIBITION

If you use imagery while in motion, it is helpful to be acquainted with Alexander's previously mentioned notion of inhibition. Inhibition is the ability to not react to a certain stimulus but rather to remain calm and keep the usual way of doing something from popping up before you've had a chance to do something new. "Inhibition is a mental skill, a mental discipline by which we can gain the time necessary to accomplish the thinking required to dominate our old manner of habitual misdirection," says Donald Weed (1990, 86), who also quotes Marjorie Barlow's definition of inhibition as "a way to drive a wedge between stimulus and response" (p. 81). Lying down in the constructive rest position is itself an act of inhibition. Without mental serenity and control, imagery cannot be used successfully while in motion.

MENTAL PRACTICE WITH IMAGERY (MPI)

Mental practice with imagery is not the easiest way to use imagery, but it is certainly a powerful one. While at rest, you visualize yourself doing a movement that you would like to improve. As in traditional mental training, you see yourself executing the movement as perfectly as possible. In MPI, you then add an image to the movement and project it onto your visualization of the imagined movement. An example of MPI would be lying down in the constructive rest position and visualizing yourself pirouetting, then adding the image of your axis becoming perpendicular to the floor.

IMAGE NARRATIVE, IMAGE BUNDLES

Imagery is used while dancing. An inner image narrative may act as spontaneous guidance. These thoughts float into your mind, sparked by your movements or by free-floating associations. They may be intuitive or learned self-corrections such as "the shoulders are level, as well as the pelvis"; "the backs of the legs relate to each other"; "the sitz bones move on the same plane." Or they may be more poetic: "Energy circulates around and through my body"; "rays of light shower down and fill me"; "my eyes gaze over the vast surface of the planet, my vision circles the immense sphere." These thoughts may occur very quickly and reside quietly on the threshold of awareness.

A dancer may bundle the effects of many images that have been practiced over time. All the images pertaining to spatial awareness are bundled under the thought "space." Other bundles could consist of images related to "flow," "align," or "center."

TRAINING YOUR ABILITY TO IMAGE

Imagery skills need to be developed similar to training a muscle. You cannot be impatient with imagery training—it works differently than most other types of training. If you practice for only two weeks using an intelligent strength training scheme, you will notice considerable improvement; this is generally not so with imaging. The mind takes more time to adapt, change, and develop its power because we are usually not aware of our specific processes of thinking. It is much easier to characterize someone's walking style than his or her thinking style. We tend to think that the mind works naturally, forgetting that it is also a part of the body, which can be more or less efficient.

If you use imagery for two weeks without noticing results, don't be discouraged. You should compare the situation to learning a language: Would you be able to read a French newspaper after studying French for only two weeks? Yet the time and effort necessary to develop imaging is well worth it. It is so beneficial that many people wonder how they ever managed without it. Also, imaging improves your mastery not only of sports and dance, but also of academic subjects.

The following exercises work on basic imagery skills using the types of imagery described above. It is helpful to have someone read the exercises to you so you can practice without having to refer to the book. You can also make a tape of the exercises. Practice in any of the positions described above.

FLASHLIGHT TRAVELS THE BODY

The purpose of this exercise is to view the space within your body three-dimensionally and also to appreciate the distances between and relationships among these spaces.

Imagine a flashlight traveling through your body. Watch it illuminate every space, nook, and cranny inside you. Start at the center of your head. Shine the light inside the back of your head, then inside the top of your head. Illuminate your chin and forehead from within.

As the flashlight travels downward, watch it casting its light on the inner surface of your neck. Move through your shoulder area into your left arm. Visualize the entire expanse of your left upper arm opening in front of you. Shine the flashlight down to your elbow, and once the light has arrived there, shine it into the palm of your hand, then watch as it lights up each finger all the way to its very tip.

When you have finished exploring your hand, travel back up through your left arm, across your shoulders, and into your right arm. Shine your light down the whole length of your upper arm, down to your elbow and beyond. When the light has arrived at the elbow, shine it down through your forearm into the palm of your hand, illuminating all the fingers to their tips.

Return up through your arm to the shoulder and begin to explore the vast expanse of your thorax and abdomen. Shine the light in 360-degree arcs and make sure you have covered the whole area, taking note of the placement of each organ. Flood your entire back with light and then shine the light at the back of your navel. Move down to investigate the entire inner space of your pelvis.

Prepare to travel down your right leg. Observe the volume of your thigh from within as you enter, and make sure you cover the whole area with your light before you move into the knee. Investigate the entire inner space of the knee, and then delve into the lower leg. Notice how the shape of your lower leg narrows as you enter the ankle. Explore your foot, peeking into the heel, the midfoot, and every toe. Shine your light onto the underside of your toenails.

Slowly retreat from your foot and leg, giving the inner surfaces a last inspection. Move back through the pelvis, which seems enormous compared to the toes, and then plunge into your left leg. Once again, observe the volume of your thigh from inside, shining the light over the entire inner surface as you move into the knee. Investigate the entire inner space of the knee before you head into your lower leg. Thoroughly inspect the inner shape of the lower leg, then glide through the ankle, brightening its interior surface as you go. Analyze the inner contours of the heel and the middle foot, then shine the light into the tunnels of each toe. Slowly reemerge from the foot and leg, giving the inner surfaces a last 360-degree inspection.

Move the light to the center of your body and turn up the brightness so that it shines into all of your extremities. As you experience the flashlight making the brightest light you can imagine, view the entire inner surface of your body and then the whole inside space of the body illuminated at once.

Turn off the flashlight and rest for a moment. Now turn the flashlight back on and make the light even brighter than before. Let the light illuminate the entire inside of the body to the tips of the fingers and toes.

Quietly turn off the imaginary flashlight and rest.

Roll to one side to get up when you are ready.

MOVEMENT WITHIN, THROUGH, AND OUTSIDE THE BODY

1. **Floating colorful balloon:** Imagine a colorful balloon. Watch it float up toward the sky. Watch it become smaller and smaller. Imagine another balloon floating down from the sky. Reach out and let it fall into your

imaginary hand, bouncing it up and down a few times. Change the color and size of the balloon. Use your imaginary hands to make the balloon spin and turn.

2. **Driving a carriage:** Imagine yourself to be the driver of a 19th-century carriage. Feel the horses pulling on the reins. Restrain the horses and guide them around a curve in the road. Feel the bumpy road beneath you and watch the trees and houses pass in your peripheral vision. Experience the sun shining on your back and the wind blowing against your face. Hear the horses whinny as their hoofs pound the cobblestones. Bring the carriage to a sudden stop by pulling hard on the reins. Listen as it becomes so quiet you can hear the horses breathing.

3. **Holding an ice cream cone:** Imagine yourself holding an ice-cream cone. Feel the weight of the cone. Notice the sun shining on the cone. Watch as the ice cream begins to melt down over your fingers. Taste the ice cream. What flavor is it? What does it feel like gliding down your throat? Feel the ice cream as it arrives in your stomach. Take another lick before it drips on the floor.

4. **Walking through the woods:** Imagine that you are walking in the woods. Smell the trees, the herbs, and the flowers. Feel the soft, spongy earth beneath your feet; hear the leaves and branches crunch as you step on them. Occasionally a ray of light warms your skin. As you arrive at a tree, feel the texture of the tree trunk. Lean against it and feel its sturdiness against your back. Continue walking through the woods. As you emerge from the woods, feel the sunshine saturate your entire body like a warm bath.

5. **Walking along the beach:** Imagine walking on a beach. Feel your feet sink into the sand; feel the sand between your toes (figure 6.6). Hear the waves breaking and the seagulls crying overhead; smell the ocean breeze. Move closer to the water and feel it sweep across your feet and ankles. Feel its refreshing coolness. Notice how the water makes the sand softer, and feel

Figure 6.6 Feel the sand between your toes.

your feet sink further into it as you walk. Run up into the dry sand and notice how it sticks to your feet.

6. **Shining stained-glass window:** Imagine yourself standing under a red stained-glass window. As the sun shines on you through the window, you are enveloped in its red glow. Change the color of the window to blue, green, yellow, purple, pink, orange, and white. What differences do you feel with each color?

7. **Flashing, mixed images:** Feel yourself smoothing a blanket on a bed. Hear the soft sound of a balloon as you let it fly off into space. Float on a water mattress. Hear a steam locomotive pulling out of a train station. Be a leaf falling from a tree. Walk rapidly down a spiral staircase. Feel your feet gliding over a slippery surface. Be a flower opening to the sun's rays. Be a basketball bouncing up and down and then swooping through the basket.

IMAGERY CHECKLIST: AM I READY TO IMAGE?

To ensure that you will reap maximum benefit from your imagery sessions, it is a good idea to review some of the factors that make imagery effective. This is especially important when you first begin to use imagery.

✔ Is this image suitable for me and the goal I have in mind?

✔ Is my intention strong? Am I motivated at this time?

✔ Do I like the image I will be using? Does it appeal to me?

✔ Do I think I can benefit from this image? Do I "trust" the image?

✔ Do I find it easy to involve at least two of my senses in this image?

✔ Does the position I am in or the movement I am doing support the image?

✔ Am I able to quiet my mind sufficiently?

✔ Is the image crystal clear in my mind?

PART

II

Biomechanical and Anatomical Principles and Exercises

*A*t times, scientific knowledge enhances art. Many great artists, such as Michaelangelo and Leonardo da Vinci, applied mathematics extensively to make their art more harmonious and expressive. Likewise, understanding anatomical imagery requires a basic knowledge of the anatomy and biomechanics of the human body.

7 Location and Direction in the Body

*B*ecause our world is three-dimensional, we define three planes for the purpose of determining direction and location within the body: the frontal or coronal plane, the sagittal plane, and the horizontal or transverse planes. Although there is an infinite number of such planes, only one median plane divides the body in half. Humans are not perfectly symmetrical, however, so the halves are not exactly the same. For example, visualize a cake of homogeneous composition (figure 7.1a). The median sagittal plane cuts the cake into equal right and left halves (figure 7.1b); the median coronal or frontal plane cuts the cake into equal front and back halves (figure 7.1c); the median transverse or horizontal plane cuts the cake into equal upper and lower halves (figure 7.1d). Two planes crossing create a line; three planes crossing create a point. If you cross the median sagittal with the median frontal plane, you create the cake's central axis (figure 7.1e); by crossing all three median planes, you find its geometrical center (figure 7.1f).

Instead of cutting up a bunch of cakes, you can also learn about how planes create points and lines by taking two sheets of paper and placing one flat on a table and the other on top at a 90-degree angle. The two sheets of paper meet along a line. If you add another paper at a 90-degree angle to the table, you will find only one point where all three papers can meet.

The geometric center of an object is not necessarily the same as its center of gravity (COG), which we will discuss later.

Figure 7.1 Plane cake.

**THE BODY
IN THREE
DIMENSIONS**

1. **Planes:** Visualize the three median planes through your body. Practice visualizing one plane at a time. Then visualize two planes at a time and the lines created by their intersection. Finally, visualize all three median planes simultaneously (figure 7.2).

2. **Intersections:** Visualize the axis of your arms and legs by intersecting their median sagittal and median frontal planes.

3. **Move in a plane:** Move your body and limbs in only one plane at a time.

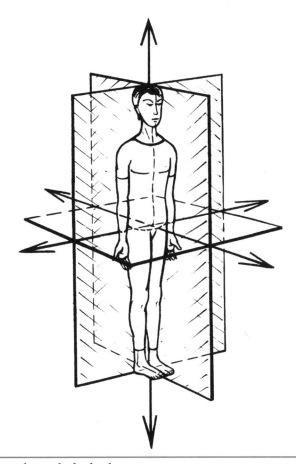

Figure 7.2   Planes through the body.

THE CENTRAL AXIS

"The impulse to turn around one's axis is found in the atom, the tornado and the human baby at birth. It is eternal without origin," writes Heinrich Kosnick (1978, 58). As we have seen, the central axis (CA) can be found geometrically by intersecting the median sagittal and median frontal planes. Although the CA is a metaphor that is very helpful for attaining good alignment, it is merely a functional concept.

YOUR CENTRAL AXIS

1. **Searchlight:** Visualize a miniature searchlight positioned between your feet shining a bright, contained beam of light up through your central axis. Imagine the light shining out the top of your head. The point where the light touches the ceiling should be directly above the point where it originates on the floor.

2. **Guitar string:** Visualize your central axis as a guitar string extending from a point centered between your feet to a point at the center of the top of your head. Give the string an imaginary pluck and see and feel its vibration in the core of your body. Hear the sound of the string as it vibrates. What is its tone?

3. **Rolling**: Lie on your side on the floor. Roll on the floor as if you were a cylinder. Roll to one side, then the other, maintaining your focus on the central axis.

4. **Path of the axis:** To a great extent, the central axis passes through organs rather than bony parts. Its approximate path is up between the sitz bones and through the pelvic floor, the bladder area, the small intestine, the left lobe of the liver, the right atrium of the heart, the pulmonary trunk, and the esophagus. These organs can be thought of as contributing to the functional axis by virtue of their contractile and hydrostatic properties and weblike fascial interconnectedness along these central areas of the body.

BODY GEOGRAPHY

Anatomists use specific terminology to define direction and location within the body. There are two basic ways of doing this: by describing either your absolute position or your relative position. Assume that you are in the Empire State Building (ESB) in New York City. To describe your location, you could say that you are in the ESB (absolute location). You could also say that you are in the building on the southeast corner of 34th and Park Avenues (relative location). Anatomically, an absolute description of a location would sound like this: "Let's look at the iliac crest (top of the hip bone)." A relative description would be "The pubic bone lies medially (toward the center of the body) to the hip joint" (figure 7.3).

Figure 7.4 depicts the relative locations in the body—superior/cranial (above), inferior/caudal (below), anterior, ventral (to the front), and posterior, dorsal (to the back).

These terms can be thought of in relation to the three planes discussed above: In the frontal plane, you can distinguish between a medial (inside) direction and a lateral (outside) direction as well as a cranial (upward) and caudal (downward) direction. In the sagittal plane, you can distinguish between the ventral (front) and dorsal (back) directions as well as between the cranial (upward) and caudal (downward) directions. In the horizontal plane, you can distinguish between the ventral (front) and dorsal (back) directions as well as the medial (inside) and lateral (outside) directions.

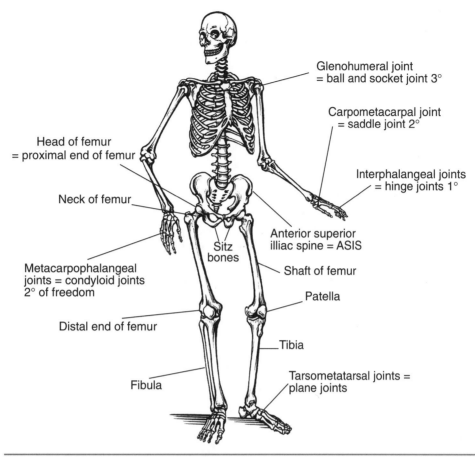

Figure 7.3   The human skeleton.

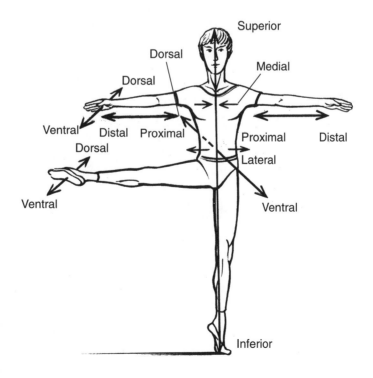

Figure 7.4   Directions in the body.

Descriptions combining several of these terms are common in anatomy: The anterior superior iliac spine (ASIS) is a prominence located on the forward and upper part of the ilium.

Proximal and distal are another set of important relative terms. Proximal means closer to the center of the body; distal means farther from the center of the body. A body part proximal to another is closer to the center of the body. The proximal end of the femur, or thighbone, is the rounded head that sits in the acetabulum, or hip socket. The distal end is the one that forms the upper part of the knee and contacts the shinbone.

Now back to the ESB one last time: If I am on the top of the ESB, I am higher than a person on the twelfth floor, but the person on the twelfth floor is higher than a person on the first floor. Therefore, even though the femur head is the proximal part of the femur, the hipbone is proximal in relation to the femur as a whole (see figure 7.3 and 7.4 again).

It is important to be able to distinguish between movement initiated from the proximal and the distal ends of a body part. When you imagine that the tips of your fingers are leading your arm through space, you are initiating distally. You are initiating proximally if you are thinking of the movement of the arm originating in the shoulder joint. Distal initiation tends to lead you out into space; proximal initiation facilitates centered movement. Usually dancers prefer one type of initiation. A mime uses distal initiation to mimic the existence of outside objects, such as an imaginary wall. Figure 7.5 shows a dancer who has just initiated at the most proximal point in her body: her center. She is imagining herself to be an octopus propelling itself backward by shooting water out from the center of its body.

Photo by Mark Skolsky.

Figure 7.5   Initiation from center.

JOINT MOVEMENTS

Joints allow the limbs to move in the aforementioned planes. The hip and the shoulder have ball-and-socket joints that permit motion in all three planes (anatomically called three degrees of freedom). The interphalangeal joints of the fingers allow for motion in one plane only. Rather than relying on these planes, anatomy defines joint motion in relation to the body no matter how you stand.

In flexion (to bend), the bones move in the sagittal plane around a transverse joint axis (side-to-side axis), bringing the ventral sides of the limbs closer together. Extension, from the Latin *extendere*, "to pull apart," is the opposite motion in the same plane and around the same joint axis. (See figure 7.1b'.)

Abduction (to lead away) moves a body part away from the midline of the body in the frontal plane around a sagittal joint axis (front-to-back axis). Adduction (to lead toward), the opposite motion, brings a body part closer to the midline in the same plane and around the same joint axis. (See figure 7.1c'.)

Medial rotation around the longitudinal axis (vertical axis) takes place in the horizontal plane and rotates the body part toward the front midline of the body. Lateral rotation around the longitudinal axis takes place in the horizontal plane and rotates the body part toward the back midline of the body. (See figure 7.1d'.)

Circumduction (to lead around) combines all the plane motions. Circumducting your arm will describe a cone shape in space.

Getting used to these terms may be a nuisance initially. However, they are not just an indispensible aid in describing location and direction in the body; they also offer an excellent exercise for training the mind's imaging skills.

8 Force, Gravity, and Mass

*F*orce produces, stops, or changes motion; no movement can occur without it. Forces always work in pairs. If you push against a wall (force number 1), the wall must be pushing back against your hand (force number 2). If this were not the case, your hand would simply go through the wall. Because force is involved continuously throughout every movement, even when you seem to be standing still, understanding force will increase your ability to make intelligent choices for alignment.

FORCE VECTORS

Most of the time, we experience force as a push or a pull, such as the pull of gravity. Forces are also at work within the body; for example, a contracting muscle exerts force on the tendons and bones. A force can be visualized as an arrow, called a vector. The vector shows the object of the force, its direction or action line, and its magnitude. The larger the force, the longer the arrow.

Force is also needed to stop a moving object. If no external force acts on it, the object will move forever. Here on earth, of course, friction and air resistance prevent objects from moving in the same direction indefinitely. The following sections describe various types of force. Contact forces and inertia are discussed in the context of Newton's laws.

Gravity

On earth, gravity is always present, pulling us toward the center of the planet. Without gravity, we would float away. If the earth did not resist our being pulled toward its center, we would sink through its surface (figure 8.1).

Figure 8.1   Gravity.

Of all the external forces you must contend with, gravity is the most important because it is always there, influencing your alignment. Every time you climb a flight of stairs or get up from a chair, you are overcoming the force of gravity. Astronauts floating in space can lose significant muscle and even some bony mass, and usually have difficulty walking after landing. Even if you remained in bed for months you would not suffer this degree of muscle loss here on earth, because each movement you make—even the slightest motion of your head or body—is training your musculature. Gravity keeps us in a permanent weight training room, our bodies being the highly articulated barbells. Therefore, the way you move *most of the time* is the most important part of your alignment training, not your occasional training sessions. Instead of letting gravity "bring us down," we need to make it our ally.

SENSING GRAVITY

The way we sense gravity depends on our relative position. If the bones of your leg are aligned with the vector of the gravitational force, as in standing, you are more likely to experience this force through your bones. If you are lying on the floor with your legs outstretched, you will more readily sense the effect on your muscles.

SUBTLE MUSCLE RESPONSE

Stand in a comfortable position. Shift your head slightly forward and notice the reaction in the musculature of your neck. Next shift your head slightly toward the back and notice any changes in the muscle tone of your neck. Then shift your head slightly to the side and notice how your neck muscles react. Finally, focus on your entire body. Watch for the little movements—the slightest twitching of your fingers, the swaying motion of your body as you stand. Notice how even slight changes in alignment change the activity of your muscles.

Elasticity

The more we stretch an elastic band, the greater the elastic force pulling the band together again. When we compress a spring, we also feel elastic force. Connective tissue and muscles possess a great amount of elasticity, allowing for springiness, bounce, and rebound.

EXERCISING ELASTICITY

Think of your bones, muscles, and connective tissue as very elastic, making your alignment responsive and adaptable, not rigid or fixed. As you leap, visualize your bones and muscles releasing their elastic energy. As you land, think of yourself rebounding like a bouncing ball and being propelled back up into the air. Now try the opposite and, as you jump, think of your bones as rigid and your muscles as ropes with no elasticity. Compare the difference in height attained with each jump.

Buoyancy

For an object to float, an upward force must be exerted on it; otherwise it would sink through the fluid. This upward force is equal to the weight of the fluid displaced by the object. We have all submerged a ball in water and felt it pushing upward against our hands. If we let go of the ball, it will surge upward, propelled by the force of buoyancy.

EXERCISING BUOYANCY

Femur heads as buoys: Stand comfortably with your knees aligned in the same sagittal plane as your feet. Visualize the heads of your femurs as buoys, floating on water (figure 8.2). Each buoy pushes up against your pelvis, supporting it. Your pelvis floats easily on the buoys. Float your pelvis down on the buoys as you bend your hip, knee, and ankle joints. Float your pelvis up on the buoys as you stretch your hip, knee, and ankle joints.

Try to think of the buoys initiating the movement. As the water level goes down, so do the buoys, which causes your hip, knee, and ankle joints to bend. As the water level rises, the buoys float upward, causing your hip, knee, and ankle joints to stretch. Try to think of the force that moves your pelvis upward as coming from the buoys pushing into your hip sockets.

Imagine the buoys moving up and down equally on both sides; keep them on the same level in your mind's eye. (This exercise will help correct a pelvis that is habitually tilted to one side, provided the condition does not result from one leg being longer than the other.)

Stand on your right leg only and think of the right buoy supporting your pelvis. Next stand on your left leg only and think of the left buoy supporting your pelvis. Once you have a feeling for this strong, yet gentle support of the femur heads in the hip sockets, try walking while visualizing the image.

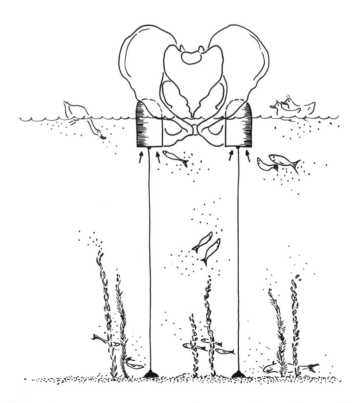

Figure 8.2   Femur heads as buoys supporting the pelvis.

Friction

Friction exists wherever two surfaces touch, glide, or roll over one another. One surface tends to work against or resist any motion of the other surface. This resistance at the contacting surfaces is called frictional force. The magnitude of this force depends on both the roughness of the contacting surfaces and the pressure between them. Friction is important in contact improvisation and partnering.

Walking and running require adequate friction. We have all experienced dancing on a floor with too little friction, causing us to slip, slide, and tighten our muscles to create more pressure against the surface. Conversely, a sticky floor has too much friction, preventing turns and causing the knees to twist. A dancer's best friend is a floor with ideal friction. Although imagining a sticky floor to be slippery won't change the floor, it may be very helpful in changing the way you deal with the floor.

IMAGING FRICTION

Imagine that the space surrounding you has varying levels of friction. What is it like to move through a sandstorm, through water, or through the emptiness of outer space with no friction whatsoever?

MATTER AND MASS

Matter is that which occupies space. Mass is the quantity of matter an object contains. It is not the same as weight. When you place an object on a scale to weigh it, you are measuring both its matter and the force of gravity on the object. The same object would weigh more on Jupiter and less on the moon. Astronauts (and we're not talking Michael Jordan) can jump nine feet high on the moon with all of their equipment on their backs.

A flowerpot will sit on a windowsill until an outside force pushes it in a certain direction. It is stable because the reaction forces of gravity-on-pot and windowsill-on-pot cancel each other out (figure 8.3). If the flowerpot were pushed off the windowsill by gale-force winds, the combination of its mass and gravity would turn it into a dangerous projectile hurling toward the ground. If the flowerpot were floating in outer space, without gravity, it would not create any force. If it were to bounce off a passing spaceship, the contact force could provide enough energy to send the pot on an everlasting voyage through space.

The Center of Mass

The center of mass is also called the center of gravity (COG). The COG of a geometric object such as a homogeneous sphere is identical to its geometric center. This holds true as long as the mass is equally distributed within the sphere. Figure 8.4a shows a perfect sphere made of homogeneous cork. Here the COG and the geometric center coincide. If the same perfect sphere were made half of cork, half of lead, the COG of the sphere would be within the lead section, but the geometric center would still be in the same place (figure 8.4b).

Figure 8.3   A flowerpot on a windowsill will sit there until an outside force pushes it in a certain direction. If the pot were to bounce off a passing spaceship, the contact force could provide enough energy to send it on an everlasting voyage.

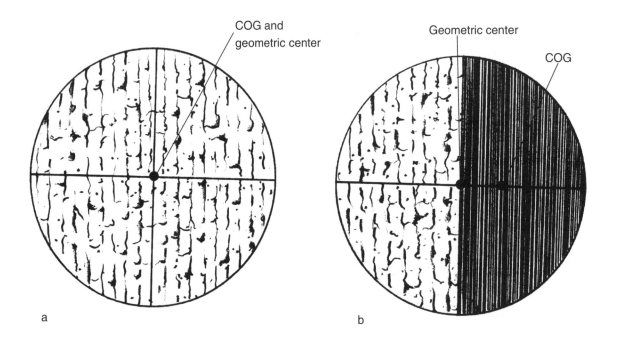

Figure 8.4   (a) A perfect sphere made of homogenous cork. The COG and the geometric center now coincide. (b) A perfect sphere made half of cork, half of lead. The COG is in the lead section, but the geometric center remains in place.

Assuming a human being is a single solid object, its COG lies approximately in front of the second sacral vertebra. However, an individual's COG depends on his or her build and alignment. If a man's torso is very long and muscular in relation to his legs, his COG will be relatively higher.

Gravity acts on the entire mass, although for simplification, it is depicted as acting on the center of gravity, as if all mass were concentrated at that point. Therefore, the COG can lie outside of an object. Strangely enough, the COG of a hoop is in the space in the middle of the hoop. If the pelvis thrusts forward in relation to the rest of the body, the COG may lie within or even behind the sacrum. Bending to the left moves the COG to the left. If you bend far enough, the COG will be situated outside of your body.

Figure 8.5 shows how the COG travels in relation to the body. In figure 8.5a, the COG is identical or close to the geometric center (depending on body build). In figure 8.5b, the arms are being lifted while the upper body is bending to the side; therefore, the COG moves up and to the side. In figure 8.5c, the arms are lifted higher and the upper body is bent farther to the side; thus the COG is even higher and farther to the side, outside the body.

To create good alignment by focusing on the COG, it is helpful to think of the body as composed of individual masses: the head, torso, pelvis, and legs. The structure is most stable when the COGs of these masses are located over each other in the same vertical line and when the COG is low (as long as the supporting surface doesn't diminish). Thus, with a lower COG, less effort is required to maintain the balance of an inherently unbalanced system, such as the upright human body. This is the building-block postural model.

Knowing where your center is does not mean that you are centered (have control over where your center is placed when you move). Being able to move through connecting steps without constantly recentering is important in dance and gymnastics. In a piqué arabesque, you should be able to place your center over the

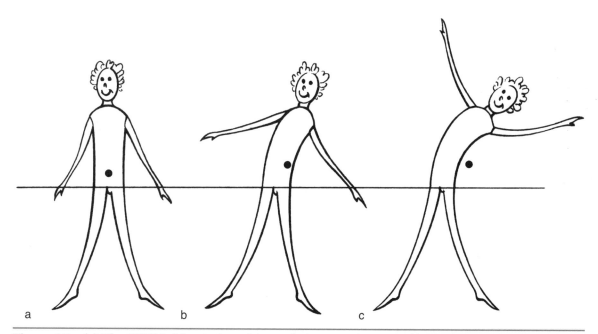

Figure 8.5 (a) The COG is identical or close to the geometric center (depending on body build). (b) The COG moves up and to the side. (c) The COG is outside the body.

supporting foot in one fluid and direct motion. This can only be done with a secure sense of your body's center.

1. **Finding the COG:** You can approximate the COG of an object through trial and error. The point where a pencil balances on your finger is just below its center of gravity. If you suspend an object from its center of gravity, there will be no resulting rotation. Try to find the COG of this book.

2. **Changing the location of the COG:** As you move, try to visualize the changing location of your COG. The center of the body is usually in the pelvic area, even if the actual center of gravity is momentarily located elsewhere. Central initiation may "ex-center" the body, sending the COG outside of the body. Initiating from center, the dancer we saw in figure 7.5 hurls her pelvis back, but her center of gravity does not move back nearly as much because she throws her arms and legs forward. Think of your center of gravity in normal standing alignment as "neutral" (figure 8.5a).

   As you move, your center of gravity "leaves" this neutral point (figures 8.5b and c). Visualize the relationship between the neutral point in your body and the actual location of your center of gravity. Merge your COG with the neutral point once again. The interaction between the neutral point and the actual location of COG is similar to the rebound of a yo-yo, with the hand holding it representing the neutral point. The COG moves away from and back to the hand. Improvise with this idea until you become more familiar with the concept of COG.

3. **Concentric growth rings around COG:** Image the feeling of centering by visualizing yourself as the core of a tree, surrounded by concentric growth rings. Note how the rings become smaller and smaller as they approach your center. Feel the power concentrated around your center.

Line of Gravity

The action line of the force of gravity, or the line of gravity (LOG), points vertically down toward the center of the earth. If your LOG falls outside your base of support, you will fall over. Daredevil motorcyclists cross deep gorges with ballast attached to their cycles so that it hangs below the rope they are driving over. This ballast causes the COG of the combined driver/cycle/ballast system to be below the point of support (the wire). It may appear as if the cyclist is delicately balancing the cycle *on* the wire, trying to direct the LOG over the wire, although, in reality, the system as a whole is *hanging* from it. This creates a much more stable balance because the low COG tends to right the cycle.

Lifting the arms overhead is destabilizing because it raises the COG. Rarely do you see a circus artist crossing a wire with his or her arms overhead. For the same reason, turns with the arms overhead are more difficult to balance.

WORKING YOUR LINE OF GRAVITY

1. **Balance on one leg:** After you have tried this with both legs, imagine your body to be filled with sand. Jump up and down a few times and let the sand settle down toward your legs and feet. Now stand on one leg again and see if it is easier to balance while using this image.

2. **Tightrope walking:** If you have the opportunity, try walking over a tightrope (even a log will do). Imagine your COG dropping down toward the supporting surface. Notice if this image makes it easier to balance.

BALANCING YOUR LINE OF GRAVITY

In figure 8.6, the pirouetting dancer visualizes a heavy ballast beneath the ground attached to her LOG as part of her overall mass. The ballast lowers her imaginary COG, making her more stable and upright. The ballast also helps correct the LOG (make it perpendicular to the ground). The minute changes in alignment that occur in response to the image will suffice to create the desired effect. Try using this image for any balance or turn. Once the low COG kinesthesia is established, the metaphorical image can be discarded.

Figure 8.6   Imaginary ballast to lower the COG.

CHAPTER

9 The Laws of Motion and Force Systems

*M*otion takes place in accord with three scientific laws discovered by Sir Isaac Newton. Evan Tsang, a student at Caltech, pointed out that Newton's law of inertia only became known because the physicist was able to "make the creative leap to a world without friction." Tsang stated: "If you couldn't imagine it, you could never come up with these ideas."

NEWTON'S FIRST LAW OF MOTION: THE LAW OF INERTIA

We experience the effects of inertia when the car we are riding in suddenly accelerates and we are pushed back into our seats. If the car comes to a sudden stop, we are pitched forward because we stay in motion. The tendency of an object to resist changing state, to remain at rest or to keep moving, is called inertia. To move any part of your body, inertia must be overcome. If you are leaping across a dance floor, you must exert force to break your forward motion. Inertia depends on a body's mass; the larger the mass the greater the inertia.

Inertia is subjectively experienced as greater under certain conditions. A baby seems heavier when it is sleeping than when it is awake. People who think of themselves as heavy are harder to carry.

NEWTON'S SECOND LAW OF MOTION: THE LAW OF ACCELERATION

An object moves because a force is at work to make it move. The speed of the object depends on the amount of force applied to it. Speed is the magnitude of velocity without any specific direction. Velocity is the rate of change of position of an object. Any change in the speed of an object is called acceleration. Acceleration can also induce a change in direction. When the car is accelerating, you feel the seat pushing against your back because a force is being applied to your back. The amount of acceleration you experience depends on the strength of this force and your own mass. The greater the force and the smaller your mass, the more you will accelerate.

It is easier to partner a smaller, lighter dancer because the force you apply has a greater effect. Before executing a lift, you usually practice the step on your own. Obviously, when lifting your partner, increased effort is required. Because the mass of the moving system has increased, you need to exert more force. Acceleration has become more difficult. Force, mass, and acceleration are always related. If you repeat the same step without your partner, it seems easy because your muscles are attuned to moving a much larger mass.

GRAVITY EXERCISES

1. **Lifting a briefcase or large book:** For this exercise, use a moderately heavy object such as a briefcase or a large book. Before lifting it, imagine it to be very light, as light as a feather. Then lift the object and put it back down. Now imagine that the briefcase or book is very heavy. When you lift the object again, you may notice that it seems lighter. Because you have prepared your muscles to deal with the increased force, the object seems to have become lighter. This is a good injury-prevention strategy because the body is not surprised by the forces suddenly acting on it.

2. **Lifting your dance partner:** Image the weight of your dance partner just before lifting. By readying your muscles to deal with the increased forces, you increase fluidity of motion and reduce the likelihood of injury.

NEWTON'S THIRD LAW OF MOTION: THE LAW OF REACTION

Newton's third law states that for every action there is an equal and opposite reaction. Action is another word for force. A reaction is a force that acts in a direction opposite to the action. If forces act on an object without causing it to move, then all the opposing forces add up to zero resulting force.

Forces always come in pairs. As soon as two forces contact each other, reaction force is involved. If you lean two books against each other, each one is exerting force against the other. When book 1 applies a force to book 2, book 2 immediately applies a force equal in magnitude and opposite in direction to book 1.

Objects can either sit on top of, be braced against, or hang from one another. If you place one hand on the ballet barre, you and the barre exert force against each other. The ropes holding a docked ship exert force on the ship; the ship tugs on the ropes. A chandelier and the ceiling it hangs from exert force on one another.

When you are seated on a chair on the tuberosities of the ischia, or sitz bones, the chair's reaction force is less than your body weight because the chair legs are partially supported by the floor. Every step you take elicits a reaction from the ground called the ground reaction force (GRF). If the ground is able to support you, the ground reaction force is equal to your body weight. The ground pushes up against your foot with the same amount of force and along the same line of action as the downward force of your foot. If the GRF is insufficient, as on quicksand or on a thin layer of ice, you will sink out of sight. If you push rapidly against the ground with a force that is greater than your weight, the ground pushes back with a force greater than your weight, propelling you upward. The moment you leave the ground and cease to exert force against it, the ever-present force of gravity returns you to earth rather quickly. A rocket is able to escape gravity by continuing to exert force against it after blastoff. Reaction forces in the form of pulls and pushes are what create balance in partnering (figure 9.1) and are the spice of Contact Improvisation. Used inventively, reaction forces make apparently gravity-defying movements possible.

Reaction force may be imaged at any level in the body.

Figure 9.1   Reaction forces in the form of pulls and pushes are what create balance in partnering.

Adapted, by permission, from N. Serrebrenikov and J. Lawson, 1989, *The Art of Pas de Deux* (Pennington, NJ: Princeton Book Co.).

REACTION FORCE

1. **The atlas as lifesaving ring:** At the level of the hip sockets, we can visualize the reaction force between the heads of the femurs and the hip sockets. At the level of the atlas (the top of the spine), we can visualize the reaction force created by the weight of the head against the atlas. The atlas reacts with an equal force. In figure 9.2, the atlas is depicted as a lifesaving ring to metaphorically clarify the location of this reaction force. By imaging the precise location of a reaction force in the body, we can improve the efficiency of weight transfer and release excess muscular tension.

2. **The floor as "being everywhere":** If you lie on the floor and imagine that a part of the body is being supported, you are using reaction force imagery. You can facilitate the release of the shoulder blades by thinking that they are being supported by the floor. The more fully you imagine them contacting the clearly supportive floor, the more tension drops from the shoulder blades because they are reacting by "pushing" downward. This technique can be used for any body part and in any position. Komo (of "Eiko and Komo") once suggested how one can image the floor as "being everywhere" so that even when you are standing, your arm, cheek, and back rest on the floor. This image creates gentle, easy, effortless movement by giving the body part the feeling of support from the floor.

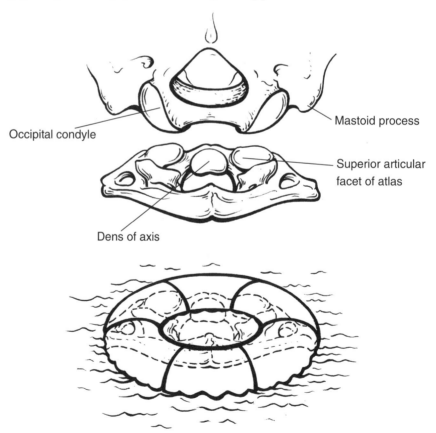

Occipital condyle

Mastoid process

Superior articular facet of atlas

Dens of axis

Figure 9.2   Visualize the atlas as a lifesaving ring to metaphorically clarify the location of this reaction force.

FORCE SYSTEMS

There are three ways in which forces can act on an object: They can be in line with each other in a linear force system (figure 9.3a); they can be at an angle to each other in a concurrent force system (figure 9.3b); or they can be parallel and at a distance from each other in a parallel force system (figure 9.3c). In a complex system, a combination of the above forces is likely to be acting on an object.

Concurrent Force Systems

Two or more forces that act on the same point of an object but are not in line with each other are part of a concurrent force system. When the vectors of two such divergent forces are added to each other, the sum is the *resultant* force. The action lines of the shaft and the neck of the femur are separate force vectors. Their resultant force is the seventh of Sweigard's (1978, 195) nine lines of action, a line of force from the center of the knee to the center of the hip socket (figure 9.4).

Figure 9.5 shows three force vectors being exerted by a male dancer to stabilize a female dancer on his shoulders. The force vectors arise from the contact of hand against hand, knee against shoulder, and shoulder against knee. The male dancer's effort is lowest when the female dancer's COG is balanced over his COG. This alignment of COGs occurs when the resultant force vector is in line with both dancers' LOG.

Muscle fibers often point in directions that diverge from the actual resultant pull of the muscle. In pennate muscles, those with fibers arranged like a feather, the individual fibers lie at an angle relative to their tendons. Together, however, the fibers form a concurrent force system with a single resultant force called the total muscle force vector, or the action line of the muscle. When a muscle con-

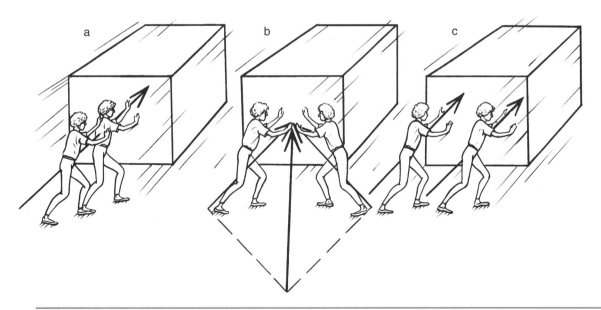

Figure 9.3   (a) Two forces in line with each other—a linear force system. (b) Two forces at an angle to each other—a concurrent force system. (c) Two forces parallel and at a distance to each other—a parallel force system.

tracts, at least two force vectors (two pulls) are created: one at its origin (proximal end) and one at its insertion (distal end).

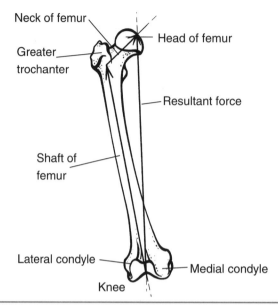

Figure 9.4   The resultant force is Sweigard's seventh line of action, a line of force from the center of the knee to the center of the hip socket.

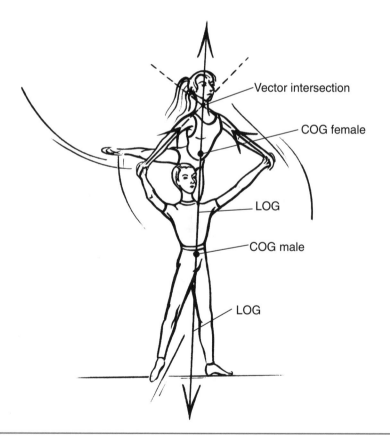

Figure 9.5   Three force vectors being exerted by a male dancer to stabilize a female dancer on his shoulders.

Adapted, by permission, from N. Serrebrenikov and J. Lawson, 1989, *The Art of Pas de Deux* (Pennington, NJ: Princeton Book Co.).

1. **Shortening or lengthening the action lines:** The action lines of a muscle can be imagined to shorten or to lengthen. In a deep stretch, you can imagine the action line of the muscles or muscle group being stretched (becoming longer). To aid the process, you can imagine the action line of the opposing muscle or muscle group shortening.

2. **Lengthening the back of the leg:** A common image in dance is to visualize the back of the leg lengthening, as in a grand battement. This image helps elevate the leg by aiding the release of the muscles that extend the hip joint and flex the knee. This, in turn, improves the ease of hip flexion and knee extension.

Parallel Force Systems

If the forces acting on an object are parallel to each other and lie in the same plane, they are part of a parallel force system. Levers are examples of parallel force systems.

The closer a weight situated on a lever is to the center, or fulcrum, the less force is needed to counterbalance the weight. Our intuitive understanding of this principle is why we instinctively know not to carry our shopping bags away from our bodies (figure 9.6a). The closer they are, the less work is needed to counterbalance their weight (figure 9.6b).

If the man in figure 9.6 carries the bundle on a long stick, he experiences an increased moment force or torque. Moment force is the tendency of a force to cause rotation about an axis. It is equal to the magnitude of a force multiplied by the distance between the force and the fulcrum. In this case, the moment force would be the weight of the bundle multiplied by the distance between the shoulder on which the stick rests and the bundle. To balance this moment force, the man must pull down on the other end of the stick, creating torque with this force. Here the moment arm is found by multiplying the pulling force by the distance between the shoulders and the pulling hand. Because this distance is smaller, the force exerted by the hand must be larger for the two moment arms created by bundle-on-stick and hand-on-stick to balance each other. Any force acting on a body outside of its fulcrum or center of rotation will create a moment arm.

LEVER SYSTEMS

First described by the Greek mathematician and scientist Archimedes (287-212 B.C.), a lever is a parallel force system. Levers were among the first machines used by humans to haul water and to lift heavy objects. A lever can amplify force, change its direction, or make a force work at a distance from where it is applied. As we all know, the way to move a heavy boulder is to place a long rod supported by a smaller stone under it. By exerting force from afar, you amplify

Figure 9.6   (a) If the man carries the bundle on a long stick, he experiences an increased moment force or torque. (b) The closer to the body the weight is carried, the less work is needed to counterbalance it.

its effects and move the boulder more easily. A small mouse can move a large piece of cheese at a great distance from itself using a lever (figure 9.7). The bones and joints of the body are considered lever systems.

A lever consists of two forces acting around a pivot (also called a fulcrum): the effort force (EF) and the resistance force (RF). The distance from the EF to the fulcrum is the force arm (FA), and the distance from the RF to the fulcrum is the resistance arm (RA). In dancing, muscles are often the EF and gravity is the RA.

First-Class Lever: The Seesaw

In a first-class lever (figure 9.8), two forces are applied on either side of an axis, creating rotation in opposite directions. Pilobolus Dance Company uses "seesaw" partnering with a dancer in the middle carrying one behind, and a dancer in front resting on the outstretched legs of the dancer behind. Besides the obvious forces being generated by the two children in figure 9.8b, there are less apparent ones at play. Because contact creates force, the fulcrum touching the seesaw and gravity are also forces to be considered. (Remember that gravity is always acting on an object, even if it is in the air.)

The seesaw is a very versatile lever. It can be used to lift a heavy weight with little force or to move a weight a great distance with just a small movement of

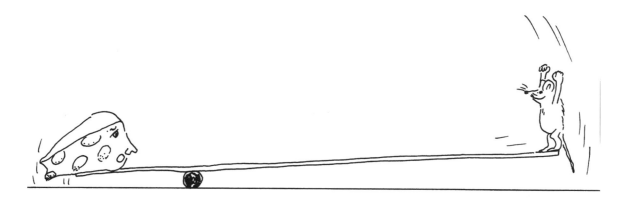

Figure 9.7   Using a lever, a small mouse can move a large piece of cheese at a great distance from itself.

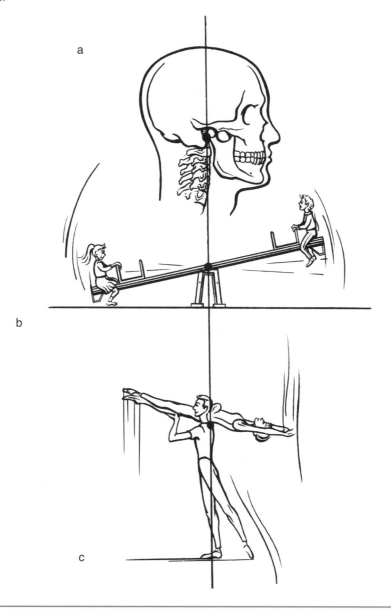

Figure 9.8   First-class levers.
Adapted, by permission, from N. Serrebrenikov and J. Lawson, 1989, *The Art of Pas de Deux* (Pennington, NJ: Princeton Book Co.).

the force arm. In figure 9.8c, the male dancer uses his hands (effort force) to balance the weight (resistance force) of the female dancer. In figure 9.8a, we can see that the head sitting on the cervical spine is a first-class lever. The atlas, the uppermost vertebra of the spine, serves as a fulcrum. Ideally, only minimal work is required for the muscles to balance the mass of the head equally around the axis of the fulcrum. As the COG of the head is slightly above and in front of the atlas, a slight muscular effort will be needed to counterbalance this weight. If the head is habitually held forward, the muscles of the neck will need to work harder to maintain balance, causing a "muscular imbalance" (figure 9.9a). Holding the head over the axis of the fulcrum reduces muscular effort, increasing muscular balance (figure 9.9b). Other first-class levers in the body are the vertebrae balancing on top of each other, the pelvis balancing on the heads of the femurs, the femur balancing on the tibia, and the tibia balancing on the talus. Sweigard (1978) points out the importance of balanced first-class levers for the maintenance of correct alignment.

Figure 9.9 (a) Muscular imbalance. (b) Holding the head over the axis of the fulcrum reduces muscular effort, increasing muscular balance.

FIRST-CLASS LEVERS

Head as a seesaw: Visualize the head as a seesaw balanced on the atlas (the uppermost bone of the spine). Allow the head to balance easily on its fulcrum. Remember what it was like to sit with a friend perfectly counterbalanced on a seesaw. Transfer that feeling to your head.

Second-Class Lever: The Wheelbarrow

A second-class lever such as the wheelbarrow (figure 9.10b) is efficient because the resistance force is between the fulcrum and the effort force, so the length of the effort arm exceeds that of the resistance arm. Although this lever produces efficiency and strength, it has a drawback: The effort force must always move over a greater distance than the resistance force. Also, if the effort force moves upward, the resistance moves upward as well.

The foot can be considered a second-class lever as it pushes off the ground to lift the weight of the body upward (figure 9.10a). In this case, the ball of the foot is the fulcrum; the effort force is applied by the calf muscles via the Achilles

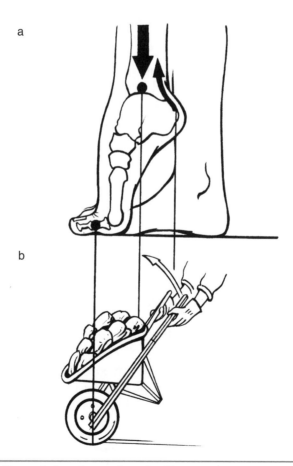

a

b

Figure 9.10   Second-class lever, the wheelbarrow.

tendon at the posterior heelbone. The resistance force is the weight carried on top of the long arch of the foot. When a dancer is in a full relevé and the LOG falls momentarily in front of the ball of the foot, the system can be considered a first-class lever because the weight and force are on opposite sides of the fulcrum. Therefore, from demi-pointe or full-pointe, the foot shifts from a second- to a first-class lever. If a dancer's arch does not permit a demi-pointe that allows for the ankle to be over the ball of the foot, the effort force of the calf muscles increases greatly because the entire weight of the body must be constantly counterbalanced. Mechanically efficient, second-class levers per se are not found within the human body because they would require lengthy muscles reaching to the distal ends of the bones, transforming the body into a cumbersome mass.

DEMI-POINTE AS A LEVER

In the demi-pointe position on one foot, feel your weight shift slightly in front of, then behind, the fulcrum. Image the ankle perfectly aligned over the ball of the foot, creating minimal effort in the muscles of the lower leg.

Third-Class Lever: The Crane

Here the EF is closer to the fulcrum than to the resistance. Although this is not the most efficient configuration, most bony levers in our body are of this type. Therefore, carrying a weight in your hand requires considerable muscular force (see figure 9.11a). However, the advantages outweigh the loss of force by saving weight and allowing the distal ends of the bones to move rapidly through space. A small contraction of a muscle at the proximal end of the bone near the fulcrum creates a large arc through space at the distal end of the bone. Efficiency is sacrificed for the ability to proceed through space in an elegant and rapid fashion.

ILIOPSOAS FLEXES THE THIGH

Stand in parallel position. Visualize the line of action of the right psoas muscle from the top inside of the femur up the side of the spine to the twelfth thoracic vertebra. The most important hip flexor, the iliopsoas, inserts very close to the fulcrum of its third-class lever, the hip joint. Initiate thigh flexion by seeing this muscle pull up on the femur. Imagine that this muscle can move the knee in space like a crane moving its shovel. Remember that the force for the movement is being applied very close to the hip joint. Once you have experimented with this kind of initiation, visualize a string attached to your knee. Imagine that this string is the force that lifts the thigh and initiates thigh flexion. In effect, the thigh has become a more efficient second-class lever. Let the string move the knee around in space. Once you have experimented with this image, lower the leg and compare the sensations created by the two images. Which image made it easier to lift the thigh? Which image made it easier to move the knee through space? (The iliopsoas is discussed in more detail in chapters 10 and 11.)

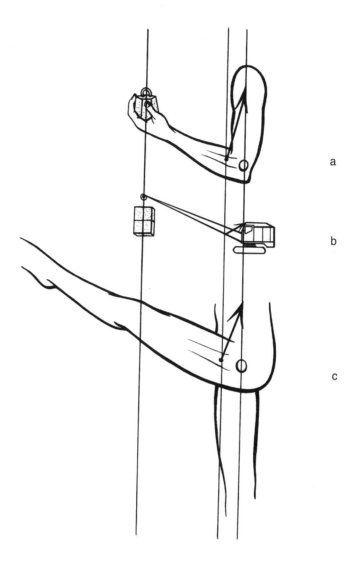

Figure 9.11 Third-class lever, the crane.

Mechanical Advantage

The length of the effort arm relative to the resistance arm determines the mechanical advantage, or the efficiency, of a lever.

$$MA = \frac{\text{Length of effort arm}}{\text{Length of resistance arm}}$$

In second-class levers, the effort arm is longer than the resistance arm, yielding a mechanical advantage greater than one. Third-class levers have effort arms shorter than their resistance arms, yielding a mechanical advantage less than one.

IMAGING THE MECHANICAL ADVANTAGE

Try the following images as you perform a grand battement (high leg kick). Is it possible to change the body's leverage to improve our efficiency? Although we can't move the attachments of the muscles to gain longer effort arms, we can imagine efficiency.

1. **Counterweight:** When your leg is going up, image the trochanter (the prominence at the proximal end of the femur) dropping down the back of the leg as a heavy counterweight (figure 9.12). In this way, you transform the third-class lever into a more efficient first-class lever.

2. **Billiard ball:** Think of your leg as hollow and, as it moves upward, imagine a billiard ball starting at your foot and rolling down through your leg toward the socket.

3. **Gust of wind:** Think of your foot being propelled upward by a strong gust of wind.

4. **Imaginary hand:** Think of an imaginary hand pushing your foot upward.

5. **String:** Imagine a string is attached to your foot and is lifting your leg.

   (See also *Dance Imagery for Technique and Performance.*)

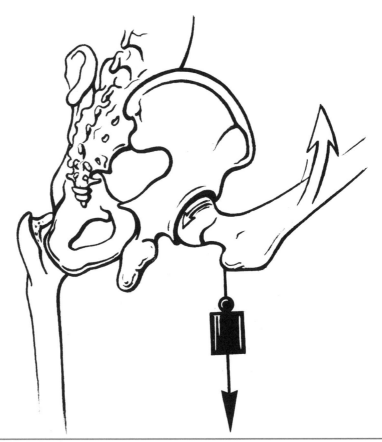

Figure 9.12   Image the trochanter dropping down the back of the leg as a heavy counterweight.

Moment Arm

When two children sit on a seesaw, they exert force against the seesaw at a 90-degree angle. If the muscles in the body were to exert force on the bones, the levers of the body, at such an acute angle, they would have to point outward, perpendicular to the bone. The action line of most muscles is actually almost parallel to the bones to which they attach. Because the force is not applied at a 90-degree angle to the lever, the lever arm is the distance between the action line of the muscle and the joint center or axis of rotation. This distance, called the moment arm (MA), is the shortest distance between the axis of rotation and the line of action of the muscle.

The body uses various mechanisms to create a pulleylike effect, altering the muscle's force vector and therefore the MA. The pulley diverts the action line of the muscle away from the axis of rotation, creating a longer lever on which the muscle can act. The patella (kneecap), for example, forms part of the quadriceps tendon before it inserts into the tibia. This increases the distance between the tendon and the axis of rotation. The longer the lever, the greater the force.

MOMENT ARM FORCE

1. **Kneecap float:** Avoid thinking of pulling your kneecap inward or backward as you extend your knees when coming up from a plié. Instead, imagine a widening motion, as if the kneecap were floating perpendicularly away from the femur as you extend the knee (figure 9.13).

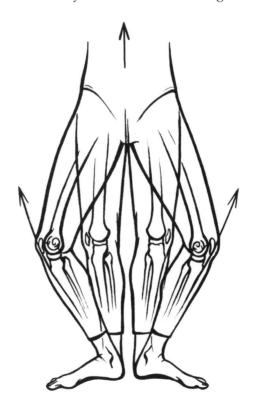

Figure 9.13 The patella gliding on the femur diverts the action line of the muscle away from the axis of rotation, creating a longer lever on which the muscle can act.

2. **Space behind kneecap:** As you extend your leg coming up from a plié, imagine the space behind your kneecap increasing, creating a little cushion of air for the kneecap to glide on.

3. **Psoas string walk:** Visualize the iliopsoas muscle as two strings inserted at the minor trochanters. The strings detach from their origins on the spine and remain attached at their insertion to the minor trochanters. Watch as the strings drop forward to become horizontal to the ground. The strings are now pointing outward, vertical to the bone. Let the strings pull the femurs forward alternately, leading you out into a walk.

Angular Motion

A pirouette is an ideal example of angular motion. As discussed previously, turning force is called torque. The mass of the turning object defines the moment of inertia, or the body's resistance to change in angular motion. Torque arises from a force couple, which consists of two equal and opposite parallel forces acting on a body. It is the prerequisite for a change in angular momentum. In preparing to turn, the dancer's feet are placed at a distance, ready to push against the floor. The floor then pushes back with an equal and opposite force. The greater the distance between the pushing feet, the greater the torque. Obviously, a pirouette beginning in fifth position requires more muscular force for the same number of turns than one beginning in fourth position.

To lengthen the amount of time that force is exerted against the floor, dancers often execute a preparatory motion with the arms and upper body. Once the force has been exerted against the floor and the dancer is turning, the angular momentum will remain constant or diminish due to friction against the floor. Since angular momentum is the product of moment of inertia and angular velocity, the dancer can increase velocity by reducing inertia. As discussed previously, inertia depends on the mass of the body and, in the case of moment of inertia, its distribution relative to the axis of rotation. If the mass is far from the axis, the moment of inertia is larger. The larger the shape, the greater the moment of inertia. Obviously, a pirouette in passé requires less force than one in arabesque. A pirouetting dancer instinctively reduces inertia and increases velocity by bringing the arms closer to the body. To decrease velocity and end the turn, the dancer increases inertia by opening the arms away from the body.

ANGULAR MOTION

1. **Particles and pirouette:** Visualize your body as composed of many particles making up a mass (although it does not sound very flattering). In a pirouette, the particles can be brought closer to the rotational axis to increase the velocity of rotation or moved farther from the rotational axis to decrease the velocity of rotation.

2. **Magnetic axis:** In a pirouette, imagine the axis to be a magnet. To increase the velocity of your turns, the magnet attracts the surrounding mass. It is important that the mass is attracted to the axis equally from all sides, or the axis itself will be disturbed.

ENERGY CONSERVATION

Sometimes it seems as if energy disappears. A bouncing ball goes up and down, the height decreasing with each bounce until it stops. Did the energy vanish? No; it was converted to another form of energy. As the ball moved, some of the energy was used to push the air aside and some was converted into heat as the ball hit the floor. This is known as the law of conservation. A system may undergo many changes, but some measurable quantity of the system never changes.

A seesaw can convert energy from one form to another. When the mass on one end of the seesaw goes up, the mass on the other end comes down. The higher mass has more potential energy. In this case, it is gravitational energy that is being conserved. The mass that rises gains gravitational energy; the mass that falls loses gravitational energy.

In a normal standing position, the head has more potential energy than the hips or the knees because the head has the longest distance to fall to the ground. If it were to fall, it would have the most kinetic energy. In a vertical leap, once you leave the ground against the resistance of gravity, you are moving through space and have kinetic energy. While you are going up, kinetic energy is reconverted into potential energy, and the higher you go, the greater the resulting potential energy. This energy was created by the contraction of your muscles, allowing the bones to leverage against the floor. At the top of your leap, you stop moving for a moment because you have no more kinetic energy—it is now potential energy. The ability to do work is there but is inactive at that moment. As you descend, the energy is reconverted.

When you execute a battement, chemical energy in the muscles transforms into kinetic energy as the muscles contract. This energy is then used to move the bones as levers. The levers gain potential energy as the leg rises into the air. Elastic energy is created as the elastic components in the muscles, tendons, and connective tissue are stretched. As the leg pauses for a moment before going back down, its potential energy peaks. As the leg comes down, it transforms elastic and potential energies into kinetic energy.

These physics principles indicate how to create efficient movement. When dancing, we usually want to convert a high ratio of our energy into the kinetic form. Of course, there is no way to avoid losing energy in the form of heat and no way to avoid its accompanying and cooling perspiration. But some dancers look like they've just run the New York City Marathon after a warm-up or barre work. Feeling very tired after a dance class is not necessarily a measure of success. A good class should leave you feeling flexible and coordinated, not tense and cramped.

POTENTIAL FALL AND KINETIC REBOUND

Try a Doris Humphrey fall and rebound exercise to experience the change between potential and kinetic energy. You begin the fall with a lot of potential energy and turn it all into kinetic energy as you fall. When you break the fall with your legs, you leverage more energy into the system to move back up and convert your kinetic energy into potential energy as you return to vertical. (See also *Dance Imagery for Technique and Performance*.)

THE ABILITY OF MATERIALS TO RESIST FORCE

Whenever a force is applied to a material such as metal, wood, or rubber—or in the human body, bone, muscle, or tendon—the material may change its size or shape. Strain is defined as the deformation of a material relative to its original shape; the term stress describes all the reaction forces created within the material when subject to external forces. The ability of a material to resist force depends on its structure. *Tensile strength* is the degree to which a material can resist being pulled apart. Two equal external forces acting along the same line and in opposition cause tensile stress. The tensile strength of a string is its ability to carry a weight before tearing apart. The opposing forces on the string arise from the weight hanging on the string and the place where the string is attached.

Compressive strength is the degree of resistance to being compressed. Two external forces acting on opposite sides and in the same line against an object cause compressive stress. When you stand up, your bones resist being compressed. If your bones could not resist compression, your body would spread into a sci-fi-like blob on the floor due to the attraction of gravity. This would happen to you on Jupiter, bones or no bones, because the gravitational force there is so much greater than on Earth. In our bodies, bones are best at resisting compressing forces. Tendons, ligaments, and muscles are built to resist tensile forces. If this were not so, your arms, which are primarily held in place by ligaments, muscles, and tendons, would drop to the ground due to the continuous pull of gravity.

Other forces in the human body include shear, torsion, and bending. Experienced at the fulcrum-lever contact area in imbalanced first-class levers, shear causes a body surface to slide over an adjacent surface. Such bending occurs when a load is placed on a supported beam. The magnitude of bending depends on the load's weight and the distance between the load and the supports. Bending is a combination of shear, tensile, and compression stress. Torsion develops when forces act on a rod or shaft that tend to twist it; again, tensile, compression, and shearing stresses are at work.

Just as the above-mentioned forces are working in the human body, any structure made by humans exemplifies these forces at work. Bricks in a wall resist compression. Cross beams transfer the weight of a floor to the walls. The beams need to resist bending, so if one starts to bend, a brace must be installed (figure 9.14). In much the same way, we reduce our risk of injury by refining our alignment and movement patterns to help keep harmful stresses and strains at bay.

Even the lungs provide a certain amount of support. At the *Gymnasium* I attended in Switzerland, we played soccer in a rounded structure called the *balloon*. Based on the principles discussed above, this sizable outdoor gymnasium without walls or cross beams was supported by slightly increased atmospheric pressure inside the plastic walls. The plastic cover needed to resist being pulled apart; a hole would make the structure collapse. The hull of the balloon was the structure's tensile element. The weight of the cover was resisted by the air, which, if it is contained, resists being compressed like a wall.

ABILITIES TO RESIST FORCE

Take a small rubber band and stretch it until it breaks to discover its maximum tensile strength. It reaches maximum at the moment just before it breaks.

Figure 9.14   Traditional Swiss house braced by wooden beams.

CHAPTER

10 Joint and Muscle Function

A change in the body's alignment is always associated with adjustments in the joints and muscles. The dynamic approach to alignment is not about holding joints or muscles in certain positions, for this would be fixed alignment, quite the opposite of what we are trying to achieve. By understanding how they work, we can use imagery to create a balance in our muscles and joints that is strong, yet fluid, ready at any moment to send us into coordinated action.

JOINT TYPES

Joints are divided into two types: synarthroses (joints without sinovial fluid) and diarthroses (joints with sinovial fluid), popularly considered movable joints. Synarthroses are further divided into fibrous and cartilaginous joints. The sutures of the skull are fibrous joints connected by thin fibrous tissue that allow for only slight motion at birth and in infancy. The joint between the pubic bones, the pubic symphysis, is an example of a cartilaginous synarthrosis.

A diarthrosis enables free movement of the two adjoining bones. The joint is encapsulated in lubricating sinovial fluid and covered with cartilage. Joint receptors within the capsule transmit information on the status of the joint to the central nervous system. Hinges and pivots are diarthroses with movement capability in one direction. The interphalangeal joints of the fingers are hinges, and the atlantoaxial joint in the neck is a pivot joint around which the atlas rotates.

Condyloid and saddle joints have two degrees of freedom. The knuckle joints are condyloid; the thumb knuckle is a saddle joint. Ball and socket joints, such as the hip, and plane joints, such as the carpals at the base of the hand, have three degrees of freedom.

Joint surfaces are either convex or concave. The ball of the hip joint belongs to the upper leg bone, the femur, and is convex. The socket of the hip joint belongs to the pelvis and is concave. If the end of a bone is convex, as in the femur, the shaft of the bone will move in the opposite direction from the surface of the ball (figure 10.1a). This means that if you lift your knee, thus lifting the shaft of the femur, the surface of the ball will move downward. The opposite holds true for the socket of the hip joint. Because the socket is part of the pelvis, it moves in the same direction as the pelvis. If you tilt your pelvis forward, the socket moves forward as well (figure 10.1b).

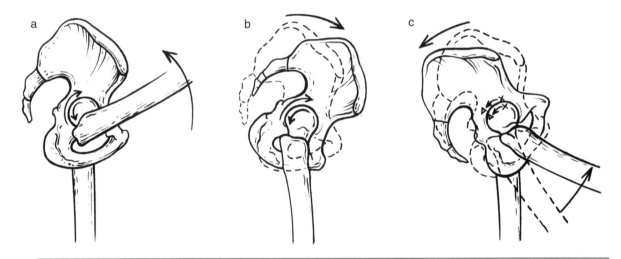

Figure 10.1   (a) If the end of a bone is convex, the shaft of the bone will move in the opposite direction from the surface of the ball. (b) Since the hip socket which is part of the pelvis is convex, if you tilt the pelvis forward, the socket moves forward as well. (c) If the rotation of the head of the femur is insufficient, the pelvis will tuck to accommodate the continuing elevation of the leg.

IMAGING JOINT MOVEMENT

Stand on one leg and lift your knee until your thigh is horizontal to the floor. Lower your knee again. Now perform the same motion but focus on the ball in your hip socket moving downward. You may notice that it feels different to lift the leg in this way. Try lifting the knee one more time, but this time visualize an imaginary string attached to your knee, lifting it up as the ball in your hip socket becomes heavy and drops downward (figure 10.2).

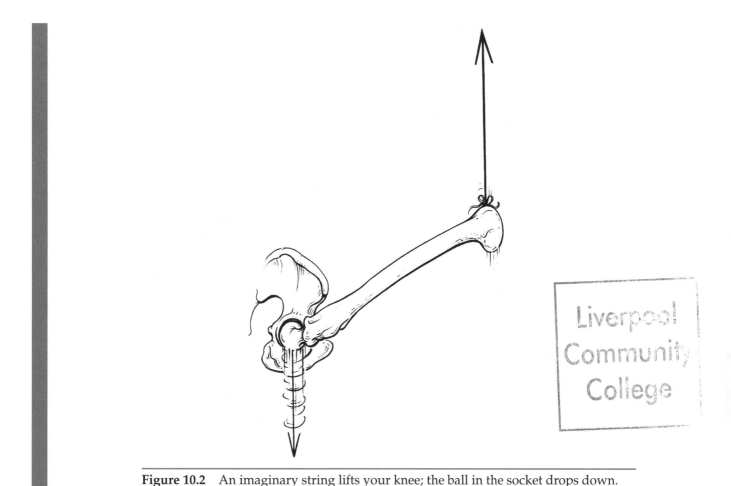

Figure 10.2   An imaginary string lifts your knee; the ball in the socket drops down.

Joint Surface Interaction

Joint surfaces can change their relationship to one another in three different ways. The shoulder or glenohumeral joint exemplifies all three. One joint surface can rotate over another, similar to the tires of a car spinning on ice without traction (figure 10.3a). Here the contact point of the ice remains constant while the contact point of the tire is constantly changing. A joint surface can roll over another like a tire rolling on a road (figure 10.3b), the contact point of each surface changing equally. One joint surface can slide over another as the tires of car slide over an icy road when the brakes lock up (figure 10.3c). The contact point of the tire remains the same while the contact point of the ice changes. Only in the case of the wheels spinning on ice does the axis of the wheel remain in place; in the other cases, the axis moves, creating a so-called instantaneous axis of rotation (IAR). In many cases, joint motion is a combination of gliding and spinning—the IAR moves in an arc through space (see figure 10.4).

   Lubrication is essential for joint functioning, decreasing wear and providing nourishment for the cartilage. In figure 10.5, a water fountain designed by Christian Meyer of Munich shows how effective such a system can be in bearing weight. A 1,000-kilogram (2,250-pound) granite ball rests within a perfectly aligned granite socket in a layer of water issuing from a deep underground source. The water

Figure 10.3 A joint surface can: (a) rotate over another, as when the tires of a car spin on ice without traction; (b) roll over another like a tire rolling on a road; (c) slide over another as the tires of the car slide over an icy road when the brakes lock up.

Adapted, by permission, from J. Zuckerman and F. Matseu, 1989, *Basic Biomechanics of the Muscoskeletal System* (Baltimore: Williams and Wilkins).

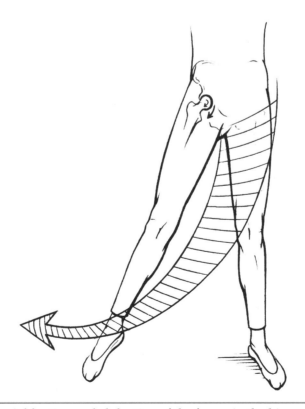

Figure 10.4 Adduction and abduction of the femur in the hip socket traces an arc.

creates sufficient lubrication and hydrostatic lift so that children can easily set the otherwise heavy ball into rotary motion.

Figure 10.5   A granite ball rolls within a perfectly aligned granite socket in a layer of water issuing from a deep underground source.

In rotation, the joint surfaces move in opposite directions to each other (counterrotate). This may be confusing at first because the eye usually sees the movement of only one joint surface, when in reality, both are moving relative to each other. Figure 10.6 may help in visualizing this phenomenon. The bottom of a ship is depicted as the ball of the joint, and the water surrounding the ball is the socket. As the ship lists to the right, the convex hull glides to the left. The water beneath it rushes to the right, gliding along the hull of the boat. Although the surface of the ocean is still horizontal, the water has changed position relative to the bottom of the boat.

In a grand battement en avant (high leg kick to the front), the head of the femur spins in its socket. Ideally, the spinning action in the joint suffices for the full extension of the leg. If the rotation is insufficient or gets stuck, the pelvis will tuck to accommodate the continuing elevation of the leg. Tucking will bend the supporting knee (see figure 10.1c).

This situation is comparable to turning a doorknob. If you hold the knob loosely, your hand will simply glide over it without turning the knob (figure 10.7a). Tightening your grip on the knob will arrest the gliding motion and turn the knob (figure 10.7b). Likewise, tightening the joints will prevent easy gliding of the leg into high extension. This situation is depicted in figure 10.1c for the hip joint. The X shows two opposing points on the head of the femur and the socket of the pelvis. Instead of the Xs moving in opposite directions, or counterrotating as would be the case in a spin, they move in the same direction to point delta. Therefore, elevation of the leg has caused the pelvis to tilt backward. Ease of joint motion can be promoted by imaging the ball spinning easily in the socket.

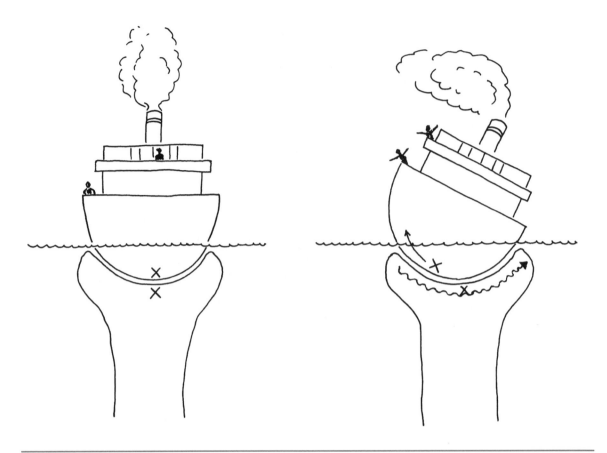

Figure 10.6   As the ship hull glides to the left, the water beneath it rushes to the right, gliding along the bottom of the boat.

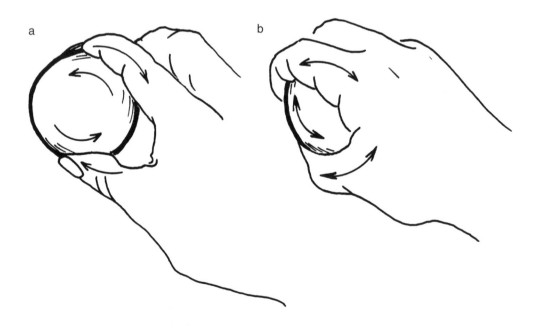

Figure 10.7   (a) Gripping a knob loosely, your hand will simply glide over it. (b) Gripping a knob tightly arrests the gliding and turns the knob.

IMAGING JOINT SURFACE INTERACTION

1. **Counterrotation in the hip socket:** As you lift your knee, focus on the relative motion of the ball and socket. As the knee moves up, visualize the dorsal surface of the ball moving downward (see figure 10.1a). Although the concave surface of the hip socket seems to be stationary, it moves relative to the surface of the ball of the femur. Because the surface of the ball moves downward, the visualized relative motion of the socket is upward. As the knee moves downward, visualize the dorsal surface of the ball moving upward and the surface of the socket moving downward.

2. **Spin, glide, and counterrotation in abduction/adduction of the hip socket:** Move your leg out to the side (abduction) and then move it back in (adduction). In abduction, there is both a downward gliding motion of the ball in the socket and a spin and counterrotation of the socket. The IAR traces a downward and outward arc. Think of this arc on a much larger scale and project it onto the motion of the entire leg (see figure 10.4 again).

To cover all joint possibilities, imagine the upward movement of the concave socket (counterrotation) as occurring slightly before the downward motion of the head of the femur. This syncopation will help stabilize the joint in space.

Kinematic Chains

If you bend your knees (plié), the ankle and hip joints bend as well. Any motion in the ankle joint (while standing) will result in motion in the knee and hip joints. The bones are linked in a closed kinematic chain—movement in one joint elicits movement in the neighboring joints. With both feet on the ground, the legs are confined by two firm boundaries, the floor and the pelvis, making the legs part of a closed kinematic chain. If the foot is not on the ground, the motion of the knees may or may not involve the hip and ankle joints; this is an open kinematic chain.

Range of Motion (ROM)

Every joint has a normal range of motion (ROM). Limitations on ROM may stem from bony deformations or cartilaginous or ligamentous restrictions. In most cases of restricted ROM, the muscles crossing the particular joint are tight. This is why stretching to increase ROM is so prevalent among dancers. Excessive ROM without sufficient muscular strength may result in injury because the joint is not protected by the stabilizing action of the muscles. Dynamic alignment increases ROM by reducing muscle tightness while providing stability.

BONES

Bones are the densest form of connective tissue in the body. In addition to producing white and red blood cells in their marrow, they protect internal organs; for example, the ribs protect the heart and lungs and the skull protects the brain. Stanley Keleman (1985) refers to bones as "inner honeycombs." Although the mineral content of bone is similar to that of marble, it also contains collagen fibrils for elasticity (Juhan 1987). A demineralized bone can be bent, as if made of rubber, and will rebound into its original shape. Thus, bones can resist high degrees of compression, tensile, and shear forces.

The body contains 200 bones of all shapes. There are short bones in the hands and feet, long bones in the legs and arms, flat bones in the skull, bones with airy compartments in the sinuses, and so on. The long bones are hollow, increasing their resistance to breakage. The sesamoids in the feet act as pulleys and shock absorbers. Some bones (such as vertebrae) do not fit into any of the above categories.

Bones consist of several layers that differ significantly from each other in structure and function. Their outer covering is called the periosteum, a tough protective membrane. You can feel this slippery, skinlike covering by placing your finger on the front of your shinbone and moving it around. The next layer of the bone is the dense and compact cortical layer; it is the essence of the bone, its hardest part. Further toward the center is the cancellous or spongy layer with a platelike structure called the trabeculae (small beams). The trabeculae are situated along the lines of force through the bones and aid in supporting the joints. The trabeculae arise in response to stresses in the system (figure 10.8), creating force lines similar to the iron girders of the Eiffel Tower or the curving braces in an archway (see figure 12.21).

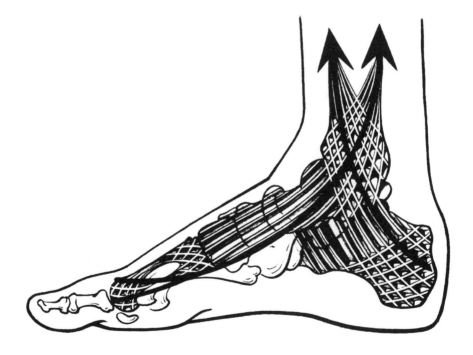

Figure 10.8   The trabeculae are force lines similar to the curving braces in an archway.

Similar to coral, the interior of bones consist of many interconnected channels and structures designed to support weight efficiently. Doctors have even been able to use coral in rebuilding bones after injury.

The innermost strata of the bone is the soft marrow, which is continuously producing new blood cells. Even as you read this chapter, millions of new blood cells are being born.

Bones are not at all fixed in shape. Depending on the forces that they are subject to, they can change in contour and remodel themselves. Just as a wind-blown tree adapts to stresses (figure 10.9), so too will bone remodel itself according to compression and pulling. A furniture mover's bone mass increases; the bone in a ballerina's second toe thickens. The pull of muscles on bones creates bulges such as those on the major and minor trochanters.

Most bones can be viewed as spiraled along their long axes. A classic example is the femur, which spirals inward as viewed from the top downward (see figure 11.13). The leg bones are actually a set of counterspirals; the shinbone spirals outward and the foot spirals inward. Ribs are interesting because they are both curved and spiraled. These shapes lead to imagery that can help us with spiraling motions such as in the shot-put, discus throw, or spiral turns.

Figure 10.9   A wind-blown tree adapts to stresses.

EXERCISING THE BONES

1. **Body hangs on bones (walking, standing, sitting):** Place all your weight on your bones by thinking of them as a clothes hanger that the rest of your body can hang on like a well-pressed suit. It is easy for the bones to perform this task; they remain light and buoyant as the body casually drapes over them.

2. **Muscle sleeves (improvisation):** Think of the bones as arms within their sleeves made of muscles. It may help to think of the muscles as being made of silk or a similar soft material. Wiggle the bones inside their sleeves, imagining that the two can move independently. Allow the sleeves to slide over the bones. It is easiest to begin this exercise by actually moving an arm while using the image. It takes practice to use the image effectively without any movement. Try this image with different parts of the body and notice where it seems more difficult to create the sense of bones being separate from muscles, where it feels like the sleeves are stuck to the bones.

3. **Reach with your bones, reach with your muscles (improvisation):** As you reach out into space, think of your bones leading the way as if they were eager to move out and explore the space. As you experiment with various areas of the body, notice where it is easier to let the bones initiate movement and where it seems more difficult. Is it possible to think of the finger bones moving out into space? The tailbone? The top of the skull? Now practice the opposite: Instead of the bones, which have "lost interest" in moving out into space, the muscles now lead the way.

4. **Core initiation:** Practice initiating movement from the core of your bones. This is the soft part, the marrow. It seems unusual to think of bones as having a soft component, let alone thinking of this area as moving you through space. However, you may notice that in this softness lies a certain power.

CONNECTIVE TISSUE AND FASCIA

Connective tissue makes a community out of structures placed in each other's vicinity. If you removed everything except the connective tissue, you would still recognize the body's shape. Consisting of bones, ligaments, tendons, and fascia, connective tissue creates form, fills space, transfers mechanical force, envelopes, and supports. Because it is viscoelastic, it can return to its original shape after deformation and dampen shearing forces.

Bone, the densest form of connective tissue, can withstand the highest compressive loads. Connective tissue is the packaging of all our body surfaces. Fascia, the layer next to the muscles, is like a very tough sheet that separates, connects, and encases. Our muscles would spread out like a glob of honey without fascia. That is why imagery of melting, spreading muscles is not far-fetched. Fascia also connects and organizes the spatial arrangement of our organs, hanging them from the ceiling of the diaphragm, as with the liver, or hammocking organs between bony support systems. In this equal partnership, the organs support the surrounding structures with their hydrostatic and muscular properties.

Tendons transfer the force of the muscles to the bones. Ligaments are the ropes and pulleys of the body, securing the joints, limiting joint motion where necessary, and stabilizing structures. Tendons and ligaments have high tensile strength and, in normal activity, have a large "reserve" of this strength. Like bones, ligaments and tendons can remodel depending on the strains to which they are exposed.

MUSCLE

A muscle is a large bundle of fibers held together by small sheets, which in turn are held together by a larger enveloping sheet. The functional unit of a skeletal muscle, a muscle designed to make us move through space, is fiber. Every fiber is basically a small contracting machine that can exert force on the bones to which it is attached by shortening itself.

Innervation

A special type of nerve cell, the alpha motor neuron, signals the muscle fibers to contract. All muscle fibers connect to a single alpha motor neuron, a motor unit, which is the smallest part of the muscle that can contract independently. When the fibers receive a command signal, they can do only one thing—shorten. This doesn't mean that the whole muscle shortens. If only a few muscle fibers receive the command to shorten, no perceptible movement occurs in the muscle. The few fibers that are working may not suffice to contract the whole muscle. We can compare this situation to a team of husky dogs hooked up to a sled. If only one of the dozen or so dogs attempts to pull the sled while the others are sound asleep, the sled will not move forward.

For a muscle to contract, motor units need to fire repeatedly. The more motor units activated, the stronger the movement. If you are thinking of a movement without doing it, or you are hesitant about doing it, you will activate some motor units, but not enough to make you move.

Types of Contraction

Three types of contraction are commonly described: concentric, eccentric, and isometric. Concentric and eccentric contractions are dynamic, involving movement through space of the bony levers to which the muscles are attached. If you hold a weight in your hand and slowly bend your elbow to lift it upward, your biceps and other upper arm muscles shorten and contract at the same time, as expected. This is a concentric, or shortening, contraction. If you lower the weight, the muscles are still contracting to keep the weight from falling out of control, but they are getting longer in breaking the fall of the weight. This is called an eccentric, or lengthening, contraction. If you simply hold a weight with your elbow bent, the muscles work without lengthening or shortening. This is an isometric, or constant-length, contraction. The term contraction can actually be confusing. Literally, an "eccentric contraction" means "away from center, pulling together," in other words, a contradiction in terms. Some authors are therefore replacing the term muscular contraction with muscle action, which makes more sense.

SLOWLY LET GO

When your upper thigh quadriceps muscle straightens your knee, it is performing a shortening, or concentric, contraction. In a plié, this same muscle must break your fall by eccentric action. As your knee bends, the quadriceps lengthens while contracting just enough to break your fall. Visualize the muscle slowly letting go. You can compare the sensation to the notion of carefully lowering a bucket into a deep well. You may also think of the muscle as slowly stretching taffy.

Prime Movers, Synergists, and Stabilizers

For every joint movement there are muscles that produce this motion called the movers or agonists. If you want to bend your elbow, then certain elbow flexor muscles are the so-called prime movers because they are the most important movers. The muscles that oppose this movement are called the antagonists. In a passé motion the iliopsoas is the prime mover, because it is the strongest hip flexor. Sometimes certain muscles join forces to produce a certain effect; they are called synergists.

The agonist sends an inhibiting signal to the antagonist so that it can perform its function. Just as a ship cannot pull out of the harbor if it is not released from its ropes, an agonist cannot move if it is not released by its antagonist. This process is called reciprocal inhibition, a mutual relaying of tension states so that the muscles can work in harmony.

If joint stability is needed, such as in the standing leg in the grand battement, then co-contraction may occur, in which both agonist and antagonist contract simultaneously. These muscles are now acting as stabilizers to maintain posture and continuity of motion. Stabilization does not always mean that a part of the body is being fixed in a non-moving position, but may occur dynamically throughout a motion cycle.

BRUSHED INTO LENGTH

Aid the movers by seeing the antagonists as long and released. In a battement, développé, or any extension, visualize the underside of the arm and leg being brushed into length (figure 10.10).

Figure 10.10   In a battement, développé, or any extension, visualize the underside of the arm and leg being brushed into length.
Adapted, by permission, from a photo by Steven Speliotis.

The Stretch Reflex

Complex movement would not be possible without an automatic pilot constantly adjusting our posture. This automatic pilot consists of reflexes that underlie our consciously guided movement. Sherrington (1964) writes: "The reflex is independent of consciousness even at first occurrence. It does not emanate from the 'ego'" (p. 156). We have all reflexively withdrawn our fingers from a hot plate or flame. The body acts before we can think about it, producing rapid movements to prevent us from injuring ourselves. If the doctor's hammer taps the proper point, the knee straightens due to the stretch reflex. The so-called muscle spindles and the Golgi tendon organs monitor the length of a muscle to keep it from being injured by overstretching. To permanently increase muscle length through stretching, this reflex must be circumvented. Reflexes, righting reactions, and equilibrium responses underlie all successful, effortless movement. Primitive reflexes are with us from birth; righting reactions that control alignment come into full bloom at about one year of age. Equilibrium responses maintain balance from the time we first walk (Cohen 1993a).

Muscle Tone

Tone (from the Greek *tonos*, meaning tension), the basic level of muscular tension, determines the body's density. Your basic muscle tone is lower when you sleep and higher when you are very active. Without muscle tone, the body would collapse; conversely, excessive tone blocks movement. A baby's muscles feel soft, resilient, and rubbery to the touch because they are free of excessive tension. Some people seem to be in a constant state of high muscular tension, whereas others are in the opposite state—flaccidity. Often we find differing tension states in the body, such as tense shoulders with high tone and midsection with low tone. Similarly, varying styles of movement require varying degrees of muscle tone. The pre-Breakdance robot style of dancing, for example, was definitely a high-tone affair.

Gerda Alexander (1976), founder of the body therapy system called "Eutonie" ("eu" means harmonious in Greek), sought to create an optimal balance of tone in the entire body. Testing her students' basic sensibilities to tone by having them make drawings and clay models of their own bodies, she found little correlation between the results and the person's body type, even among dancers. She suggests correcting this "Dys-tonie" or unbalanced tone in the body through modeling, drawing, movement exercises, lying and rolling on balls or chestnuts, among other things.

The more you can change the level of tone in your body at will, the richer your expressive possibilities. Improvisation is a way to practice this ability. Balanced tone is one of the goals of dynamic alignment. Most people need to increase tone in the center front of their bodies, which includes the abdominal and deep pelvic muscles. This in turn helps create the foundation for reducing tension in the shoulder and upper chest areas.

EXERCISING MUSCLE TONE

1. **Changes in tone:** Move like a robot and then like a flowing river. Imagine supporting a heavy weight and then gliding through a silk curtain. Be an oak tree resisting the wind and then a leaf being tossed by the wind. (See also *Dance Imagery for Technique and Performance*.)

2. **Lying on chestnuts:** Gather a bunch of chestnuts or marbles and spread them on a towel. Lie down with the back of your body on the chestnuts and imagine your back melting down over them. If this hurts, use soft rubber balls, or place the chestnuts under areas that do not hurt until some of the tension in your back recedes. (Do not do this exercise if you have an acute attack of back pain; only use it as a preventive measure.)

Muscles Crossing Joints

Muscles only affect the joints they cross. Some muscles cross one joint, and others cross two joints, often creating opposing actions. Two-joint muscles are most efficient when they can shorten at one joint and lengthen at the other; otherwise they may develop what is called active insufficiency. The rectus femoris muscle, for example, originates at the hip and attaches below the knee. It flexes the hip and extends the knee, making it easier to perform a développé than a straight leg lift. If the knee is stretched as you lift the leg, the rectus needs to shorten both at the hip and at the knee, causing an active insufficiency. Simply stated, there is less "shortening power" left if the knee is extended as you lift the leg. If the knee is bent, the rectus can concentrate its contractile power on the hip. By learning how to change muscle balance toward more active relative use of the iliopsoas in leg extensions, you can avoid active insufficiency in the rectus femoris.

Extending the leg to the back in arabesque lengthens the rectus femoris at the hip and shortens it at the knee, lending optimal function to this two-joint muscle. When you bend the knee, as in attitude, the hamstrings shorten over both the back of the hip and the knee. If you continue to bend the knee in this position, you will notice that the hamstrings become actively insufficient, sometimes even cramping.

EMPHASIS ON ILIOPSOAS

The purpose of this exercise is to emphasize the deep-lying iliopsoas in a hip flexion. Lift and lower your knee and notice what this action feels like. To activate the prime mover for hip flexion, the iliopsoas, use an indirect approach, reducing your reliance on the secondary movers such as the rectus femoris. As you lift your knee, imagine the place where you are creasing your hip to be very foldable, soft, and melting. Now lower your knee. Perform the action once again in your mind's eye only, focusing on a very malleable, soft creasing at the hip. Lift your knee again and notice any changes in sensation. Lift your other knee and notice the difference between your legs.

Control Over Individual Muscles

Learning how to control individual muscles is so difficult that it can usually only be done with the visual and auditory feedback of a biofeedback machine. We humans would have been extinct long ago if we had to instruct every individual muscle to move. It would have taken forever to escape from an attacking predator (figure 10.11), with disastrous results for humanity (figure 10.12). Body therapies would not exist if we had such control because everyone could optimally adjust every muscle. We would never need massages, but most of the day would be spent organizing our muscles.

Figure 10.11   Human beings would be long extinct if they had to instruct each individual muscle to move. It would have taken forever to escape from an attacking bear.

Figure 10.12   . . . with disastrous results for humanity.

Muscular interdependence is important to remember when using muscle imagery. For example, if you image an action line of a muscle as lengthening, you will influence not only that individual muscle but all coacting muscles such as synergists and antagonists.

Muscle Balance and Posture

Ideally, muscles not required to perform a movement should not be involved. But are there any such isolated movements? Just lifting your arm to the side causes subtle changes throughout the body. Your breathing pattern changes slightly, and even the muscles of the legs need to adjust. Muscles stabilize one part of the body against the movement of another and constantly perform midmovement corrections to maintain balance. All of these actions should happen efficiently, without excess strain.

Dynamic alignment helps us achieve this goal by balancing the muscles in our neutral position (easier said than done). I have already pointed out the importance of well-balanced, first-class levers for alignment. To simplify for clarity, muscles acting on a bone can be visualized as a tent or drape attached over a central pole. If the muscles are tight, the bone is held rigidly in place (figure 10.13a). If the muscles are flaccid, the bone sways and lacks control (figure 10.13b). If the muscles are imbalanced, tight on one side of the joint and flaccid on the other, the bone loses alignment (figure 10.13c). Ideally, the muscles should be neither too tight nor too flaccid.

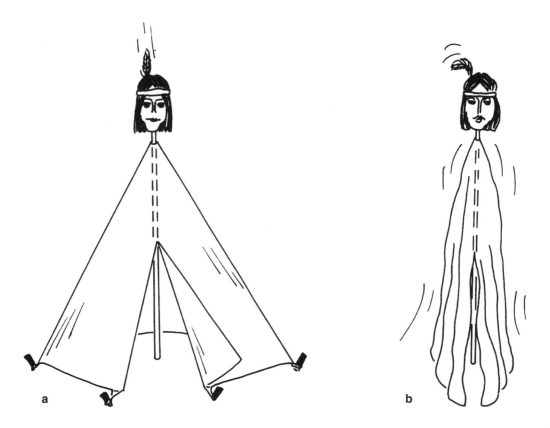

a   b

(continued)

Figure 10.13   (a) If the muscles are tight, the bone is held rigidly in place. (b) If the muscles are flaccid, the bone sways and lacks control.

c

Figure 10.13   (c) If the muscles are imbalanced, tight on one side of the joint and flaccid on the other, the bone loses its alignment.

Can alignment be corrected by strengthening some muscles and weakening others? To create balance, you could lengthen a habitually shortened muscle and strengthen a weak one. A good knowledge of muscle function is necessary to improve balance with such exercises, and even then success will be limited to creating a temporary and "rough" balance. Sweigard (1978) points out that any exercises to increase the strength of weak muscles will also increase the strength of strong muscles. Unless you change your basic habits, body image, and movement patterns, you are going to reinforce your old imbalances indefinitely. Some somatic therapies, such as Vojta-Reflexlocomotion, emphasize that agonist-antagonist training is not very helpful because it leads to an overexertion of individual muscle groups. Vojta (1992) contends that a plan for the ideal posture preexists within the brain, and that all you need to do is create the correct stimulation to bring it into existence.

MINIMAL AMOUNT OF HOLDING

Hold a one- to two-inch stick or rod in one hand and lower it perpendicularly to the ground. If you grasp it tightly, it will stay in its position. Determine the minimum effort needed to keep the stick from falling. Do the same exercise with your left hand and compare the ease with which each hand accomplished the task.

Discovering Muscular Imbalances

There are several ways to begin noticing muscular imbalances in your body. One is simply to palpate an area on one side of the body and compare it in muscle thickness and density to the same area on the other side. The neck is a good place to start because many of us hold our heads slightly to one side. Put your fingers on both sides of your neck and see if you notice any differences between the muscles on the left and right sides. Compare your findings with your preferred motions of the head: Does it seem more normal to tilt the head slightly to the right or to the left? Does it seem more normal to turn the head to the right or to the left to look behind you? Usually, if you prefer to look to the right, that is also your better turning side in dance, influencing muscle chains all the way down to the feet.

DISCOVERING MUSCULAR IMBALANCES

Standing up from a chair and sitting down again is another way to detect muscular imbalances. Put your right leg in front and your left in back and stand up and sit down again. Repeat with your left leg in front and your right leg in back. Do this very slowly and notice the differences between the sides. Catch yourself during the day and watch how you stand up and sit down. Most likely you use similar patterns and reinforce them, continuously. (See "Discovering and Correcting Leg Patterns" in chapter 11.)

How Movement Habits Create Muscular Imbalances

In dance, it is important to be equally strong on both sides of the body. Balance of strength may be more important than overall strength. We are usually aware which is our "better" supporting leg and which leg is "better" in extension, and sometimes try to correct the situation. But if your only action is to strengthen and stretch, and you don't attempt to change your nondance movement habits, you will not be entirely successful. Don't work on your alignment only in dance class. When dancers listen to the teacher during class, their true alignment patterns often emerge, patterns surprisingly different from their "dance alignment." True improvement in alignment is not possible by focusing on and artificially maintaining alignment only during class.

Muscle Chains

Muscle chains are separate muscles with different origins and insertions but similar lines of action. The left internal oblique stomach muscles and the right external oblique stomach muscles form a muscle chain, as do the right internal obliques and the left external obliques. These particular muscle chains support complex rotary and spiral actions throughout the body. Although their connection is not otherwise obvious, muscle chains connect the arm to the pelvis. Anteriorly, the ascending fibers of the pectorals are in line with the internal obliques and the psoas of the opposite side. Posteriorly, the latissimus dorsi connects the arm to the spine and the lumbar fascia. Its fibers are generally in line with the external obliques and the gluteus maximus of the opposite side. Imaging muscle chains creates strong kinesthetic connections throughout the body, which can manifest in feelings of envelopment, three-dimensionality, and general interconnectedness. This is helpful in spiral turns, but when visualized, these sensations are helpful in many actions, even in standing.

MUSCLE CHAIN

Lying on the floor with one arm overhead, visualize a diagonal muscle chain through the body, from the biceps, ascending pectoral, and serratus anterior and crossing the midline of the body diagonally to the inner obliques and psoas (figure 10.14).

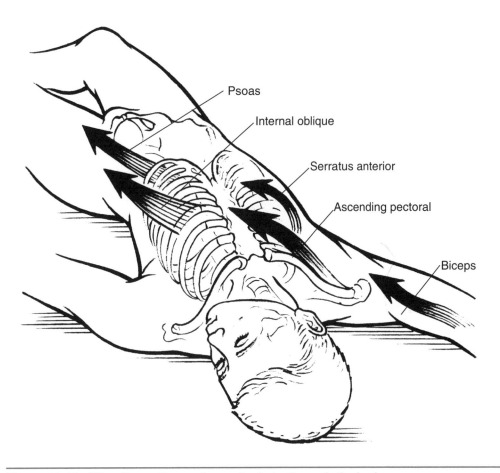

Figure 10.14 Visualize a diagonal muscle chain through the body.

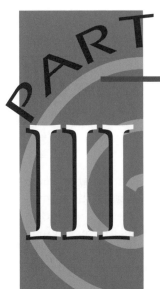

PART

III

Anatomical Imagery Exercises

*D*ynamic alignment requires a knowledge of anatomy—the location and status of your joints, the tension states of your muscles and organs, the numerous connections between the muscles, bones, and organs, and the shapes and inner volumes within you—to give the mind a vast array of options for improving and adjusting alignment.

A complete survey of anatomy is beyond the scope of this book. In preparing this section, I have focused on the particular needs of the dancer and movement specialist in relation to proper alignment of the musculoskeletal system. Other body systems are mentioned where appropriate.

Although I have subdivided the discussion into the major anatomical groups and their associated imagery exercises, these subdivisions should not be considered absolute because every part of the body is in some way connected to every other part. If you pull on the leg of someone lying in the supine position, the person will feel it in his or her neck. The connective tissues transfer the mechanical force all the way through the body.

Because of these interconnections, images relate to each other. For example, using an image that influences the sacrum and the joints between the sacrum and the pelvis, the iliosacral joints, creates a reaction on the other side of the pelvis, at the pubic symphysis. The image used for the back of the pelvis may be "widening" or "spreading," whereas the experience at the front of the pelvis may be "connecting" or "integrating." Thus, imagery helps us create a unified experience of the body by heightening awareness of these interactions, bringing us closer to the experience of dynamic alignment.

It always helps to touch the accessible anatomical landmarks. Tracing bony outlines aids the visualization process by creating a tactile map of these parts in one's own body. Working with a partner enhances the benefit of many of these exercises. Beyond personality, posture, and fingerprints, every bone and muscle makes us unique.

A person skilled at using imagery creates a synergistic effect, enhancing the effectiveness of each area by visualizing two or more images simultaneously. For example, visualize the shoulders and sacrum widening as the central axis becomes perpendicular to the floor.

I introduce each image with a name suggestive of its purpose and the position or movement in which it may be practiced. These positions are not absolute. You may substitute standing, walking, or improvising if it suits you.

CHAPTER 11

The Pelvis, Hip Joint, and Company

*L*et's start in the center of the body, where life itself begins. The pelvis is the hub of the body, a center of stability and originator of motion. Any large action in space necessitates a weight shift of the pelvis. Due to its large mass relative to the rest of the body, pelvic misalignments cause significant reactions up and down the body chain. The pelvis mediates between the legs and the spine, cushioning excess impact from below before it can reach the delicate spinal cord. The strongest muscle in our body, the gluteus, attaches to the pelvis, and many other large muscles either attach or cross through it. Cradled within, we find our deep abdominal organs lending tone and interconnectedness to the pelvis. Much like a slanted bowl of fruit in a renaissance painter's still life, the hydrostatic and fluid qualities of the organs mesh with the bony, muscular, and ligamentous elements to create a balanced whole (figure 11.1).

THE PELVIC ARCHES

The pelvis, meaning "basin," is composed of two halves, each comprising three bones: the ilium, the pubis, and the ischium (plural: *ischia*), or sitz bones, from the German "Sitzbeine," which means "bones to sit on." (For this text, I have adopted the German term for its metaphorical-practical connotations.) Until the age of three, these three bones are still separate.

Figure 11.1 Imagine the pelvis as a fruit bowl filled with fruit.

Viewed anteriorly, the pelvis appears to be an arched structure similar to an ancient Roman, Greek, or Chinese bridge. Arched structures are so stable that many ancient examples remain intact today, including two that the Romans built 19 centuries ago to bring water to Segovia, Spain, and Nimes, France. Competitors entered the ancient Olympic Games, chronicled from 776 B.C., through a sacred arched entrance that still stands—a true marvel: naked stone touching naked stone without mortar binding the individual pieces together. The blocks are narrower at their lower ends, forming thick wedges similar in shape to the sacrum. If you stand on such an arch, the wedges push harder against their neighboring stones, increasing the stability of the structure. The central stone, called the keystone, seems to hang in midair, buttressed by the equal forces coming from the adjoining stones (figure 11.2).

The pelvis actually contains two arches: a higher, main arch in the rear and a second, lower arch in front. The keystone of the posterior arch is the sacrum, which forms the base of the spine. Its smaller counterpart in front is the *pubic symphysis* (grown together; see figure 11.18). The adjoining "stones" of the symphysis are the pubic rami; *pubes* (strong) refers to the lower torso (figure 11.3).

Strength in the lower abdominal area is indeed critical in dance. Often the posterior arch is overused while the anterior arch, the strong pubic symphysis, is neglected. By widening across the entire front of the pelvis, instead of isolating the action from the hip socket when turning out, we spread the front arch, weak-

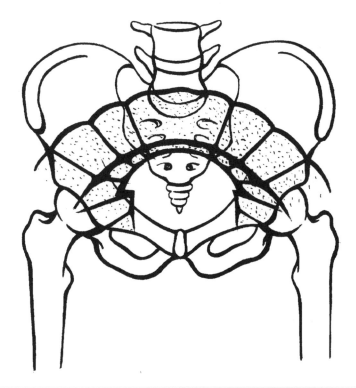

Figure 11.2 The pelvis appears to be an arched structure similar to ancient Roman, Greek, and Chinese bridges.

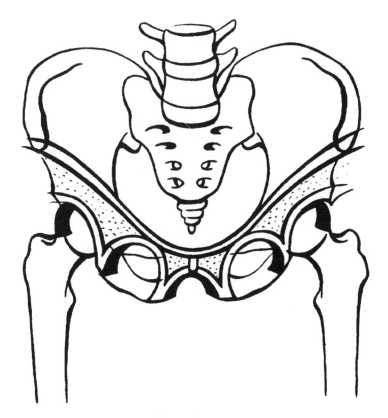

Figure 11.3 The lower arch in front of the pelvis is formed by the pubic bones.

ening the structure. The trabeculae, structures within bone that transfer the force (internal braces of the bone), reveal the "correct" path of the weight through the pelvis: from the sacrum to the pubic rami and sitz bones, to the dome and central area of the acetabulum (hip socket). This holds true for sitting as well as standing, except that while seated, the force is transferred to the sitz bones instead of the hip socket. In sitting, however, there is a tendency to drop the pelvis posteriorly and round the back, putting excessive stress on the back arch and lumbar spine. Allowing weight to travel into the pubic rami invigorates the front arch. As mentioned, isolating the turnout in the hip sockets allows the pubic arches to direct their force in the opposite direction of the turnout motion toward their keystone.

IMAGING WITH THE PELVIC ARCHES

1. **Pelvic structures:** The structures of the pelvis that can most easily be contacted are the crests of the ilia. Trace your fingers downward from the lowest ribs to find the iliac crests, following them to the front of the body until you've reached the anterior superior iliac spines (ASIS) (see figure 11.18). If you glide your fingers down and diagonally toward the center of the pelvis, you arrive at the location of the hip joints, which cannot be directly palpated because they are covered by musculature. From there, continue downward and inward to discover the pubic rami. Now move your fingers horizontally toward center, where they will meet above the pubic symphysis.

   If you follow the iliac crests to the rear, you encounter the posterior superior iliac spines (PSIS; see figure 11.21). Below these spines is a depression that marks the top of the sacroiliac joint. These are the dimples you can see above the buttocks. From there, continue vertically downward, reaching under the buttocks to discover the large bony prominences called sitz bones. Between the sitz bones but slightly higher, you will find the tailbone or coccyx. If you place your thumbs on the iliac crests and reach down the sides of your legs with your fingers, you will find other large bony prominences, the greater trochanters of the femur.

2. **Theraband® buttress (standing, walking):** To experience the effect of the arches on the keystones, tie a Theraband® (a broad rubber band used for conditioning exercises) tightly around your pelvis at the level of the greater trochanters. Both standing and walking, you may notice a lifting sensation through the center of the pelvis as the bracing arches push against their keystones. If you do this with a partner, the buttressing person must exert some effort to create the same effect as a Theraband®.

3. **Sacrum drops:**

   a. **Constructive Rest Position (CRP):** Visualize the shape of the sacrum lodged between the ilia. In your mind's eye, you will be working on creating motion between the ilia and the sacrum. Visualize the sacrum dropping toward the floor; think of it as being heavy. You may want to add an auditory component and imagine hearing it "plunk" on the floor, or hearing it "splash" as you think of it falling into water. Notice that you are creating motion between the sacrum and the ilia, and that there is space between these bones. This image is greatly enhanced by the simultaneous or alternate visualization of the tailbone lengthening downward (see the discussion on the spine in chapter 13).

   b. **Standing:** Visualize the sacrum as a wedge between the iliac bones. Watch this wedge drop lower between the adjoining bones. Think of the sacrum as having weight. Perform a small hopping motion to reinforce the feeling of dropping the sacrum.

4. **Sacral ferry (CRP, standing):** Visualize the sacrum floating down to wedge between the iliac bones, similar to a ferry boat coasting into its dock. The ferry needs to be centered to connect with its dock. See the dock (the ilia) guide the ferry into perfect alignment (figure 11.4).

Figure 11.4 The sacrum floating down to wedge between the iliac bones.

PELVIC IMBALANCES

An arch is no better than its foundation; the deeper and more stable the roots of the foundation, the more stable the structure. The choice of materials is the key to success. Where large forces interact, the pelvis is composed of reinforced bone, ligaments, and fascia, whereas other areas are built less solidly. An example is the iliac bone, which is thick and reinforced at its crest and around the hip joint, but its inner portion is thinner. Strong ligamentous ties connect key areas.

The organs are active components in the pelvis. Their weight increases the buttressing effect, making the arches stronger and providing internal hydrostatic support. If the thrust coming up through the legs is unequal, the keystones will unbalance, causing compensatory strains all the way up the spine. To avoid such imbalances, it is important to improve pelvic alignment.

The pelvis can be tilted anteriorly, posteriorly, laterally, or twisted. In the latter case, the right and the left pelvic halves are not on the same anterior-posterior plane. If the PSIS is higher on the right and the ASIS is higher on the left, the right pelvic half is twisted forward in relation to the left half (figure 11.5). These

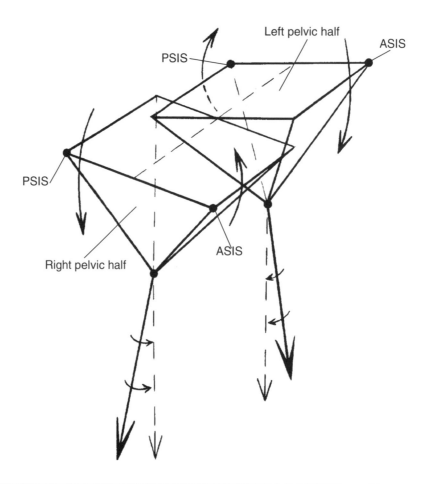

Figure 11.5 Imagine the pelvis to be made of two separate halves in the shape of inverted pyramids.

events can be visualized by making fists with your hands and placing them next to each other. Each hand represents a pelvic half. Remaining side by side, the fists can be tilted equally sideways, forward, or backward. In the case of the twist, however, one of the fists is tilted farther forward than the other.

Pelvis imbalances can be caused by habitually putting more weight on one leg than the other. This creates muscular imbalances, which influence the equality of the pelvis. Most people have one standing leg—a leg they prefer to rest their weight upon that generally feels more stable—and a gesture leg—the leg they prefer to use for expression in space. Imbalances also may result from differences in leg length. As Sweigard (1978) warns, these asymmetrical patterns may show up in a dancer's choreography.

DISCOVERING AND CORRECTING LEG PATTERNS

1. **Discover your leading leg:** Notice which leg takes the first step when you start walking. If you consciously observe yourself during the day, you will notice that most of the time, the same leg initiates a walk up or down a flight of stairs. The back leg is accustomed to pushing, the front leg to

leading out into space. This trains the legs and pelvis halves in different ways.

2. **Discover your balancing leg:** Put one leg on a chair, then step onto the chair and balance for a moment on one leg. Repeat the action with the other leg. Which leg accomplished the task with less effort and enabled you to stay more centered?

3. **Correct quadriceps imbalance:** With your back to a chair, move forward about one foot and place your feet next to each other. Now take a step backward and sit down very slowly. Repeat the action with the other leg. Compare the difference in feeling between sitting down with your left leg versus your right leg in back. Sitting down requires more eccentric muscle effort of the back leg's quadriceps group. If you habitually sit down with the same leg in back, you create unequal conditions in your legs through many repetitions over a lifetime or even a year. This quadriceps imbalance can be one of the factors causing a twist in the pelvis.

4. **Practice your "weaker" side:** Whenever possible, reverse your habitual leg initiations in standing up, sitting down, and stair-climbing patterns.

IMAGING BALANCE

1. **Water level (standing position):** Visualize a carpenter's level placed on the crests of the ilia. Check whether the position of the air bubble in the level is to the left or right of center. Imagine the crests of the ilia leveling off, causing the air bubble to move to center.

2. **Horizontal pelvic alignment:**

   a. **Second position plié to tendu à la seconde:** Visualize a horizontal line connecting the iliac crests and another horizontal line connecting the hip sockets. The iliac crests are fairly easy to palpate at the top and sides of the pelvis. The hip sockets can be visualized behind the midpoint of the inguinal band, above and slightly lateral to the sitz bones. Visualize these two lines remaining parallel to each other and horizontal to the floor as you move from second position plié to tendu à la seconde (figure 11.6). It is also helpful to visualize these lines being horizontal in other movements, such as chassé or pirouettes. If you add lines connecting the left iliac crest with the left hip socket and the right iliac crest with the right hip socket, you create a square shape, which can also be used as a visual alignment grid for the pelvis. The square does not tilt to any side as you move from second position plié to tendu à la seconde.

   b. **Standing:** Visualize the heads of the femurs as buoys floating on water (see chapter 8, figure 8.2). These buoys support your pelvis. Your legs are the anchor lines, your feet the anchors. Since the water is level, so are the buoys and the pelvis they carry. The pelvis hovers easily suspended on the strong support the buoys provide. If the surface of the water descends (as in a plié), the pelvis floats downward equally balanced on both buoys. As the water level rises, the buoys push the pelvis

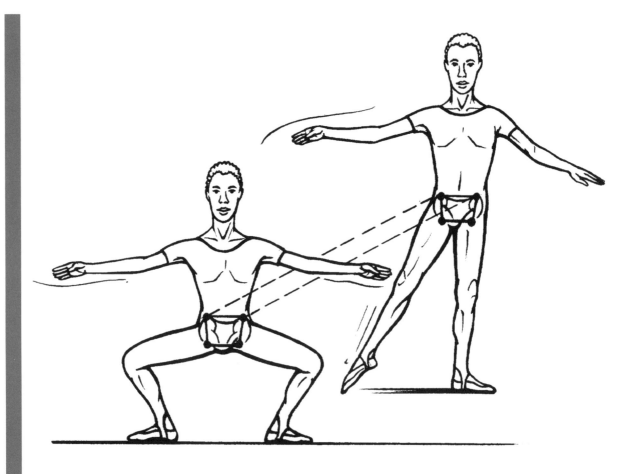

Figure 11.6   Visualize a square created by these four points.

back upward with equal force. If the right side of the pelvis is higher than the left side, visualize the buoy on the left pushing up with increased force, and vice versa. If the pelvis is tilted anteriorly, visualize both buoys pushing up with increased force as your tailbone releases downward.

3. **Sagittal pelvic alignment (standing, walking):** Visualize two spotlights located at the hip sockets. These lights should be directed horizontally to the front. If the lights are shining upward, lower them to horizontal; if they are shining at the floor, raise them to horizontal. The spotlights can be substituted for eyes that are looking forward in a horizontal plane. (Adapted from Sweigard.)

4. **Pelvic alignment in extension (extension, développé):** Imagine the pelvis as a bowl. Imagine this bowl hanging from your central axis. Let the rim of the bowl be in the horizontal plane. As you extend your leg, do not tilt the bowl, do not lift any side of the bowl, and do not drop any side of the bowl.

5. **Untwisting the pelvis:** Imagine the pelvis to be made of two separate halves in the shape of inverted pyramids. Your sitz bones are the points of the

pyramids. Shoot a beam of light out of both points. You may find that the beams are pointing in different directions. Ideally, both beams should point vertically downward. Watch the beams adjust until they are both in the same frontal plane. If the beams won't adjust in your imagination, don't force them to. Notice the difference between the beams, and try the exercise again after you have gained more experience working with the pelvis (see figure 11.5).

THE PELVIC POWERHOUSE

The body's center of gravity is located approximately in front of the second sacral vertebra. As mentioned, the largest muscles of the body attach or pass through the pelvis, our muscular powerhouse. The body is fortunate in having its power so placed: Coordinated muscle action involves the center of the body; balletic lines pass through the center of the body. The pelvis balances the considerable weight of the upper body on two fairly narrow shafts and must be strong before a baby can begin to walk. Unless these muscles are perfectly balanced and synchronized with the rest of the body, we cannot make delicate weight shifts. The pelvis is the site of the Graham technique's contraction, reverberating out to the extremities. Certain invertebrate animals, such as the octopus, move by contracting and shooting water out from their centers, propelling them backward through space like a rocket (see chapter 7, figure 7.5).

The physical center is crucial for attaining a centered mind. Meditative practices of both Eastern and Western religions imbue the *hara* or *tanden*, located below the navel, with special significance. In *Hara, the Vital Center of Man*, Durkheim (1992) demonstrates the importance of this center both in Eastern and Western thought, quoting some of the teachings of Okada Torajiro, who taught *Seiza*, a practice based on sitting:

Pull your strength into one point, your lower abdomen. Your posture is bent, because your mind is bent. Like a five-story Pagoda—this is how immaculate your posture should be. Your feet are the firewood, the stomach the oven. Why do your feet hurt? Because you have no strength in your lower abdomen. (p. 205)

Okada said *Seiza* cured him of his weakness and sickliness as a youth. Ohashi (1991) points out in *Reading the Body:*

My teacher, Master Shizuto Masanuga, used to tell us that when diagnosing and massaging *hara*, we must become a mother with a samurai's mind. That means [while] we are eminently gentle, we are at the same time focused, directed and alert. (pp. 116-117)

Being gentle, yet focused, directed, and alert, is certainly valuable in dance.

**EXERCISING
THE PELVIC
POWER-
HOUSE**

1. **Pelvic geyser (sitting, standing, improvising):** Imagine the pelvis to be the source of a powerful geyser. Feel its profound energy potential. Visualize an eruption of the geyser—first bubbling, then shooting upward through the body (figure 11.7).

2. **Teeterbabe (in motion):** Imagine your pelvis suspended in a teeterbabe. The legs dangle; all the weight is controlled at the pelvis (this image is used in the Erick Hawkins technique). I would like to point out that children need to learn to walk in their own time and should not be put into walkers or teeterbabes to make them walk sooner; however, this does not mean that this image is not useful for adult dancers.

3. **Climbing harness (in motion):** Those who have done mountain climbing can imagine the pelvis suspended in a climbing harness.

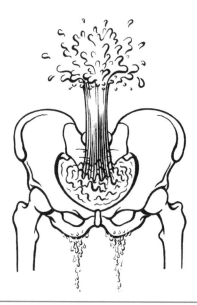

Figure 11.7   Imagine the pelvis to be the source of a powerful geyser.

THE PELVIC FLOOR

The pelvic floor is delineated by four bony landmarks: the two sitz bones, the pubic symphysis, and the coccyx (tailbone). Connective tissue and muscle form layers like a lasagna, with stratas of connective tissue and muscle. The levator ani muscle forms the internal part of the pelvic floor, attaching to the pubis in front and the obturator internus fascia and the coccyx in back. The pubococcygeus portion of the levator ani attaches to both the tailbone and the pubic symphysis, not unlike a hammock suspended from these two points. These muscles create a safety net, a last supportive resort for the pelvic organs (figure 11.8). The pelvic floor relates functionally to the thoracic diaphragm and experientially to many other areas, such as the first rib circle and the top of the head. The pelvic floor is a psychologically delicate area to work with due to its intimate relationship with the organs of reproduction and excretion; however, the activity of the pelvic floor is important for pelvic alignment, ease of motion of the femur in the hip socket, and balance of the entire spine. An active pelvic floor creates deep support for erect posture, allowing elongation of the spine and freeing the shoulder girdle, neck, and head. Experiencing the pelvic floor also helps improve alignment at a deep level, creating higher and better controlled extensions of the leg.

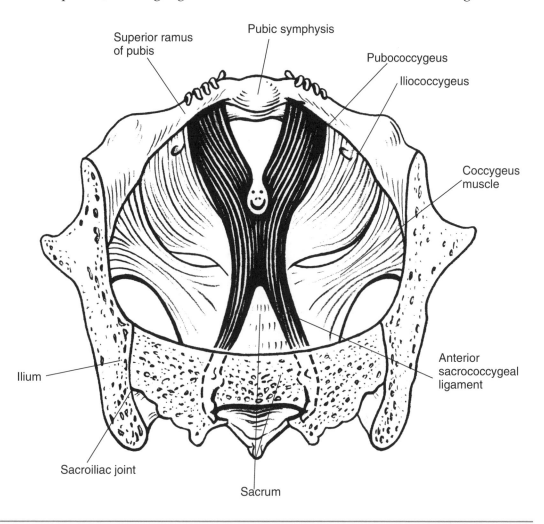

Figure 11.8 The pelvic floor creates a safety net, a last supportive resort for the pelvic organs.

ACTIVATE THE PELVIC FLOOR

1. **Increase tone (sitting):** Image the four points that delineate the pelvic floor: the sitz bones, the pubic symphysis, and the coccyx. See them extend away from each other as you inhale and move closer together as you exhale.

2. **Increase tone (improvisation):**

   a. **Trampoline:** Visualize the four bony landmarks that delineate the pelvic floor. Imagine a trampoline suspended from these four points. Picture a large ball or any object of your choice bouncing up and down on this trampoline. Do some small jumps without fully leaving the floor, and imagine your pelvic floor to be bouncing up with the ball on top of it. Discover what you must do to make the ball rebound vertically from the trampoline.

   b. **Drum:** Imagine that the pelvic floor is the surface of a drum. Feel it vibrate and resonate. (If you wish, you can play drumming music, ideally with a deep bass drum, to enhance the image of the resounding pelvic floor. African drums are usually suitable.) Initiate your motion through space from the vibrating pelvic floor. Experiment with leaps and turns as well. See the lift in the leap as a reaction against the striking of the pelvic floor. Feel the impact of the landing in your center and the reverberations of the plié (figure 11.9).

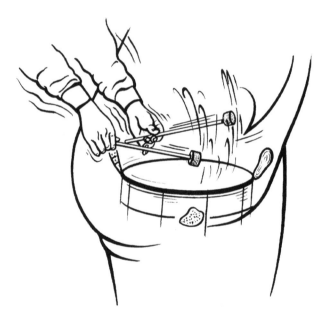

Figure 11.9   Imagine that the pelvic floor is the surface of a drum.

3. **Flying carpet (improvising, climbing stairs, standing up and sitting down, plié, all vertical-level changes of pelvis, including vertical and traveling leaps):** Imagine the pelvic floor to be a flying carpet that lifts and supports the pelvis and torso as you move. The flying carpet supports the pelvis gently and frees the legs.

4. **The pelvic floor cylinder:**

   a. **Relate the pelvic floor to first rib circle (standing, vertical-level changes of body):** Visualize the pelvic floor circle. Visualize the first rib circle. Imagine a cylinder connecting the two circles. Picture this cylinder as vertical. Together the pelvic bowl and the ribs create an oval shape that surrounds this cylinder. Imagine the three-dimensionality of the cylinder and the oval shape (figure 11.10).

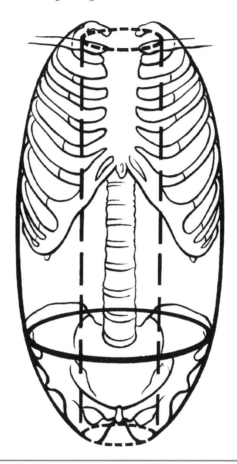

Figure 11.10 Imagine the cylinder created by connecting the pelvic floor circle and the rib circle.

    b. **Ascending and descending vibration:** Remembering exercise 2b, you can think of the upper and lower circles as two opposing surfaces of a cylindrical drum. Imagine the upper and lower drum circles vibrating in unison. It may be helpful to make a humming sound. Think of the lower drum surface (pelvic floor) sending its vibrations up through the body to the upper circle (first rib circle). Imagine the upper drum surface sending its vibrations down through the body to the lower drum surface.

5. **Activating thoracic and pelvic diaphragms using sound (small jumps):** Start without fully leaving the floor. Allow a deep "huh" sound to emerge from the air passing through your throat without straining your vocal cords. Visualize the thoracic diaphragm bouncing up and down, creating sufficient airflow through the vocal cords to create a deep, wide sound. Imagine this sound reverberating with the pelvic floor. Let your shoulders and arms hang; do not tense your abdominal muscles. As you continue to bounce, add the image of shaking your tail down to the ground. The feeling is similar to shaking an old-fashioned mercury thermometer down to zero.

THE SITZ BONES

Prehistoric man obviously sat on the bottom of his pelvis. Over time, this habit, combined with the pull of the hamstrings on the same spot, produced a significant bulge convenient for sitting—the sitz bones. Even today, one can observe the people of remote tribes in New Zealand and Africa sitting this way. Another group of people that still spontaneously sit this way are young children (see chapter 6, figure 6.5). The sitz bones kept the vital organs of excretion, digestion, and reproduction from being too close to the cold, hard floors of our ancient habitats. Without sitz bones, you'd practically be sitting on your bladder.

Padded chairs are a relatively recent phenomenon. On hard surfaces, people were not likely to lean back onto their tailbones (coccyx), as many of us do today when sitting. I once tried sitting on a medieval king's throne for a few minutes and must say that it is one of the fastest ways to appreciate correct sitting alignment on your sitz bones (figure 11.11).

As mentioned earlier, babies and toddlers sit on their sitz bones in perfect alignment, usually until age three, when they may start adopting the postural habits of their not-so-perfect parents. The sitz bones can be visualized as miniature legs, their little feet providing an excellent opportunity to learn how to balance the pelvis without creating unnecessary tension farther up along the spine. The sitz bones can be likened to the heavy ballast bulbs of sailboats that keep them upright, even in the worst of weather (one hopes). Without its ballast, a sailboat would capsize immediately. The way in which we normally sit affects our overall alignment, especially if we spend a lot of time in this position. If the sitz bones are pointing downward, the pelvis is perfectly upright and aligned. The fluid concept of a ship's ballast will help us reach this goal in a dynamic, nonrigid fashion.

Figure 11.11   Sitting on a medieval king's throne for a few minutes is a good way to appreciate correct sitting alignment on your sitz bones.

ACTIVATING YOUR SITZ BONES

For the following exercises, choose a chair with a level surface and a height that allows your thighs to be approximately parallel to the floor, creating a 90-degree angle between your thighs and your torso. If the chair slants downward toward the rear, your pelvis will tend to rock backward, making it difficult to sit atop your sitz bones.

1. **Visualizing your sitz bones (sitting):** Place your hands under your pelvis and feel the weight of the bones on your fingers for a moment. Notice how close together they are. Try to visualize the spatial relationship between the sitz bones and the hip sockets, which are only a few inches above, slightly forward and to the side. Notice if you are placing equal weight on both sitz bones.

2. **The sitz bones as the base of the pelvis—activating abdominal, deep pelvic, and pelvic floor musculature (sitting):**

   a. **Rocking sitz bones:** Rock forward and backward on your sitz bones. Rock very fast and feel the pelvic and stomach muscles begin to come alive. Slow down until you are barely moving. Finally, sit still and visualize yourself rocking.

   b. **Planting stick sitz bones:** Think of your sitz bones as planting sticks. Imagine the sticks pushing into the soft earth beneath you.

   c. **Swinging cuckoo clock weights:** Imagine the sitz bones to be the heavy weights that hang from a cuckoo clock. Let them hang down and swing front to back.

   d. **Elevated sitz bones:** Repeat the following on both sides. Put your weight on one sitz bone and lift the other. Picture the elevated sitz bone hanging down like a heavy weight.

   e. **Melting sitz bones:** Imagine your sitz bones melting down toward the chair. Flex one leg at the hip socket and lift the knee without lifting your pelvis. Repeat several times on both sides.

   f. **Dropping femur head:** Once again, imagine your sitz bones melting down toward the chair. Visualize a string attached to one knee and extending vertically upward. Flex at the hip socket and imagine the initiation for the leg lift coming from the string attached to the knee. Visualize the head of the femur dropping down and into the hip socket as the knee rises.

3. **Release tension in the buttocks, lower spine, back of the legs (standing):** Hold your buttocks with both hands and pull them straight up without tilting your pelvis forward. Hold for a minute, then let go slowly. As the buttocks slide down, visualize them melting all the way down the back of your legs to your heels.

THE HIP JOINT

The hip joints, which are of the ball and socket variety, are responsible for transferring the thrust of the legs to the pelvis. The hip joint has three degrees of freedom: flexion/extension, abduction/adduction, and internal/external rotation. More stable and less mobile than the shoulder joint, the hip joint is pushed to its maximum flexibility in dance.

Mees (1981) points out the great likeness in shape between a right pelvic half and a left shoulder blade, and vice versa, suggesting greater functional relationship than is immediately apparent. The hip sockets are located at the front of the pelvis and are angled downward, whereas the shoulder sockets are clearly located at the sides of the upper torso. This is an important distinction, as we usually think of the hip sockets as being farther apart than they are and the shoulder sockets as being closer together (to the front, hunched shoulders) than they are. The fastest animals on earth are slender as viewed from the front or back, with hip sockets or acetabula very close to each other.

Men's acetabulae are generally closer together than women's, giving men a biomechanical advantage for the transfer of force from the legs to the pelvis (but from the point of view of energy consumption, women are more efficient). The greater distance between the hip sockets in women creates a wider birth canal between the iliac, sitz bones, and pubic bones.

The weight of the spine rests in a vertical plane that is behind a vertical plane through the hip sockets, forming a cartlike structure in the torso. The legs can be visualized as horses pulling the cart, with the cart hinged to the backs of the horses. The strap connecting the cart to the horses (the pelvis to the upper legs) is the iliofemoral ligament. Also called the Y-ligament, because it is shaped like an inverted Y, this ligament prevents us from falling straight backward off our horse. When you pick up an articulated skeleton, forgetting that it lacks a Y-ligament, the torso and head tumble to the rear. Dance training tends to lengthen the Y-ligament, permitting increased external rotation and extension of the leg, such as seen in arabesque.

The largest bone in the body, the femur, receives the body's weight on its two ball-shaped heads. Rather than being straight, the femur has a short neck leading to the greater trochanter. This angulation of the neck on the shaft increases the buttressing effect on the pelvic arch and enhances range of motion. A straight femur would reduce the range of motion in the hip joint and make muscle attachment difficult.

The femur slants toward the midline of the body at its base. The wider the pelvis, the greater the slant. If we think of the shaft and neck of the femur as a two-force vector, we can determine the resultant mechanical axis of the femur (see chapter 9, figure 9.5), what we visualize to achieve correct leg alignment. Looking down the length of the femur from above, we see the angle formed by an axis through the femoral neck and an axis through the femoral condyles (figure 11.12). The angle of torsion averages 15 degrees (Norkin and Levangie 1992) in adults but is greater in children, which is why toddlers often walk with somewhat turned-in legs. Generally speaking, the smaller the angle of torsion, the greater the turnout.

In leg flexion and extension, the movement of the femoral head within the acetabulum can be visualized as rotation, but all movement in the hip socket involves some gliding of the femur head in the acetabulum. In flexion, as the leg

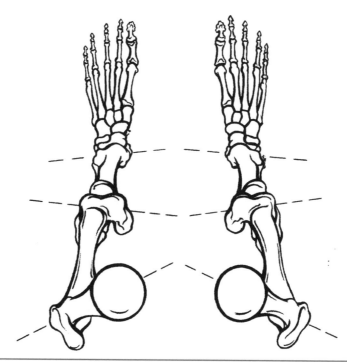

Figure 11.12   The angle of torsion formed by an axis through the femoral neck and an axis through the femoral condyles.

moves up in grand battement, for example, the head spins backward (if it were to roll, it would roll toward you). In extension, as the leg comes down in grand battement, the head spins forward (and would roll away from you). Rotation, abduction, and adduction are also joint movements composed of rolling, spinning, and gliding motions.

IMAGING LEG ALIGNMENT

1. **Leg alignment (standing):** Put your finger on your middle toe. As though your finger had paint on it, brush up the front of your leg and create an imaginary colored line extending from your middle toe, through the center of your ankle, up the front of your lower leg, over the kneecap, over the thigh, and into the hip socket. Repeat the action and visualize the central axis of your leg passing through the center of the anklebone, the lower leg, the knee and thigh, and into the hip socket. Finally, imagine your pelvis balanced equally on both femur heads (figures 11.12 and 11.13).

2. **Hip creasing (sitting):**

   a. **Piece of paper:** Place one foot, or at least the heel portion of the foot, onto the chair on which you are sitting. Visualize the crease at front of your hip socket becoming very deep. Think of the fold occurring as easily as a fold in a piece of paper. Facilitate this image by imagining the sitz bones lengthening to the floor and the back widening. Repeat the exercise with the other leg. (Adapted from Andre Bernard.)

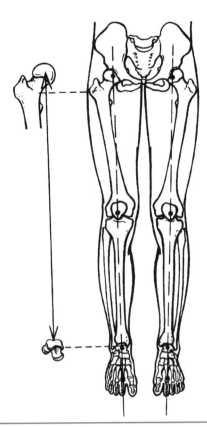

Figure 11.13   The central axis of your leg passing through the second toe, center of the anklebone, the lower leg, the knee and thigh, and into the hip socket.

    b. **Cloth doll:** Imagine yourself to be a cloth doll with your legs attached to your torso by a thin seam. Fold your upper body down over your legs and let your torso rest on them. Visualize deep, foldable hip creases. Remain in this position for a moment. Slowly roll back up through each vertebra of your spine. Initiate the action from the end of your spine, letting the coccyx drop down toward the floor.

3. **Femur head billiard balls (standing up, sitting down):** Imagine your femur heads to be billiard balls. As you stand up, visualize the billiard balls rolling up through your hip sockets and out the back of your pelvis. As you sit down, imagine your hip sockets giving the billiard balls a shove back down to your ankles. Once you can clearly visualize this action, add the image of a shower of warm, soothing water releasing any tension in your back (figure 11.14).

4. **Isolation of hip joint action in turnout:**

    a. **Supine:** In the supine position, with your knees bent at a 90-degree angle and feet flat on the floor, let your knees slowly drop to the sides. Visualize the head of the femur rotating in the hip socket and watch the pubic rami push in the opposite direction toward the pubic symphysis. As the right femur externally rotates, visualize the right pubic rami pushing in the opposite direction toward the pubic symphysis. As the left femur externally rotates, visualize the left pubic rami moving in the opposite direction toward the pubic symphysis. Once you have arrived in your

Figure 11.14 The femur heads as billiard balls and a warm, soothing shower releases tension in your back.

     maximum turnout, internally rotate your legs and bring them back to the parallel position.

    b. **Standing:** As you externally rotate your legs, image the pubic rami moving toward each other.

    c. **Cogwheel image (supine, standing):** The relationship between the turning-out and pubic rami actions can be visualized as two cogwheels counterrotating. As the outer cogwheels (the femur heads) externally rotate, the inner cogwheels (pubic rami) internally rotate. As the outer cogwheels internally rotate, the inner cogwheels externally rotate (figure 11.15).

5. **Acetabulum controls femur (improvisation):** Imagine the hip socket to be like a hand holding the head of the femur. This hand moves the femur with gentle pushes and tugs to initiate leg movement.

6. **Pelvic ball on femur heads (standing, improvisation):** Imagine the pelvis to be an air-filled ball supported by the femur heads. Visualize the ball bouncing easily on the femur heads. Visualize the femur heads pushing gently against the ball, balancing it (figure 11.16).

7. **Femoral head spin:**

    a. **Battement:** Imagine that you are looking at the femur head from the rear. Visualize the motion of the femur head in the hip socket as the leg

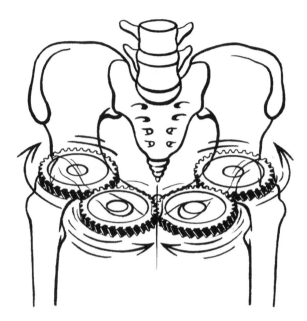

Figure 11.15   As the outer cogwheels (femur heads) externally rotate, the inner cog-wheels (pubic rami) internally rotate.

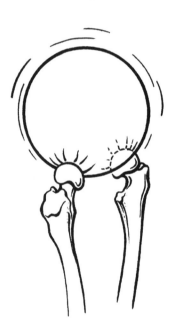

Figure 11.16   The pelvis is a ball bouncing easily on the femur heads.

elevates in grand battement. Watch the femur head spinning backward. As the leg reaches its highest point, see the femur head glide or drop downward within its socket. (See also chapter 10, figure 10.2.)

b. **Countering the socket:** As the leg elevates in battement, focus on the rear surface of the hip socket. Watch this surface move up in relation to the head of the femur as your leg and foot move up. Watch this surface move down in relation to the head of the femur as your foot moves down.

c. **Combination (grand battement):** Combine exercises a and b by thinking:

When the leg goes up: "The back surface of the socket and the foot move up, the femur head glides down."

When the leg goes down: "The back surface of the socket and the foot move down, the head of the femur glides up."

THE ILIOPSOAS

Mabel Todd (1972) contended that the psoas is probably the most important muscle in determining upright posture. The psoas major attaches to the twelfth thoracic and five lumbar vertebrae. One could say that it lies cuddled up on both sides of the massive lumbar vertebrae. Although it does not attach directly to the pelvis, it joins forces with the iliacus, which arises from the inside of the ilium. Via a common tendon, these muscles reach down to the minor trochanter on the medial side of the proximal femur (figure 11.17). Since the psoas and iliacus work in conjunction with each other, they are referred to as the iliopsoas. As the prime flexor of the hip joint, the iliopsoas is crucial for achieving high leg extensions, as well as for achieving deep hip flexion or creasing at the hip socket. Usually the potential of the iliopsoas is not fully exploited for hip flexion, even though this is a common movement in dance. Instead, the more superficial and less powerful hip flexors, such as the rectus femoris and sartorious, are overused. Additional complications arise if the external rotators of the femur, the obturator and piriformis muscles, do not properly balance the psoas (Todd 1972).

The internal and external obturators connect the greater trochanter to the pubic and ischial rami and the obturator foramen at a point above the psoas. The piriformis connects the ventral surface of the sacrum with the greater trochanter near the internal obturator (figure 11.18). Balanced action of the left and right piriformis muscles is essential to spinal function, since the sacrum forms the base of the spine and inequality of tension between them would eventually produce a change in sacral alignment.

In the closed kinematic chain (standing on both legs), contraction of the obturators pulls the front of the pelvis downward. In a forward tilted pelvis the weight transfer between the heads of the femur and the pelvis is less efficient. The psoas displaces forward together with the lumbar spine. This extension of the lumbar spine causes increased shearing forces in the lumbar-pelvic junction just as the psoas arrives in a less efficient position to support the area. Since the obturators are important deep external rotators, dancers tend to have tight (contracted) obturators, which increases the tendency of the pelvis to dip forward. The dancer can counteract this tendency by tensing the stomach muscles in an effort to pull up the front rim of the pelvis. This sets tension against tension and restricts the functioning of the diaphragm.

We come full circle if we consider the diaphragm's downward extending crura as closely related to the psoas. The psoas can also be followed upward through the muscle groups on the dorsal aspect of the spine. The inferior fibers of the trapezius muscle attach to the spine of the twelfth thoracic vertebra, whereas the

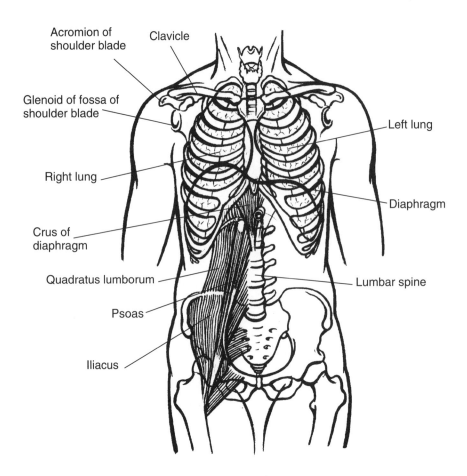

Figure 11.17 The psoas major attaches to the twelfth thoracic and five lumbar vertebrae.

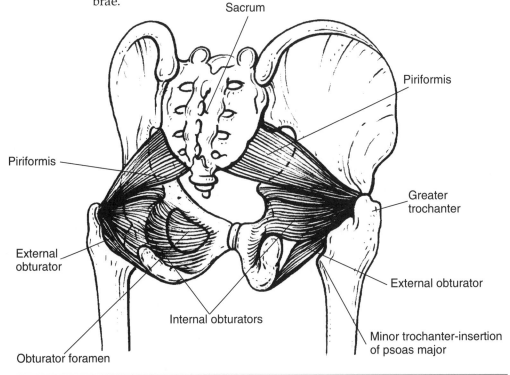

Figure 11.18 The internal and external obturators and the piriformis.

superior fibers of the psoas attach to the body of the twelfth thoracic vertebra on the ventral side. The trapezius extends all the way up to the back of the skull, conveying the effect of the psoas to the top of the body.

Rather than simply stretching or strengthening the iliopsoas muscle group, we must balance the entire pelvis and its related structures. Even the condition of the closely allied organs, such as the kidneys, may influence the psoas, and vice versa. Of course, if the psoas is very shortened, it pulls the lumbar spine forward in the closed-chain standing position, and the increased lumbar lordosis may cause lower back pain. In this case, a correctly executed deep psoas stretch usually brings immediate relief. Imagery can be used to aid the stretch but imagery alone, even if applied diligently, would take too long to remedy the shortened psoas, allowing further damage over time.

Tightness in the deep rotators also affects the closely related pelvic floor musculature, disrupting the relationship between the pelvic floor and the diaphragm. This disruption weakens the abdominal wall through its antagonistic relationship with the diaphragm. The stomach muscles, which can act as spinal flexors, must work with the lumbar back extensors to maintain pelvic balance and adequate psoas function. Once the psoas is awakened, the flattened abdominal wall coveted by so many dancers happens all on its own. The all-important lift of the pelvis is also gained through efficient iliopsoas action. Once the iliopsoas regains its role as a pelvic stabilizer, less artificial holding of the abdominals is required. The following exercises focus on the deep external rotators and psoas, one of several paths to efficient use of the iliopsoas group.

EXERCISING THE ILIOPSOAS

1. **Hip creasing:**

   a. **Fishing pole (CRP, legs not tied together):** Imagine the leg to be a fishing pole. The lower leg is the string and the foot a fish. The handle of the fishing rod is in the hip socket. Pull the fish (foot) out of the water by initiating the action from the handle. As you perform this action think of your back and especially the lumbar area spread on the floor (figure 11.19). (Adapted from Sweigard.)

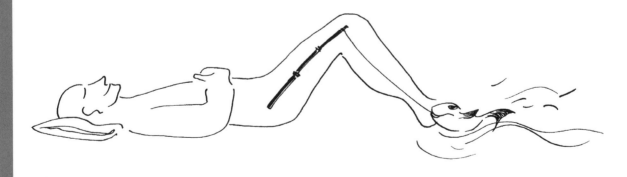

Figure 11.19   Pull the fish (the foot) out of the water by initiating the action from the handle.
Adapted, by permission, from L.E. Sweigard, 1974, *Human Movement Potential* (New York: Harper and Row).

b. **Minor trochanter string (supine, standing):** Imagine a string attached to the minor trochanter. Initiate the hip-folding action by pulling the string toward the head in a direction that is perpendicular to the floor. (Also see chapter 9, figure 9.12c.) Don't grip the stomach. Drop the back, especially the lumbar area, and neck, to the floor like soft cloth.

c. **Knee string (supine):** Imagine a string attached to the knee. Pull the string horizontally toward the head to make the leg flex at the hip socket. When the leg returns, let the string lower the foot to the floor very slowly. While you perform these actions, imagine the psoas flowing down next to the spine like a river.

d. **Spreading iliacus (supine):** In your mind's eye, picture the iliacus muscle located on the ventral, concave surface of the iliac bone. As you flex the leg at the hip socket, imagine the iliacus spreading out and widening across this surface.

2. **Obturator foramen breath circle (supine, sitting, standing):** Visualize the rounded opening between the pubic and sitz bones (called the obturator foramen) in your mind's eye. As you exhale, imagine your breath passing through this opening, allowing it to become soft and permeable. As you inhale, picture the breath circling around the sitz bones. During exhalation, image that the opening is the ring of a soap bubble blower. Blow through the ring from inside to out and visualize a bubble expanding outward until it pops (figure 11.20).

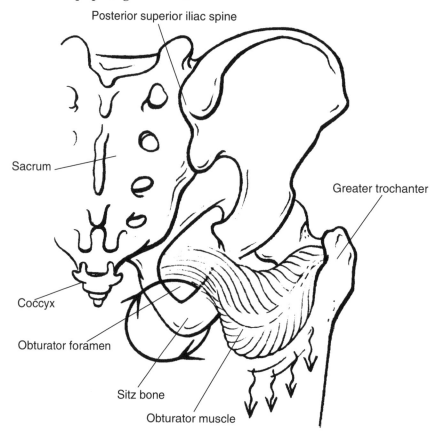

Figure 11.20   Visualize the breath circling around the sitz bones. Imagine the obturators and other deep rotators hanging and melting down over the ischial bone.

3. **Obturator melt (sitting, standing):** Visualize the obturator internus as it emerges through the lesser sciatic foramen and turns the corner to meet the back of the greater trochanter. Imagine the obturators and other deep rotators hanging and melting down over the ischial bone (see figure 11.20).

4. **Piriformis stretch (standing):** Visualize the piriformis attached to the sacrum. Watch the sacrum hang down toward the floor, suspended from the piriformis. Image both the left and right piriformis stretching to equal length like taffy or bubble gum.

5. **Femur head sinks into hip sockets:**

   a. **Supine (any movement):** Visualize the femur heads sinking into the hip sockets. (Adapted from Sweigard.)

   b. **Supine:** Imagine the femur to be a cylindrical wooden pole such as a broomstick. Visualize the pelvis as soft clay. Imagine the broomstick sinking deep into the clay. (Adapted from Andre Bernard.)

6. **Hip flexion with lower back release (standing):** As you flex your hip joint, imagine the muscles of your lower back releasing downward. Visualize the lower back muscles melting as the crease between thigh and pelvis deepens.

7. **Rib pulley (standing):** Visualize a string attached to the minor trochanter. The string loops upward over the lowest rib like a pulley. The muscles of the lower back are the pulley's counterweights. As you flex your hip joint, the lower back counterweights drop downward to pull up the femur at the minor trochanter.

8. **Psoas connects to the leg (swinging, walking):**

   a. **Leg swings from psoas:** Stand with one leg on an elevated surface so that the other leg can hang down easily. Imagine the hanging leg to be the downward extension of the psoas muscle. Swing the leg back and forth, initiating from the psoas. After practicing with one leg, take a few steps and compare the feeling between your legs. Then reverse sides and notice which leg feels more like a downward extension of the psoas, more "connected" to the psoas. As you walk or run, picture the psoas swinging your leg forward (figure 11.22).

   b. **Psoas rope:** Visualize the leg and psoas as a rope attached to the lumbar spine. Initiate a swing from various parts of the rope, the very top, center, or lower section. How does this affect the swinging motion and the hip joint? Also practice this image when walking.

   c. **Lengthening the psoas:** Stand with one leg on an elevated surface and gently swing your other leg back and forth or simply let it dangle. Imagine the weight of your leg pulling the psoas into length. The weight of the leg causes the psoas to stretch like taffy. After you have completed the exercise on both sides, practice walking with this image. Especially during the swing phase, visualize length through the psoas (figure 11.22).

9. **Psoas connects to back of the head (standing):** Imagine the psoas extending from the minor trochanter on the upper inside of the femur all the way to the occiput, the lower back portion of the skull. Imagine the legs hanging from the occiput.

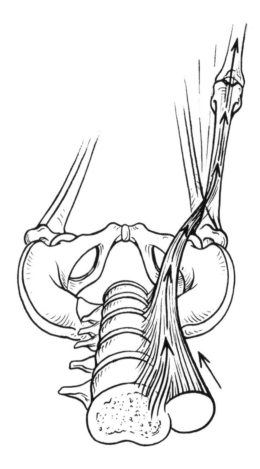

Figure 11.21 Imagine the hanging leg is the downward extension of the psoas muscle; imagine the weight of the leg pulling the psoas into length.

The pelvis is the intermediary between the upper and the lower body. It serves as a relay station for the forces traveling up from the legs and for the weight of the upper body traveling in the opposite direction. It is therefore a center of coordination and movement initiation, while absorbing excess shock and providing protection for the lower abdominal organs.

CHAPTER 12

The Knee and Lower Leg

*T*ry the following experiment: Take hold of two pencils near their pointed ends and place the flat ends against each other. Now push the pencils together. It is rather hard not to allow the pencils to slip away from their joint contact. Now hold the pencils further in so that your grip is much closer to the contact point of the pencils. If you push the pencils together now, you will notice that it is much easier to keep them joined because you have reduced the leverage. This is what the knees are faced with: Placed between two long bones or levers that amplify the forces arriving from above and below they are required to supply great stability and flexibility as well. The knee solves its dilemma in several ways; one is sheer size and another is rather ingenious. Deep sockets provide stability as can be seen at the hip, but they ultimately limit flexibility. Therefore the knee has devised sockets that add depth (the menisci), but above all can distort and "move" to another spot during flexion and extension to increase the range of motion of the joint.

The fibula and tibia of the lower leg have a sort of David and Goliath relationship, at least from the point of view of sheer bulk and strength. The tibia transfers 90 percent of the weight from the knee to the foot; its proximal end provides the lower articulating surface of the knee, which the fibula is not part of, and its distal end provides most of the upper articulating surface of the ankle joint. Why do we need the rather delicate fibula? While the tibia is occupied with transferring weight, the fibula is free to make delicate and rapid adjustments at the ankle joint without jeopardizing the transfer of weight which is essential for maintaining integrity.

Try the following experiment: Cross your right leg over your left so that your right foot is dangling in the air. Place the fingers of your left hand on your inner ankle bone and the fingers of your right hand on the outer ankle bone of your right foot. The inner ankle bone is the distal end of the tibia, and the outer ankle bone is the distal end of the fibula. While moving your foot in a variety of ways, you will notice that the inner ankle bone moves less than the outer. Especially when your foot performs rapid gyrations, the outer ankle bone seems to "dance around" in comparison to the calmer inner ankle bone. Now place your finger on the proximal head of the fibula located to the outside and below the knee. This is the location of the proximal tibiofibular joint. Place the fingers of your left hand on the proximal end of the tibia just below the inner border of the knee. This time as you move your foot at the ankle joint you will feel the motion of the fibula while the tibia remains nearly motionless. Repeat the experiment on the left side.

THE KNEE

The knee joint is called a double condyloid joint because of the two rounded bulbs called condyles at the lower end of the femur. The condyles, which resemble two adjacent tire halves, face the two shallow convex surfaces of the tibial plateau (figure 12.1). The knee joint has two degrees of freedom: flexion and extension around a transverse axis and rotation around a vertical axis. The latter movement is only possible when the knee is flexed sufficiently, ideally about 90 degrees, due to ligamentous restrictions in the extended position. This is why you can screw your knees into a better fifth position when you are in plié and end your career when you straighten.

The knee needs to remain flexible while supporting most of the body's weight. Theoretically, stability could be achieved through rigidity and flexibility through remaining lax, but both are out of the question for the knee. The solution: a large joint with adjustable surfaces. This means that the axis of flexion and extension, which passes transversely through the center of the femoral condyles, is mobile. It moves forward over the tibial plateau in extension and backward in flexion. Were the axis to remain in place, the femoral condyles would be landlocked in the center of the tibial plateau and the shaft of the femur would knock against the edge of the plateau, restricting motion.

As ingenious as this system may seem, it requires some intricate reshuffling within the joint during motion. In flexion, the femoral condyles need to glide anteriorly over their tibial counterparts, or they will roll off the tibial plateau to the rear. The reverse holds true in extension. Here is what happens in a descending plié: As the knees bend, the femoral condyles roll backward on the tibial plateau. So the condyles can continue to rotate within their grooves on the tibial plateau, they glide forward (figure 12.2). If they were to roll back without this forward gliding component, they would simply roll off the tibial plateau.

Remember that the condyles are like two adjoining tires. To better visualize the events in the knee joint as you descend in plié, imagine that as the tires begin to roll toward you, they lose their traction and slip forward on the ground and spin

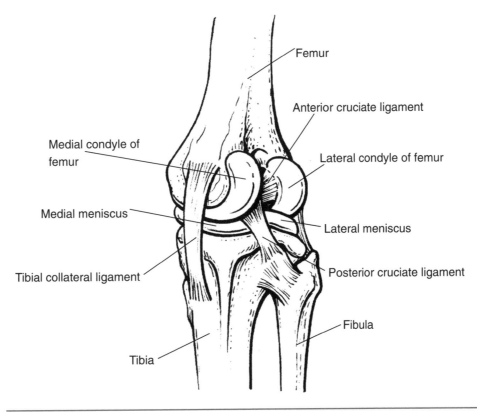

Figure 12.1   A right knee viewed medially and posteriorly.

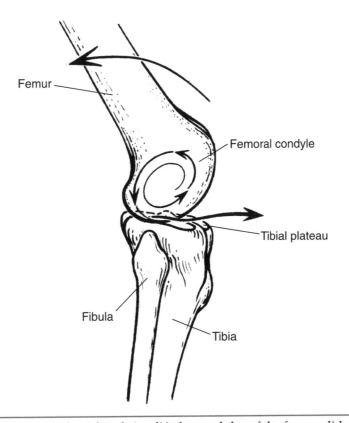

Figure 12.2   As the right knee bends in plié, the condyles of the femur glide forward so they can continue to rotate within their grooves on the tibial plateau.

(figure 12.3a). The surface of the tibia moves backward in relation to the condyles of the femur. As you straighten from a plié, the opposite occurs—the tires begin to roll away from you. If they were to continue in this fashion, they would roll off the front of the tibia, so they slip backward on the tibia and spin (figure 12.3b). Here the tibia moves forward in relation to the femoral condyles to support the anterior portion of the femoral condyles.

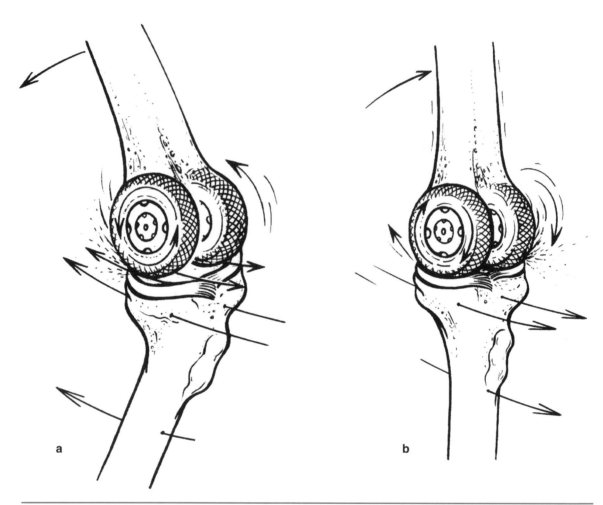

Figure 12.3   (a) Tires roll toward you but lose their traction and slip forward on the ground and spin. The surface of the tibia moves backward in relation to the condyles. (b) Tires roll away from you, slip backward on the tibia, and spin. The tibia moves forward in relation to the femoral condyles.

   Imperfect function of the gliding actions in the knee results in increased compression and shear. Recall our discussion of the doorknob in chapter 10. Tightening the grip on the knob will prevent motion between your hand and the knob. Similarly, if one joint surface cannot glide easily on top of another, they become stuck to each other. Neighboring joints attempt to compensate for the lack of motion, but there is still an increased chance of injury. In the weight-bearing position, the knee is part of a closed kinematic chain involving the hip and ankle joints. Therefore, improving one joint action increases the efficiency of the entire chain.

Two wedge-shaped menisci (joint disks) located on the tibial condyles increase the area of contact between the joint surfaces and reduce friction (figure 12.1). Without the menisci, the area of contact between the condyles of the femur and the tibial plateau would be tiny, producing extreme forces that could disrupt the joint surfaces.

The nature of their attachment affords the menisci a degree of adaptive motion. They actually remodel, or change their shape somewhat, to fulfill their function of increasing the contact area of the joint surfaces. You may think of them as clay with the resilient properties of rubber and an adhesiveness that keeps them beneath the femoral condyles. They distort like a piece of clay that is being modeled, yet rebound to their original shape like a rubber band. When the knee flexes, the femoral condyles roll backward on the tibial plateau, pushing the menisci ahead of them and distorting them to the rear of the knee. When the knee extends, the opposite occurs: The femoral condyles roll forward and distort the menisci to the front of the knee.

If the menisci don't move fast enough, they may get stuck beneath the condyles and tear. This can happen if the surfaces of the femoral condyles roll "uphill" on the menisci. Once again, we can use the metaphor of the car tire. If the surfaces are slippery the femoral condyles will glide easily on the mensici as they push them forward (figure 12.4). If the surfaces are "dry," the femoral condyles will roll up the menisci and compress them. Thus it is important to maintain sufficient lubrication of the knee joint by regularly moving it in both its planes of motion.

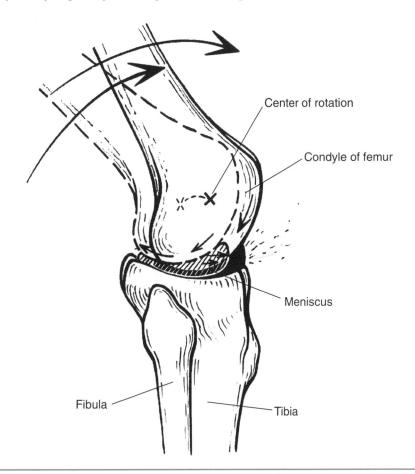

Figure 12.4 If the surfaces are slippery, the femoral condyles can glide on the mensici as they push them forward.

By providing a barrier of sorts to the femoral condyles, the menisci also aid the condyles in their gliding motion on the tibial plateau by pushing them back toward the center of the plateau. The medial meniscus, which is attached more firmly, is more vulnerable to being crushed or torn by the femur head because it cannot distort as much as the lateral meniscus. Also, the outer rims of the menisci are less firmly attached so that they distort more than the inner portion. In rotation as well, the menisci reduce friction by distorting to remain beneath the femoral condyles.

The patella acts as a pulley, increasing the force that the quadriceps muscle exerts on the tibia. The largest sesamoid bone (a bone that attaches to a tendon of a muscle like clay attaches to a string) in the body, the patella is part of the tendon of the quadriceps muscle. It increases the distance between the axis of rotation of the joint and the force vector of the quadriceps (see figure 9.14). By reducing the friction between the quadriceps tendon and the femoral condyles, the patella serves as a built-in kneepad to protect the joint from direct pressure.

The patella glides within a small (intercondylar) groove between the femoral condyles. This gliding motion is much like cross-country skiing—it's much easier if you can ski in a good track. You ruin the track by skiing on its edges or crossing it, and if the track has been distorted, the increased friction slows you down, making you work harder. Likewise, the patella must move within its groove, for if its track is disrupted, it could cause damage to both the cartilage covering the intercondylar groove and the posterior surface of the patella.

As you descend in plié, the patella moves down in its groove with the quadriceps tendon. As you ascend, it glides up in its groove. Because the quadriceps consists of four muscles, their combined pull must allow the patella to glide in its groove in flexion and extension (figure 12.5a). If, for example, the inside quadriceps, the vastus medialis, exerts more force than the outside quadriceps, the vastus lateralis, the patella is pulled medially (figure 12.5b). Similarly, in keeping with our winter imagery above, if three rows of reindeer are pulling a sled and the left row veers off to the side, the sled is pulled out of its straight course.

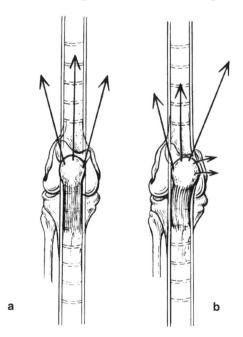

a   b

Figure 12.5 (a) Combined pull must allow the patella to glide in its groove in flexion and extension. (b) If the inside quadriceps muscle exerts more force than the outside quadriceps, the patella is pulled medially.

IMAGING KNEE FUNCTION

The following images improve knee function as well as overall leg alignment. The exercises also increase the flow of nutrients to the joint by providing better circulation of joint fluids. This is particularly important for the menisci, which do not contain blood vessels.

1. **First, touch some of the anatomical areas described above:** Bend your knee and place your finger on the sharp, bony edge at the front of your lower leg. This is your tibia. Follow the tibia upward until you reach a bony prominence. This is the tibial tuberosity where the patellar ligament attaches, which is the insertion of the quadriceps muscle into the tibia. If you place your finger on the area just above the tuberosity and stretch your leg, you will notice that the ligament becomes taut as the quadriceps pulls on the patella and the patella pulls on the patellar ligament.

   Go back to the tuberosity and place one finger of each hand on top of it. Now move one finger to the left and the other to the right and slightly upward to feel the underside of the tibial plateau, which is similar to an overhanging cliff. As you move your fingers farther and pass the ridge of the plateau, you will feel the joint space. This space is easier to feel when the knee is flexed, because the menisci are now at the back of the knee under the femoral condyles. If you stretch your knee while keeping your fingers in place, you may feel the menisci as they fill in this space. Now move your fingers inward to feel the patella. Finally, move your fingers upward over the patella and then to the outside of the knee to feel the femoral condyles.

2. **Condylar balance:**

   a. **Standing:** Distribute your weight equally on both legs. Visualize the femoral condyles of both femurs sitting on their respective menisci and tibial condyles. Imagine that both femoral condyles rest equally on their tibial condyles. Visualize the vertical ground reaction force vector located between the condyles (figure 12.6).

   b. **Balancing condylar tire pressure (standing):** If you sense that there is too much weight on the lateral condyles, visualize them as tires that are being inflated. Inflate the lateral tire until it feels like more weight has been shifted to the medial condyle. If it feels like there is too much weight on the medial condyles, inflate that tire and visualize the weight shifting over to the lateral condyles.

3. **Visualize the movement of condyles on tibial plateau (descending/ascending plié):** As the knees bend in plié, the femoral condyles roll backward on the tibial plateau. So the condyles can continue to rotate within their grooves on the tibial plateau, they glide forward (see figure 12.2). As the knees stretch, the femoral condyles roll forward on the tibial plateau. So the condyles can continue to rotate within their grooves on the tibial plateau, they glide to the rear (see figure 12.4).

4. **Movement of the tibia beneath the femoral condyles (ascending/descending plié):** Visualize the tibia gliding in the opposite direction of the femo-

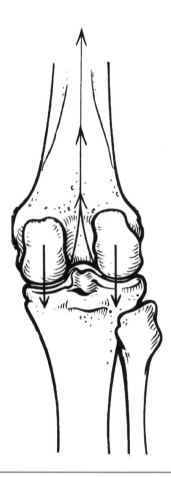

Figure 12.6   Imagine that both femoral condyles rest equally on their tibial condyles.

ral condyles. As you flex your knee, the tibia glides backward under the femoral condyles. As you extend your knee, the tibia glides forward under the condyles (see figure 12.3a and b).

5. **Meniscal motion:**

   a. **Plié:** As you bend your knees and move downward, image the menisci remodeling posteriorly to remain beneath the femoral condyles (figure 12.7a). As you move up, watch the menisci reverse direction and remodel anteriorly to remain beneath the femoral condyles (figure 12.7b). Visualize this action as very smooth and slippery.

   b. **Meniscal independence:** This time, try to imagine the menisci initiating the motion of the knee. To initiate flexion, the menisci move posteriorly; to initiate extension, they move anteriorly. (Adapted from B. Cohen.)

   c. **Life-saving rings:** To image the menisci as life-saving rings, visualize the same action as above, only now try to capture the sensation of the menisci providing lift under the femoral condyles.

   d. **Axial rotation with the right knee:** Bend your knee and use your hands to aid in axially rotating your knee. This can be done by placing your fingers on the front of the tibia and moving it back and forth. Visualize

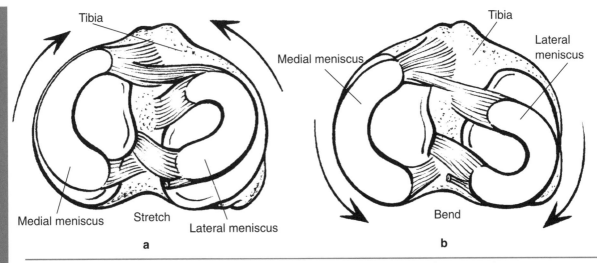

Figure 12.7   Menisci remodeling in the right knee: (a) anteriorly and (b) posteriorly.

the menisci remodeling beneath the femoral condyles. When you externally rotate the lower leg, the lateral femoral condyle moves forward relative to the tibial plateau, remodeling the lateral meniscus forward and the medial meniscus backward (figure 12.8a). When you internally rotate the lower leg, the medial femoral condyle moves forward relative to the tibial plateau, remodeling the lateral meniscus backward and the medial meniscus forward (figure 12.8b).

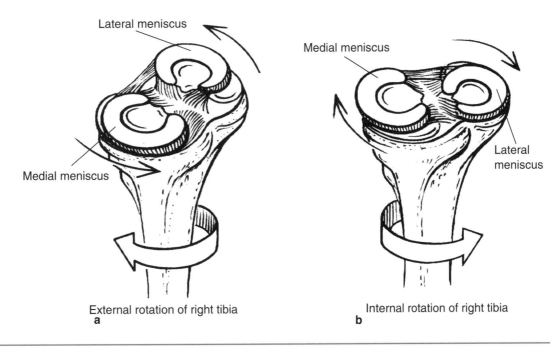

Figure 12.8   (a) When you externally rotate the lower leg, the lateral femoral condyle moves forward relative to the tibial plateau, remodeling the lateral meniscus forward and the medial meniscus backward. (b) When you internally rotate the lower leg, the medial femoral condyle moves forward relative to the tibial plateau, remodeling the lateral meniscus backward and the medial meniscus forward.

6. **Patellar motion (plié):**

a. **Wet bar of soap:** As you descend in plié, visualize the kneecap gliding easily in its well-lubricated groove like a wet bar of soap slipping in a smooth groove.

b. **Floating balloon:** As you ascend in plié, image the kneecap as a little balloon floating upward effortlessly.

c. **Pouring sand:** Imagine sand pouring out of your knees as you plié. Each leg's hip socket and knee are in the same plane as the second toes. The sand falls downward in this plane.

d. **Bilateral reins:** Visualize reins attached to both sides of the patella and reaching upward along the femur. The reins represent the pull of the quadriceps muscle. The inner and outer reins should pull with equal force in balanced patellar action. If the patella rides too far medially, the lateral rein needs to pull harder to bring the patella back into line, and vice versa.

7. **Tibial swing (lying on your stomach, knee flexion and extension):** The tibia swings around the femur as you flex and extend the knee. Imagine the centrifugal (outward) force created on the joint surface of the tibia as it swings away from the joint surface of the femur. As the lower leg continues to swing, the space increases. Figure 12.9 shows the knee extending.

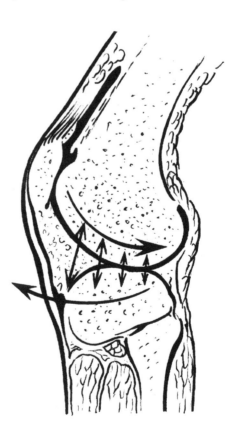

Figure 12.9   The tibia swings around the femur as you flex and extend the knee. As the lower leg continues to swing, the space in the knee joint increases.

The knees are an important part of our propulsion system. They aid us in lowering and raising our COG when required. They fulfill the dual functions of providing flexibility and stability with the help of adjustable joint surfaces, increasing the surface area of the joint while maintaining its mobility.

THE TIBIA, FIBULA, AND ANKLE

The bones of the lower leg, the tibia (shinbone) and fibula (the calf bone), form a working unit. The Latin word *tibia* (flute) elicits an image of air streaming through the bone, vibrating it and loosening the surrounding muscles. The most vertical bone of the body in upright stance and the primary weight bearer, the tibia transfers the force from the femur down to the talus, the keystone of the foot's long arch. The fibula gets it name from a pin used to fasten the toga, the loose outer garment worn by ancient Romans. The fibula does not articulate with the femur.

Besides being firmly connected at both ends, the tibia and fibula are bound together by a strong interosseous (between bone) membrane along their entire parallel length. Muscles that move the ankle, tarsal, and toe joints originate between the tibia and fibula. In dancers, these muscles may be tender to the touch due to constant use. Thus it is important to maintain their elasticity through massage, stretching, and the upcoming imagery. Todd (1972) describes the tibialis posterior muscle, with its origins below the knee, as crucial in organizing and maintaining the arch of the foot due to its attachments to the tarsal bones.

The ankle joint is located between the talus and the tibia and the talus and the fibula. It can move in one plane, flexing and extending (pointing); however, as with the knee, the axis for flexion and extension does not remain in place, providing extra mobility for the joint. Two-thirds of the top joint surface of the ankle is formed by the tibia, with the fibula providing the outer edge, creating a cavity. Together they firmly embrace the talus, allowing them to swing in the sagittal plane as if working together as an adjustable wrench (figure 12.10). Rather than bearing much weight, the fibula takes part in the pincerlike action of the ankle joint and gives it mobility. The tibial portion is like the weight-bearing palm of one hand, whereas the fibula is like the fingers of another hand making subtle adjustments, depending on the ankle joint's exact positioning (figure 12.11).

The lower surface of the ankle joint is formed by the wedge-shaped trochlea of the talus, which is wider anteriorly than posteriorly. When you plié, this wider section becomes lodged between the fibula and tibia, putting you in a much more stable position than in relevé, when the fibula and tibia embrace the narrower part of the trochlea. The talus has three inferior facets: a large lateral facet (connected to the fibula), a smaller medial one (connected to the tibia), and a superior facet. Since the fibula is located on the lateral side, its movement must be larger than that of the tibia. Both the fibula and tibia glide forward and backward along their talar facets (figure 12.10). Some researchers hold that the fibula also rotates around its longitudinal axis during ankle motion. If this is true, the ankle cannot be called a true hinge joint because its axis is variable. During dorsiflexion (lifting the top of the foot up), the fibula glides/rotates anteriorly; during plantar flexion (pointing the foot), it glides/rotates posteriorly on the lateral facet of the talus.

With each step we take, we plant a foot on the floor, causing dorsiflexion as the tibia and fibula move forward and the trochlea of the talus slides backward to-

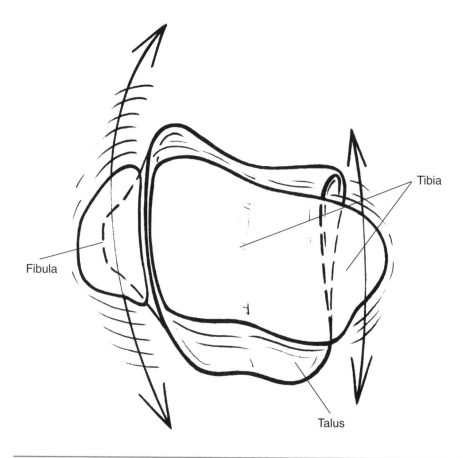

Figure 12.10   The fibula, located on the larger lateral facet of the talus, glides further than the tibia on the medial facet (bones of the left foot are shown).

ward the heel. As the foot plantar flexes in the push-off, the trochlea slides forward toward the front of the foot.

IMAGING THE TIBIA, FIBULA, AND ANKLE

1. **Ankle pincers:**

   a. **Non-weight bearing:** Hold one foot in a non-weight-bearing position and visualize the talus suspended between the tibial and fibular mortise (figure 12.11). Let the foot swing in the sagittal plane between the pincers. Imagine the pincers loosening their grip, permitting an easy swinging motion.

   b. **Relevé:** Image the opposite action of the pincers in relevé. The pincers tighten their grip and help stabilize the ankle joint.

2. **Hands adjusting talus (non-weight bearing):** Visualize the lower end of the tibia as the palm of a hand and the distal end of the fibula as fingers.

Figure 12.11   The tibia and fibula firmly embrace the talus, allowing the foot to swing in the sagittal plane.

The tibial palm supports the talus; the fibular fingers are in charge of subtle adjustments. Imagine the fibular fingers initiating movement of the foot at the ankle in a variety of directions (figure 12.13).

3. **Relative motion of tibia, fibula, and talus:**

    a. **Changing relationships:** While performing a plié, focus on the changing relationships of the tibia, fibula, and talus. As you move down, visualize the tibia and fibula gliding forward over the top of the talus. Don't forget that the tibia is mainly responsible for transferring weight to the talus. Because the fibula travels farther on the outside of the talus, the lower leg turns slightly inward with this action or, in reverse, the talus can be seen as rotating out (see figure 12.12). As you stretch your legs, watch the tibia and fibula skim backward over the mound of the talus. Because the fibula travels farther on the outside of the talus, the lower leg turns slightly outward with this action and the talus rotates in. Therefore, it is most important, especially in the downward phase, to maintain the knees aligned over the scond toes.

    b. **Talus through tibia/fibula tunnel:** Now perform the same action, but concentrate on the motion of the trochlea of the talus under the tibia and fibula. As you move downward in plié, focus on how the trochlea slips backward beneath the tunnel created by the tibia and fibula (figure 12.14). As you stretch, watch the trochlea slip forward under the tunnel formed by the tibia and fibula.

    c. **Talus through saloon doors (plantar/dorsiflexion):** As you point your foot, visualize the tibia and fibula as two saloon doors opening in front (anteriorly), allowing the talus to move forward. As you flex your foot, visualize the tibia and fibula as saloon doors opening to

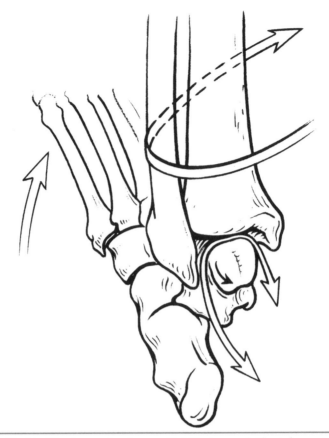

Figure 12.12   The lower leg turns slightly inward; the talus rotates out in dorsiflexion and downward in plié (left foot shown).

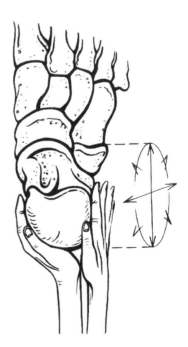

Figure 12.13   The tibial portion is like the weight-bearing palm of one hand, whereas the fibula is like the fingers of another hand making subtle adjustments.

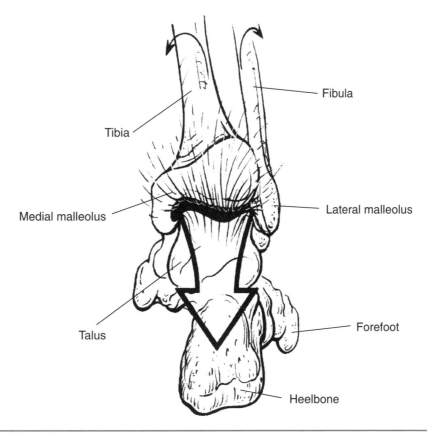

Fibula

Tibia

Medial malleolus

Lateral malleolus

Talus

Forefoot

Heelbone

Figure 12.14   As you move downward in plié, focus on how the trochlea of the talus slips backward beneath the tunnel formed by the distal ends of the tibia and fibula.

the rear (posteriorly) and allowing the talus to slide backward (figure 12.15).

4. **Membrane sail (supine):** Imagine the interosseous membrane to be a sail located between the tibia and fibula. As the wind blows between the tibia and fibula, the sail billows. Visualize the wind blowing from back to front, then imagine it reversing and making the sail billow in the opposite direction. Imagine several changes of wind direction. Sense this flapping back and forth of the sail loosening the area. It is helpful to have a partner touch the area between the tibia and fibula as you visualize this action (figure 12.16).

5. **Tarsal tendu (tendu, dégagé, plantar flexion):** As you point your ankle in a tendu, visualize a flow of energy down the front of the leg, circling the tarsal bone and continuing over the top of the foot and out through the toes. When flexing the foot, imagine the energy flowing down the back of the leg, circling the tarsal bone and continuing out the heel (figure 12.17).

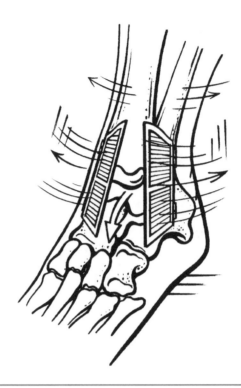

Figure 12.15   As you point your foot visualize the fibula and tibia as two saloon doors.

Figure 12.16   Imagine the interosseous membrane to be a billowing sail located between the tibia and fibula.

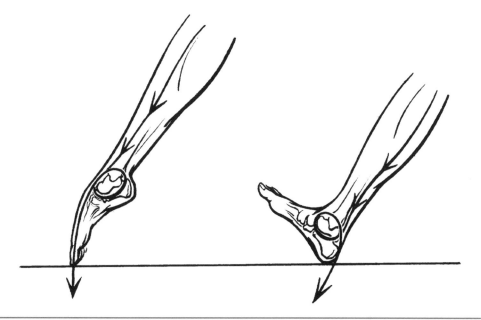

Figure 12.17   As you point and flex your ankle, visualize the flow of energy.

THE FOOT

Most feet spend their time enclosed inside leathery, bodicelike containers. For some athletes, taking off their shoes in a movement class is a novel experience. Quite a few "ahs" and "ohs" are heard as the foot is revealed to be a complex, multijointed entity and not just a lever that assists the legs in walking and jumping. Dancers are usually aware of the technical and aesthetic importance of their feet, but sadly, the most common dance injuries involve the foot. Increased awareness of alignment and balanced strength and flexibility will go a long way in preventing foot problems and increasing the foot's expressive potential.

The foot consists of 26 bones that form 25 component joints. Its duties are numerous and even contradictory in nature. The foot serves as a stable foundation, carrying and cushioning the entire weight of the body. It also propels us through space while adapting to changes in the terrain. The image of a twisted and untwisted chain explains the seemingly instantaneous transformation of the foot from a weight-bearing foundation mechanism to a lever. If you twist a jointed chain, it becomes rigid, much like the foot in its position as a lever. Untwist the chain and it becomes loose, spreading to better carry weight (author's notes taken from lecture by Irene Dowd, 1981).

The foot is subdivided in a variety of ways. Three functional sections can be described from front to back (figure 12.18). The hindfoot, or tarsus, consists of comparatively large bones: the talus (cube; the ancient Romans used to play dice with *tali*) and the calcaneus (heel). As we learned earlier, the talus (anklebone) is the transfer point of the body's weight to the foot. The midfoot or tarsal bones consist of the navicular (little boat), the cuboid (squarelike), and the three cuneiforms (wedge-formed). The forefoot consists of the metatarsals and the phalanges (toe bones). The joints between the tarsal bones can move in all planes—

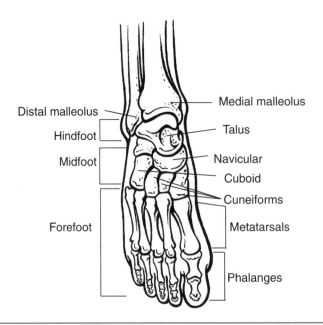

Distal malleolus
Hindfoot
Midfoot
Forefoot

Medial malleolus
Talus
Navicular
Cuboid
Cuneiforms
Metatarsals
Phalanges

Figure 12.18 The hindfoot (tarsus) consists of the talus and the calcaneus. The midfoot consists of the navicular, the cuboid, and the three cuneiforms. The forefoot consists of the metatarsals and the phalanges.

up and down, sideways, and around. The joints' surfaces can glide upon each other, distributing the impact in a multitude of planes.

The foot is like several stones held together tightly in a strong sack. Drop the sack on the floor and the stones will rearrange slightly, transferring shock to each other, equalizing any excess forces with a neighboring stone. Most likely, no individual stone will break. If, however, the stones are glued together, eliminating the ability to move in relationship to each other, some of them would break if the sack were dropped. The tarsal bones are perfectly fitted to each other to absorb and transfer forces and create a stable and enduring whole.

The foot has two basic functions: support and locomotion. These can be considered separately by dividing the foot into a heel foot and an ankle foot. The heel foot, consisting of the fourth and fifth phalanges and metatarsals, the cuboid, and the calcaneus, contacts the ground more readily and relates to the fibula and the support function. The ankle foot consists of the first three phalanges and metatarsals, the cuneiforms, the navicular, and the talus and relates to the tibia. This springy part of the foot transfers the ground reaction force to the tibia which relates it more to locomotion.

GUIDED FOOT MASSAGE

Fortunately, feet are very accessible to our hands. Most dancers have at some point massaged their tired, aching feet. The following is a guide to foot massage that will help you identify the many landmarks in this remarkably complex structure.

The inner anklebone, or medial malleolus, is an enlargement of the lower (distal) end of the tibia. The outer ankle, or lateral malleolus, is an enlargement of the distal end of the fibula. Notice that the lateral malleolus is farther down and farther to the rear than the inner malleolus. Stand with your feet parallel and notice how the lateral malleolus is farther back than the medial malleolus.

The talus (anklebone) is much harder to touch. In full plantar flexion, you can usually touch the head of the talus, located on top of the foot between the malleoli, but it recedes when the foot is dorsally flexed. Another place where the head of the talus can be touched is just below and to the front of the medial malleolus. (Anatomically, flexion refers to extreme states. Plantar flexion is toward the sole of the foot, dorsiflexion toward the top of the foot. The term flex is really dancers' slang for one type of flexion—dorsiflexion.)

In front of and below the medial anklebone (talus) and distal to the point we just touched, locate the tuberosity (bulge) of the navicular bone. Continue moving toward the toes and locate the base of the first metatarsal bone. Just below the medial malleolus, feel the small, ledge-shaped sustentaculum tali (supporter of the talus), which is part of the calcaneus (heelbone).

Touch the calcaneus on both the medial and lateral sides. Besides its large smooth posterior portion, you can feel a protrusion of the calcaneus below and in front of the lateral malleolus called the peroneal trochlea. Touch the Achilles tendon above the posterior part of the calcaneus. Glide your fingers along the outer rim of the foot toward the toes, where you will encounter a bony knob, which is the base of the fifth metatarsal bone. It is located just behind the midpoint of the outside rim of the foot. Palpate the cuboid bone between the calcaneus and the base of the fifth metatarsal. The cuneiforms form the arched instep of the foot and are best massaged with relaxed toes so that the extensor tendons do not protrude. Touch the heads of the metatarsal bones on both the dorsal and plantar sides of the foot. (This will be more difficult on the plantar side due to the many layers of muscle.) Below the head of the first metatarsal bone, palpate the part of the flexor hallucis tendon (the tendon that flexes the big toe) known as the sesamoid bones. Finally, manipulate the toe bones (phalanges) and the interphalangeal joints.

Subtalar Joint

The talus has three articulations with the underlying heelbone and one degree of freedom. Its motions are called supination and pronation. In subtalar supination (rolling on the outside of the foot), the calcaneus inverts, moving toward the midline of the body. In subtalar pronation (rolling on the inside of the foot), the calcaneus everts, moving away from the midline of the body. In these actions, there is also some motion between the talus and the navicular bone. The axis of supination and pronation is oblique, inclined upward about 42 degrees and medially about 16 degrees. The relationship between the lower leg and the midfoot can be visualized as a mitered hinge (Norkin and Levangie 1992). In figure 12.19a, the foot is depicted in a neutral position. Internal rotation of the lower leg causes pronation of the foot; external rotation of the lower leg causes supination (figure 12.19b).

In a neutral position, a line drawn down the back of the leg should not veer inside or outside as it passes down over the calcaneus. In other words, the portion of the body's weight passing down through the heel must be experienced directly at its center. In good standing alignment, the plane through the Achilles tendon and center of the heel is perpendicular to the floor.

Supination and pronation allow you to walk along a slope with relative ease. If the hillside is to your right, your right subtalar joint will be pronated and your left subtalar joint supinated, allowing your legs to remain fairly vertical. The action of the subtalar joint is also important in maintaining balance (figure 12.17c).

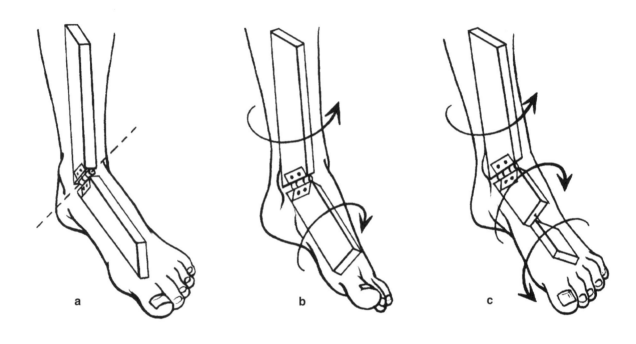

Figure 12.19 (a) The relationship between the lower leg and the midfoot can be visualized as a mitered hinge. (b) External rotation of the lower leg causes supination. (c) If the heel slips and rolls into a supinated position, the forefoot compensates by pronating.
Adapted, by permission, from C.C. Norkin and P.K. Levangie, 1992, *Joint Structure and Function* (Philadelphia: F.A. Davis).

IMAGING THE SUBTALAR JOINT

1. **Deep roots (balance on one leg):** Ask a friend to balance on one leg and observe the supination and pronation activity. If your friend closes his or her eyes, this motion will be even more evident because without the use of the optical righting mechanisms, balancing is more difficult. Now ask your friend to imagine his or her standing foot to have roots extending deep into the ground. Notice any changes in your friend's ability to balance.

2. **Heel pendulum (sitting, standing):** Feel the contact surface between your heel and the floor. Imagine the heel to be a pendulum. Visualize the pendulum swinging in and out. The pendulum's swing decreases until it hangs down toward the center of the earth. The heel is now in line with the Achilles tendon (figure 12.20).

3. **Sitz bone-heel pendulums (standing):** Extend the strings of the pendulums upward and attach them to your sitz bones. Imagine the heel pendulums hanging from your sitz bones.

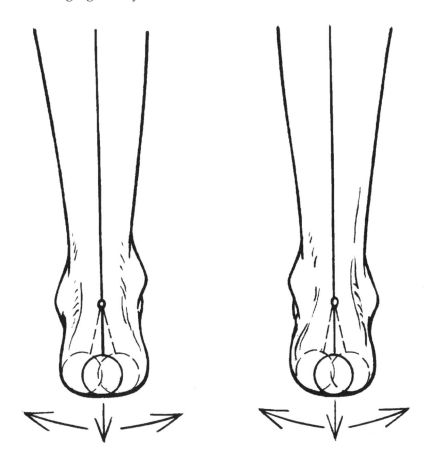

Figure 12.20   Imagine the heel to be a swinging pendulum.

The Transverse Tarsal Joint

The transverse tarsal joint is composed of the talonavicular and the calcaneocuboid joints (figure 12.21). Without the transverse tarsal joint, it would be difficult to walk across uneven ground because it mediates between the forefoot and the hindfoot. If the forefoot is forced to supinate, the hindfoot need not follow suit because the transverse tarsal joint can counter this action, allowing the heel to remain vertical. The reverse holds true as well: If the heel slips and rolls into a pronated position, for example, the forefoot can remain flat on the ground.

If the forefoot is forced to pronate, the hindfoot counters by supinating. If the heel slips and rolls into a supinated position, the forefoot compensates by pronating (figure 12.19c). This is essential if you like to walk in moccasins or barefoot, but otherwise the rigid shoes worn today all but eliminate the action of the transverse tarsal joint. This is not entirely advantageous, because it places additional strain on the ankle and knee joints.

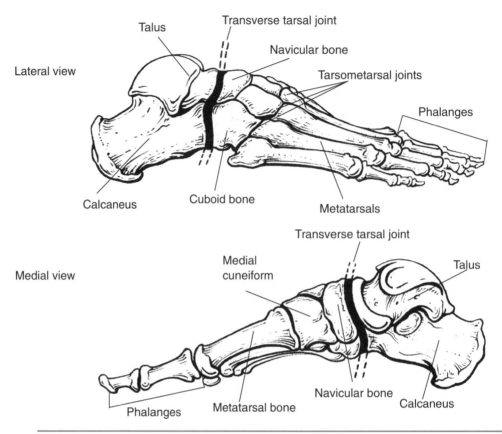

Figure 12.21   The transverse tarsal joint is composed of the talonavicular and calca-neocuboid joints.

1. **Marbles:** Place a few marbles under the medial rim of your forefoot. Notice that the heel remains on the floor. Now place the marbles under the lateral rim of your forefoot, and notice that the heel still remains on the floor.

2. **Uneven ground:** Take a walk over imaginary uneven ground. In your mind's eye, visualize a variety of odd shapes to step on and watch how your foot adapts. Now collect some objects that cannot harm your feet to experiment with—small stones, a book (you may walk along the outer edge of this book; it's included in the price). After experimenting for a while with real objects, try walking over the imaginary uneven ground again.

3. **Rubber raft:** Imagine your foot to be an inflatable rubber raft. Such a raft can readily adapt to all kinds of waves because it is able to twist along its longitudinal axis. Watch the twisting adjustments of the raft as you walk along a rocky road (figure 12.22).

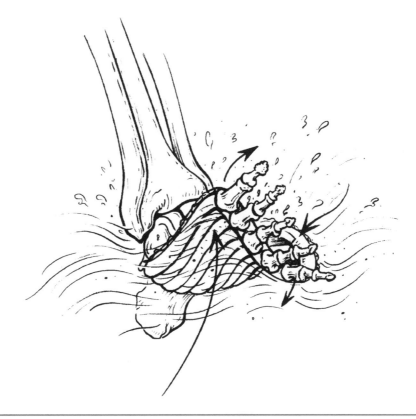

Figure 12.22   Comparing the twisting adjustments of the foot to a rubber raft.

Arches of the Feet

A multiple-arch system, much like the multiple vaults of the medieval Kloster in Kreuzlingen, Switzerland (figure 12.23), enables the foot to support the considerable weight of the body. The longitudinal arch begins at the far (distal) end of the heelbone and ends at the far ends of the first and fifth metatarsal bones, respectively (the toes are not part of the arch). The talus is the keystone of the longitudinal arch (figure 12.24). The middle cuneiform and the second metatarsal bones are the keystones of the transverse arches. The Romans seemed to have been aware of the importance of the talus as a keystone, in the physical sense as well as the psychological. In reminding someone not to fall or fail, they would say: *"Recto talo stare"* ("Stand upright on your talus").

The distal ends of the first and usually the fifth metatarsals rest on buffering sesamoid bones. In this respect, the foot is like an elongated tripod with three main contact points for weight support.

The plantar aponeurosis (neither a foot fetishist nor an obsessed home gardener) is a tough sheet of connective tissue that maintains the arches by tying together both ends of the arch, creating a bowlike tension. Compression of the bow will increase tension in the bowstring, keeping it stable and preventing excessive spreading.

Earlier we used the metaphor of a twisted chain to explain how the foot transforms from a rigid lever to a spreadable foundation. Similarly, the foot can be

Figure 12.23   A multiple-arch system much like the multiple vaults of the medieval Kloster in Kreuzlingen, Switzerland, enables the foot to support the considerable weight of the body.

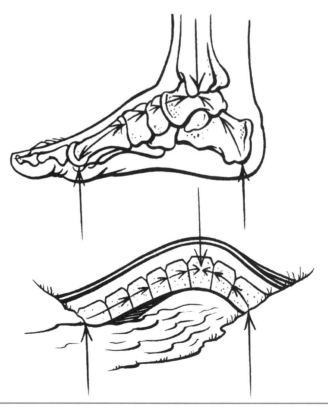

Figure 12.24   The talus is the keystone of the arch.

seen as a twisted rectangular plane. This metaphor helps in understanding the relationship between the longitudinal and transverse arches of the foot. The front of the plane consists of the metatarsal heads, which are horizontal and in contact with the floor. The back of the plane, the posterior calcaneus, is vertical (figure 12.25). When you place weight on the foot, it "untwists," flattening the arches, which involves pronation; when you push off the ground, as in a leap, the plane "twists" or supinates to act as a lever.

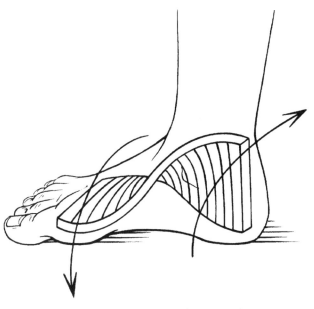

Figure 12.25 The foot can be visualized as a twisted rectangular plane.

EXERCISING THE ARCHES OF THE FEET

1. **The mediating talus (standing, walking, leaping):** Imagine the talus to be the mediator among the tibia, the calcaneus, and the navicular. It efficiently manages all incoming and outgoing forces. Like a springy rubber ball with cushioning springs attached to it, the talus receives and distributes forces. To maintain elasticity, no one side of the ball may be subject to constant extremes of pressure (figure 12.26).

2. **Foot as clay:**

    a. **Rolling your clay foot:** Imagine your foot to be a piece of clay. Roll it over a baseball or rubber ball and watch it spread in all directions. The heel spreads to the back and the metatarsals to the front and sides.

    b. **Perfecting your clay foot:** As you tendu, visualize imaginary hands remodeling your clay foot to perfection.

3. **Foot tripod (standing):**

    a. **Spreading your base:** Visualize the three contact points of the foot—the heel, the distal head of the first toe metatarsal, and the distal head of the fifth toe metatarsal—as a tripod. Distribute the weight evenly on these three

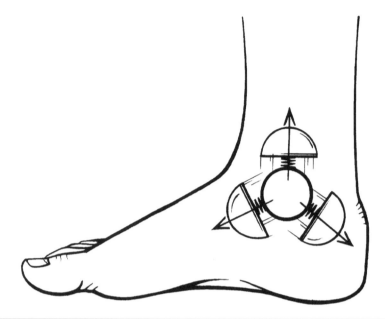

Figure 12.26　The talus is like a mediator among the tibia, calcaneus, and navicular.

points. Imagine them to be energy centers radiating into space. Imagine the points of the tripod forming a triangle. Watch them move away from each other into space, making an ever-larger triangle (figure 12.27).

b. **Integrating the tripod:** Visualize the tripod of the foot. Imagine energy originating at each corner of the tripod, merging at the apex of the vault and streaming up the center of your leg.

4. **Foot grasp:**

a. **Massage your claylike, malleable foot:** With your finger, touch the spot on the sole of your foot that you experience as its center. Try to grasp the finger with your whole foot. Enfolding the finger will help activate the muscles that maintain the arch of the foot. Imagine the finger being sucked up by the foot, all the way up between the malleoli. (Adapted from Andre Bernard.)

b. **Fingers coming up from the ground (standing, walking):** As you stand, imagine a finger coming up from the ground under each foot. Imagine your feet grasping the fingers. Each time you take a step, grasp an imaginary finger with your foot. (Adapted from Andre Bernard.)

c. **Acetabular grasp (supine, improvisation):** Simultaneously visualize the center of the foot grasping a finger and the acetabulum grasping the femur head.

d. **Spaghetti through the leg (supine, improvisation):** Imagine a long thread of spaghetti being sucked up through the center of your foot, up the center of your leg, and into the vacuumlike acetabulum.

5. **Bow and arrow:**

a. **Stand on both feet:** Imagine your feet to be bows with the bowstrings toward the floor. Shift your weight from one foot to the other and visualize the bow spreading and the bowstring becoming taut as you place

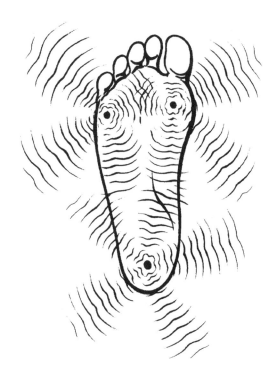

Figure 12.27   Visualize the three main contact points of the foot with the floor as a tripod.

your weight on it. Visualize the bow arching and the bowstring releasing as you take your weight off the foot.

   b. **Imagine your foot to be a bow with the bowstring toward the floor:** As you move downward in plié, notice the increasing tension in the string as the bow spreads. As you move upward in plié, notice the decreasing tension in the string as the bow arches. Now imagine that spreading the bow initiates the plié downward. Finally, imagine the arching of the bow initiating the plié upward.

6. **Three keystones (second position):** Focus on the tali of both feet and the sacrum. Visualize these three keystones simultaneously. Imagine how all three keystones are buttressed equally from both sides. Note that the pelvic arch lies perpendicular to the long arches of the feet.

7. **Foot dome (standing, feet touching in parallel position):** The adjoining arches of the foot create a vaulted structure like a cupola or the Roman pantheon (the oldest domed structure still intact). The combined tripods of the feet create six major weight-bearing points for the body. There is a small opening between the feet, just in front of the medial ankle bone. Imagine a waterspout shooting upward from the ground through the center of this cupola and continuing up between the legs. As the water falls back down, it pours down the outside of the foot, releasing the toes and outer rim of the foot into the ground (figure 12.28).

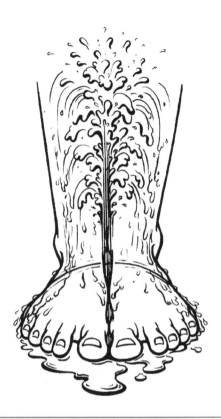

Figure 12.28   Visualize a waterspout spraying upward from between the ankles.

The Forefoot

The five metatarsals are the longest bones of the foot and are therefore an important part of its leverage system, forming a significant segment of the transverse arch of the foot. The tarsometatarsal joints also aid the transverse tarsal joint in compensatory motions of the foot.

There are 14 phalanges in the five toes—two in the big toe and three in each of the smaller toes. Rather than carrying weight, the toes should be free to make subtle weight adjustments to readily maintain balance. The joints between the metatarsals and phalanges have two degrees of freedom: extension and flexion and abduction and adduction.

As you relevé, the toes crease along the heads of the metatarsals, creating the metatarsal break, which lies along the second to fifth metatarsal heads. It is slightly oblique, allowing the weight of the body to be more evenly distributed among the toes. The plantar surfaces of these heads constitute the ball of the foot, the standing surface in demi-pointe.

EXERCISING THE FOREFOOT

1. **Metatarsals as river logs (standing, walking):** The metatarsal bones can be visualized as logs in a river, touching each other along their entire lengths. As seen from above, the logs can rotate in two direc-

tions: toward each other or away from each other. If they rotate outward, water is pushed upward between them. If they rotate toward each other, they push the water to the side. Visualize the movement of the logs as you walk. When you place weight on your foot, watch the logs (metatarsals) spread apart. As you lift your foot, watch them move closer (figure 12.29).

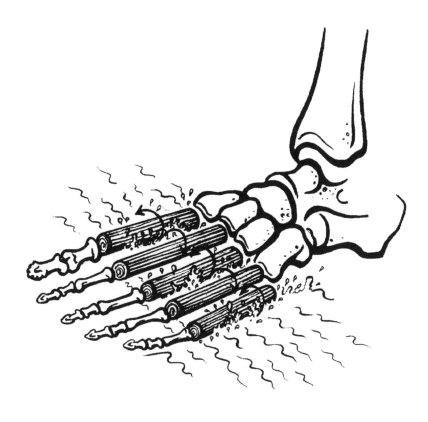

Figure 12.29   Visualize the metatarsal bones as logs in a river.

2. **Spreading toes (demi-pointe):** Imagine the toes spreading out over the floor, creating a large base of support.

3. **Metatarsal break sinking downward (demi-pointe):** As you relevé and reach demi-pointe, imagine the toes lengthening and the metatarsal break sinking into the ground. Watch the metatarsal break sink downward evenly (figure 12.30).

4. **Toes as dandelion parachutes (supine, improvisation):** Imagine the toes to be dandelion parachutes. Watch them float off the end of your foot (figure 12.31).

5. **Toes as feelers (improvisation):** Imagine the toes to be sensitive feelers, testing and exploring the space in front of them.

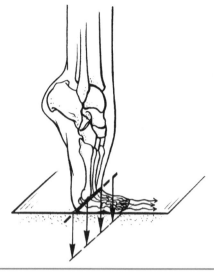

Figure 12.30   As you relevé and reach demi-pointe, imagine the toes lengthening and the metatarsals break, sinking into the ground.

Figure 12.31   Imagine the toes to be dandelion parachutes.

The foot is at once a foundation—a firm stable base of support—and a flexible, adaptable lever that can maneuver us through irregular terrain. Its multiple-arch system and the strong ties that reinforce these vaults add flexibility and bounce. Its numerous joints support us and enable us to maintain balance.

CHAPTER 13 *The Spine*

*S*pinal patterns reveal much about cultural heritage and stylistic preferences. In classical ballet, the spine is held in a very slight extension (arched); in classical Spanish dance, it is even more extended (arched); in Native American dance, it is fairly erect; and in traditional Japanese styles, it is slightly flexed (curved forward) (Barba & Savarese 1991). Modern dance employs a great variety of spinal patterns, lumbar initiations, thoracic over- and under-curves, side bends, spirals, and swings.

THE FUNCTIONING SPINE

To fulfill its varied functions, the spine needs to be both stable and mobile. As the intermediary between the upper and lower body, the spine supports and carries the weight of the head, organs, and limbs and protects the spinal cord. The vertebral column consists of 24 separate vertebrae, composite vertebrae, the sacrum, and the coccyx. The cervical spine, the highest and most mobile part of the vertebral column, consists of seven vertebrae. The thoracic spine consists of 12 vertebrae that support the ribcage. The lumbar spine consists of five large vertebral bodies whose anterior aspects touch or even pass the midline of the body (figure 13.1). The base of the spine is called the sacrum and is composed of five fused vertebrae. The coccyx, the tail of the spine, consists of four vertebral

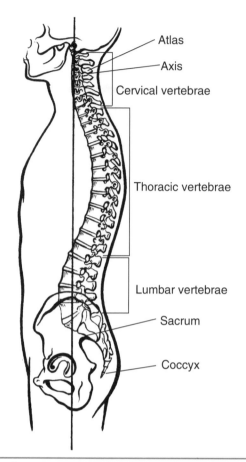

Figure 13.1   The vertebral column consists of 24 separate vertebrae, composite vertebrae, the sacrum, and the coccyx.

remnants. From the back, the spine down to the lowest lumbar vertebrae
looks like a long, slender pyramid, while the sacrum appears to be an inverted pyramid. The broad base of a long pyramid sits on the broad base of
a short and wide pyramid creating an intrinsically stable structure. From the
side, the spine has four opposing curves in the sagittal plane, which add to
its strength.

We are born with a basic convex curvature, the primary curve, of which the
thoracic and the sacrococcygeal remain intact in adulthood. Opposing curves,
necessary to sit and walk, are developed by the baby's exemplary movement
efforts. As the baby learns to lift its head, the cervical concavity develops. As it
kicks, pushes, pulls, rolls, creeps, and crawls its way through babyhood, the lumbar concavity develops.

Due to differing angles of the spinous processes (projections of the spine),
the spinal curves feel flatter to the touch than they actually are. The lumbar
spinous processes are nearly horizontal where the spine is concave; in the
thoracic concavity, they point downward. The gutters between the spinous
processes and the ribs contain powerful strands of musculature, evening out
the contour of the back so that it serves as a broad resting surface for the
body.

IMAGING THE SPINE

1. **Melting butter (supine):** Imagine the back to be a chunk of butter. Watch as it melts and spreads. (Depending on your personal preference, substitute vanilla ice cream, honey, soft snow, milk chocolate, etc.)

2. **Smoothing sand (supine):** Imagine your back to be made of chunky sand arranged in mounds. Visualize the wind blowing down your back, smoothing, leveling, and softening the sand.

3. **Primary circle (curved spine):** Imagine the primary curve of the spine continuing out into space through both the head and the coccyx. Ultimately, these curves join to create a circle. Visualize the changing size of this circle as you vary the angle of spinal flexion (figure 13.2). Imagine a tangent of this circle connecting the tailbone to the heels.

Figure 13.2   Imagine the primary curve of the spine continuing out into space through both the head and the coccyx.

PELVIS AND SPINE

The curves of the spine are influenced by the position of the pelvis. The fifth lumbar vertebra rests upon the slanted sacral table, producing intrinsic shear forces in the lower lumbar area. These forces are counteracted by bony, ligamentous, and muscular restraints, as well as by the hydrostatic pressure and tone of the abdominal organs. A line crossing the sacral table intersects with the horizontal to determine the lumbosacral angle (figure 13.3a).

Excessive forward tilt of the top of the pelvis increases the lumbosacral angle, deepening the lumbar curve, which in turn increases the other curvatures of the spine (figures 13.3b and 13.4b). Therefore, the COGs of the individual vertebrae will be less well aligned on top of each other, increasing the shear stresses at the lumbosacral and other joints of the spinal column. "Lengthening" these curves reduces these stresses; however, a back that is too straight has less shock-absorbing ability.

In the case of the anteriorly tilted pelvis, a plane defined by the ASIS and the PSIS will be tilted anteriorly (figure 13.4b). If the pelvis is tilted posteriorly the plane defined by the ASIS and PSIS will be tilted posteriorly (figure 13.4c).

Posterior tilting of the pelvis and sacrum (tucking the pelvis) tends to flatten the curves (figure 13.4c), making the spine seem flatter, but it is not an ideal approach to lengthening the spine. In the turned-out position, tucking distorts the alignment of the legs by forcing the knees forward, increasing tension in the pelvic musculature and straining the medial aspect of the knees. This not only impedes the functioning of the iliopsoas, it reduces the efficiency of hip flexion and leg extension. If you try to eliminate an old tucking habit, you will feel as if your buttocks are protruding to the rear. Although this certainly feels wrong, it is hard to repattern. A balanced pelvis is based on good movement patterns, not on the constant tensing of certain muscle groups.

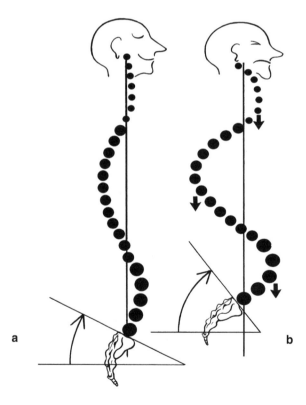

Figure 13.3 (a) A line crossing the sacral table intersects with the horizontal to determine the lumbosacral angle. (b) If the lumbosacral angle is increased, the individual COGs of the vertebra will be less well aligned on top of each other, increasing shear stresses at the lumbosacral and other joints of the spinal column.

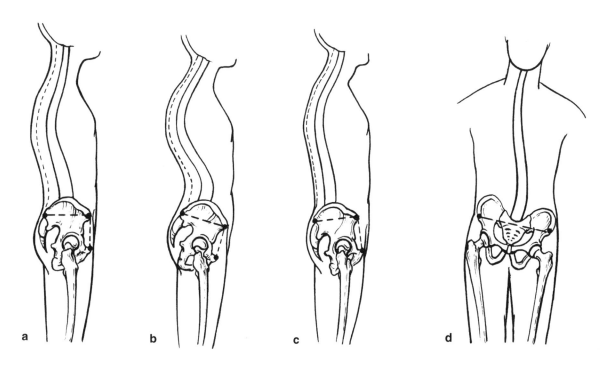

Figure 13.4   (a) The ASIS and PSIS in the same plane. (b) The PSIS higher than the ASIS. (c) The PSIS lower than the ASIS. (d) The ASIS not on the same horizontal plane.

If the pelvic crests and the ASIS are not level in the horizontal plane, the lumbar spine will deviate to the lower side of the pelvis. This forces the spine into a corrective bend to recapture its vertical alignment. Such curves of the spine in the frontal plane are called scoliotic (figure 13.4d). If the pelvic halves are twisted, the spine twists uncomfortably at its very base—certainly not the foundation of good spinal alignment.

If the pelvis is in good alignment, three points delineated by the ASIS and the front of the pubic symphysis (the joint between the two pubic bones) form a vertical plane. In this case, the ASIS and the PSIS are approximately on the same horizontal plane (figure 13.4a). Although proper pelvic alignment helps the spine to achieve balanced curves, simply placing the pelvis in the correct position is not necessarily an enduring solution. Other factors must be considered. For example, the classic closed kinematic chain of the spine supports the head at its apex, a balancing act akin to an impressive circus performance. Any changes in head positioning influence the spine.

The spine also supports various internal organs and protects the spinal cord while providing outlets for nerves fanning out into the entire body. Composed of many joints, the spine is designed for infinite combinations of movements. If the spine's potential is not fully explored regularly, its muscles, especially the short intrinsic ones, weaken.

Therefore, although achieving a visually ideal position may be an important element of efficient functioning, it is no guarantee. An improvement in spinal alignment must be dynamic, centered around motion interrelationships of bones, muscles, and organs, and include changes in the individual's body image, in which the pelvis and head play a significant part.

IMPROVING SPINAL ALIGNMENT

The images mentioned in the earlier sections (pelvic imbalances, the hip joint, the sitz bones, the pelvic floor) as well as in part IV of this book on holistic alignment will help correct pelvic imbalances, improving spinal alignment.

1. **String lifts pubic symphysis (standing, walking):** Imagine a string attached to the pubic symphysis. Watch the string pulling up and forward on a slight diagonal to lift the front rim of the pelvis. Imagine this string pulling you into a walk.

2. **Lighting designer aligns the spine (supine, sitting, or standing):** Visualize the spine as a chain of spotlights. Turn on the lights and observe their focal directions. If they shine in many confused directions, adjust them so that they all focus in the sagittal plane. Now adjust them so that they shine with equal brightness.

Concentrate on the spotlight at the center of the cervical spine. Its light should shine in the horizontal direction (perpendicular to the central axis). Focus on the spotlight at the center of the thoracic spine. Allow its light to become perpendicular to the central axis. Finally, focus on the spotlight at the level of the fourth lumbar vertebra; adjust its light so that it too is directed perpendicularly to the central axis. Focus on these three spotlights simultaneously. Watch them become parallel, horizontally aligned in the sagittal plane (figure 13.5).

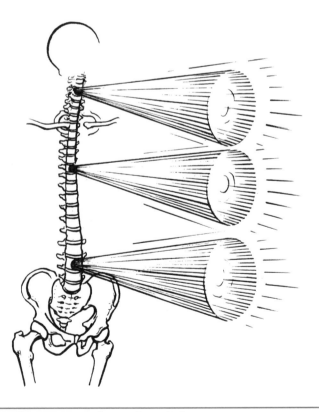

Figure 13.5   Visualize the spine as a chain of spotlights.

THE VERTEBRAE

Each vertebra consists of two main parts: a cylindrical body in front, mainly responsible for resisting compression forces, and a vertebral arch in back. The arch has four articular (joint) and three nonarticular projections; the nonarticular processes are the spinous and the transverse (figure 13.6). Only the spinous processes can be seen and palpated as the posterior part of the spine. These processes should form a line that divides the back into two equal halves. Because the spinous and transverse processes are interconnected by many short muscles, we can move the spine in a snakelike manner. If these small muscles are tight, there will be a concomitant rigidity in the larger muscles of the spine that inhibits breathing and the flow of energy through the spinal column.

Because the spinous processes are the visible part of the spine, we tend to think of the spine as being far back, when in fact the weight-bearing bodies of the vertebrae, as well as the intervertebral disks, are more centrally located. The spine also has depth. If you place your finger in your bellybutton, the bodies of the lumbar spine are only about two to four inches from the tip of your finger. Once, while in a supine position, I experienced the following spontaneous image, which gave me a feeling of depth and fluidity. My spine had become the bottom of a primal ocean. The surface of the ocean was the abdominal wall. I saw sediments made of very fine sand falling down from the surface onto the floor of the ocean, creating an ever thicker, higher, and softer coating that slowly rose to the surface of the water. This experience was a welcome counterbalance to the notion of the spine as a chain of rigid building blocks. Upon analysis, the spine has many fluid and soft aspects. The intervertebral disks contain a fluid-filled nucleus; the spinal cord is surrounded by the cerebrospinal fluid and even bone with its marrow core is fluid-like at its center. Fluidity should not be equated with weakness, however. If you ever have been knocked down by a breaking wave at the beach, you can appreciate this.

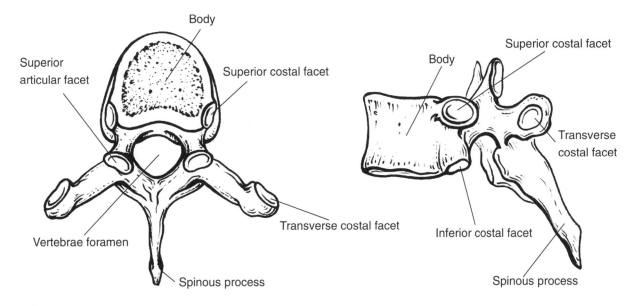

Figure 13.6   A thoracic vertebra.

EXERCISING THE VERTEBRAE

1. **Releasing the spinous processes (standing, sitting, or supine):** Visualize the dorsal spinous processes as little flags or ribbons. Imagine the wind blowing through your body from front to back, unfurling these flags. Watch the flags fluttering in the wind. Picture all the flags aligned one above the other (figures 13.7).

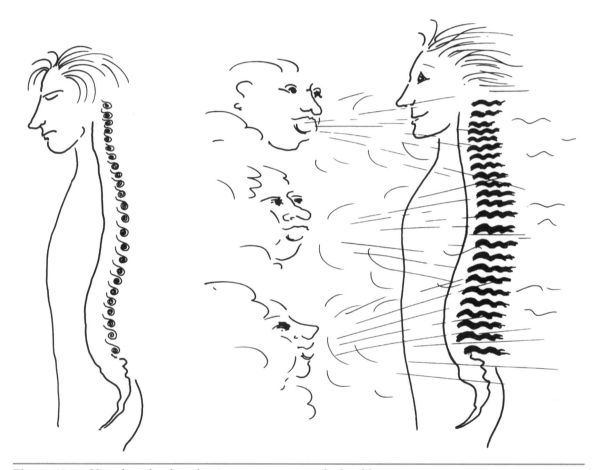

Figure 13.7   Visualize the dorsal spinous processes as little ribbons.

2. **Fluidity and subtleness of spinal movements (any position, improvisation; music optional):** Image the spinal processes as the tongues of a vibraphone. Each process creates its own distinct sound. Hear the spine-vibraphone playing. Feel the vibration of each vertebra (see figure 13.8).

3. **Fluttering transverse processes:** Imagine the transverse processes of the spine stretching sideways. Now watch as they begin to move gently, creating a downward current along the sides of the spine. This motion is similar to that of the soft, tiny hairs called cilia used by one-celled animals to move through the water (figure 13.9).

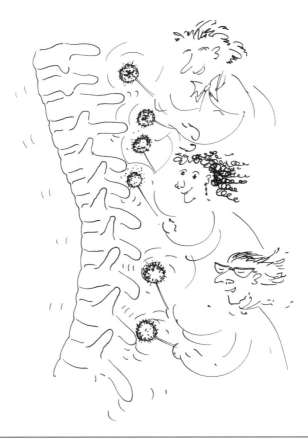

Figure 13.8   Image the spinal processes as the tongues of a vibraphone.

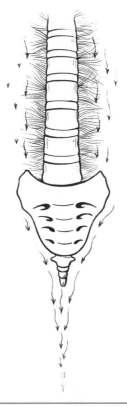

Figure 13.9   Imagine the transverse processes of the spine stretching sideways; the movement is similar to that of cilia, used by one-celled animals to move through the water.

4. **Spine as a chain of spheres/pearls:**

    a. **Awakening chain (supine, improvisation):** Lie on the floor and imagine the spine to be an interconnected chain of spheres. Watch as a single sphere comes alive with motion. At first, there is only a gentle stirring, a small rocking motion. The movement of the vertebra intensifies until it inspires its neighbors to move as well. The inspiration spreads along the entire spine until the whole chain is in motion.

    b. **Releasing pearls (supine, sitting, standing, walking):** Imagine the spine to be a string of pearls fastened by a knot at the bottom end. Visualize the knot opening and the pearls gliding off the string. As the pearls drop, watch the space between adjacent pearls widen (figure 13.10).

    c. **Pearl dance (improvisation):** Visualize the spine as a polished, glistening chain of pearls. Watch how the pearls catch the myriad colors of light. Hear the sounds the pearls make as they roll against each other.

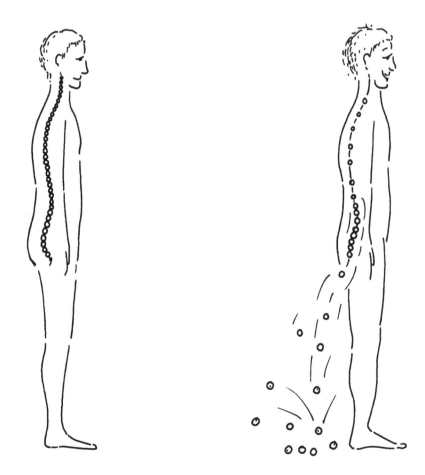

Figure 13.10   Imagine the spine to be a string of pearls fastened by a knot at the bottom end.

5. **The spine tracing through space (improvisation):** Imagine that the spine leaves a trail in space similar to a high-flying airplane's jet stream (figure 13.11).

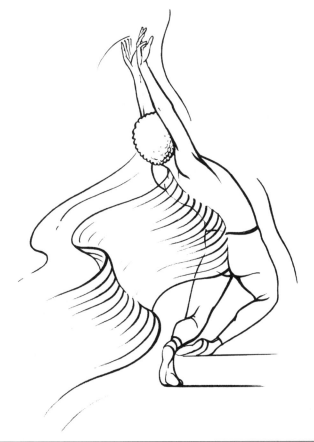

Figure 13.11   Imagine that the spine leaves a trail in space similar to a high-flying airplane's jet stream.

INTERVERTEBRAL DISKS

The intervertebral disks function as shock absorbers between adjacent vertebrae and allow for movement in all planes. Girded by the strong annulus fibrosus, the central unit of the disk, the nucleus pulposus, resembles a springy water-filled ball. In German, the intervertebral disks are called *Bandscheiben*, literally "ligament-circles." The vertebrae riding on the disks (without ligaments or muscles) can be likened to boards balancing on rubber balls (figure 13.12). This arrangement allows tilting in all planes, rotation, and a bit of gliding without the boards falling off the balls. Because it's resilient, the nucleus can store energy like a ball compressed and then released. By wrapping bands (the annulus fibrosus) around the ball, we lose mobility but improve carrying ability. The compressed ball pushes against the surrounding bands, stretching them so that they help in resisting the load. The intervertebral disks convert some of the compression stress into tensile stress through the stretching bands.

It is interesting to note that one method of earthquake-proofing a building is to place it on four spinelike segments: alternating metal cylinders (vertebrae) with more resilient rubber cylinders (intervertebral disks). Tremors are absorbed by these pillars so that the building barely trembles. Every step we take is a miniature earthquake. Part of the impact is absorbed by the legs and pelvis before it

Figure 13.12   The vertebrae riding on the disks are like boards balancing on sturdy rubber balls.

reaches the spine, but the spine buffers the residual quake before it reaches the head and the delicate brain. The motion of a dancer's head, especially when landing from a jump, reveals much about the state of his or her spine. If the dancer glides through space and lands without movement in either the neck or head, the shock has been absorbed before reaching the head. If the spine is rigid, the dancer's head will quiver.

EXERCISING INTER– VERTEBRAL DISKS

1. **Disk discoveries:**

   a. **Nucleus expands (supine):** Select a segment of the spine and imagine the nucleus to be a small ball. Observe the ball filling with liquid, pushing against the constricting bands of the annulus to expand the entire intervertebral disk. Watch as the intervertebral disk creates more space for itself by pushing the adjoining vertebrae apart. The action is similar to inflating a tire; inflating the tire lifts the car. Try to imagine that your inhalation aids the inflation of the intervertebral disks (figure 13.13).

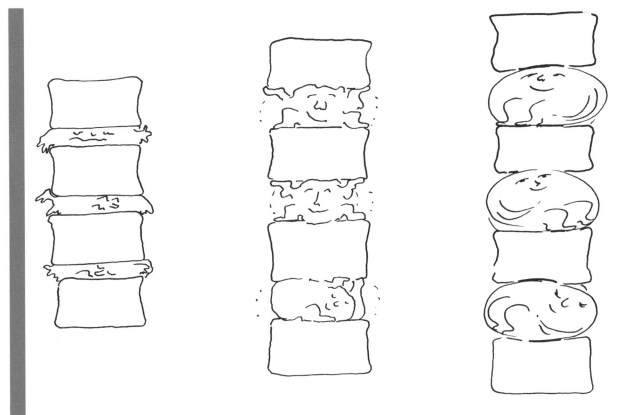

Figure 13.13   The intervertebral disk creates more space for itself by pushing the adjoining vertebrae apart.

    b. **Moving from the intervertebral disks:** Once you're finished "inflating" the intervertebral disks imagine that the spine finds its support in this soft fluid column. Try initiating movement from the intervertebral disks. How does this compare to initiating movement from the bodies of the vertebrae?

2. **The vertebrae as corks (sitting, standing):** Visualize the fifth lumbar vertebra as a cork floating in water. Imagine the sacrum hanging just beneath the fifth lumbar vertebra, increasing the space between them. The coccyx is anchored in the ocean bed. Now see the fourth lumbar vertebra as a cork floating in water, and let both the fifth lumbar vertebra and the sacrum hang downward, increasing the space between the fourth and fifth lumbar vertebrae. Progress up the spine until every vertebra has played the role of the cork. Figure 13.14, a and b, shows the eighth and twelfth thoracic vertebrae as corks.

3. **Opening the intervertebral spaces (supine, movement):** In the supine position, bend your knees and bring your legs back over your head until your toes touch the floor behind you. As you slowly roll back down, imagine each vertebra being placed on the floor individually and at a distance from the vertebrae that are already on the floor. Watch as the space between the vertebrae increases. Let the distance between them become as large as possible (see figure 13.15).

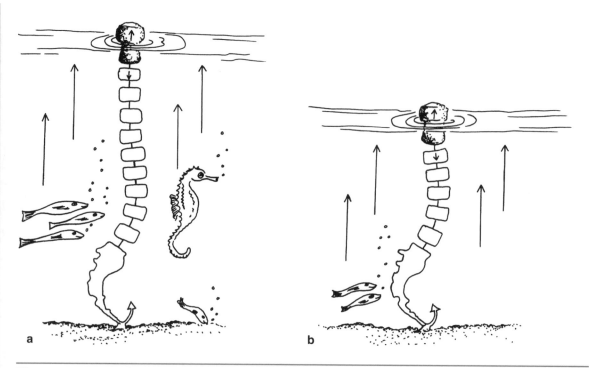

Figure 13.14   Vertebra as a cork floating in water.

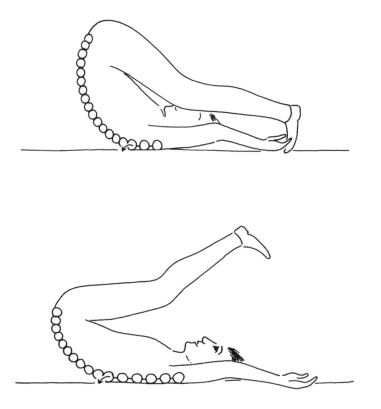

Figure 13.15   Place each vertebra on the floor individually and at a distance from the vertebrae that are already on the floor.

INTERVERTEBRAL JOINTS AND LIGAMENTS

In addition to the main weight-bearing intervertebral joints, the facet joints connect two adjoining vertebrae, preventing excessive sliding of one vertebra in relation to another. The inferior articular facet stabilizes the vertebra by preventing the superior articular facet, as well as the vertebra, from sliding forward. The right and left superior articulating facets of each vertebra connect with the right and left inferior facets of the superior vertebrae, like a necklace with two double links between stones. The facet joints lie approximately in the sagittal plane in the lumbar area; in the frontal plane in the thoracic spine, where they look like shingles on a roof; and at a 45-degree angle in the cervical spine. This arrangement favors flexion and extension in the lumbar spine, rotation and side bending in the thoracic spine, and fairly unrestricted movement in any direction in the cervical spine. Just above the lumbar vertebrae, the twelfth thoracic vertebra bridges the two sections. Its upper facet joints, like those of the rest of the thoracic spine, are in the frontal plane, whereas its lower facet joints are closer to the sagittal plane, like those of the lumbar vertebrae. This transitional area often accumulates muscular tension.

Many ligaments help stabilize the spine. The *intra*segmental system binds together adjacent vertebrae; the *inter*segmental system unifies groups of vertebrae. The anterior longitudinal ligament, an intersegmental ligament, runs along the entire length of the anterior surface of the spine from the sacrum to the second cervical vertebra. This ligament can be visualized as a long ribbon that stretches when you extend (arch) the spine and relaxes when you flex (round) the spine. The ligamentum flavum, an elastic intrasegmental ligament on the posterior surface of the vertebral canal, stretches when the spine is flexed. Thus it helps the spine move from any forward bending position into a neutral position. Metaphorically, the spine can be visualized as a long spring with interconnecting rubber bands or as a stack of tensegrity models (see chapter 2).

EXERCISING VERTEBRAL JOINTS AND LIGAMENTS

1. **Initiating from the front of the spine (improvisation):** Imagine the power to move the spine coming from its anterior aspect. Initiating movement from the front relieves the dorsal muscles of excess effort.

2. **Spinal elastic rod (improvisation):** Imagine the spine to be an elastic rod that can rebound effortlessly to neutral from any movement.

3. **Spinal brushes:**

   a. **Supine, sitting, standing:** Imagine a brush moving up along the front of the spine and another brush moving down along the back. Try seeing the two brushes working in opposition, making several strokes before moving to the next level. Feel how the brush on the front of the spine imparts some lift to the front of the vertebral bodies. The brush in back helps the muscles near the spine and the spinous processes to release downward (figure 13.16).

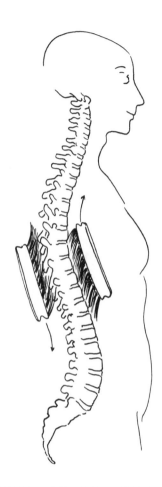

Figure 13.16   Imagine a brush moving up along the front of the spine and another brush moving down along the back.

   b. **Improvisation:** Visualize the brushes initiating spinal movement at different levels of the spine. Let the brushes interact in a variety of ways, working at the same level opposite each other or at different ends of the spine.

4. **Series of waterfalls:** Imagine a waterfall pouring down the back of the spine. Every spinous process is a ridge over which the waterfall cascades on its downward course. Imagine the water splashing between every crevice and ridge created by the transverse and spinous processes and the superior and inferior articulating processes.

RIB CAGE AND SPINE

Most of the elliptically shaped ribs connect to the spine at two different points. The first through tenth ribs connect to a socket created half by the upper vertebra and half by the lower vertebra. Ribs 11 and 12 articulate with one vertebra only. The first through tenth ribs also articulate with the transverse process of the vertebrae. Anteriorly, the first through seventh ribs connect directly to the sternum (breastbone). Ribs 8 through 10 connect to the sternum indirectly via the costal cartilages above them, and ribs 11 and 12 float unattached to the sternum. The ribcage makes the thoracic spine the most stable but least flexible portion of the spine. The lower ribs slant upward toward the spine at an increasing angle. Each pair of ribs braces the spine from either side, lifting it and actively supporting it. The lower ribs are approximately three times as wide as the first rib, creating a conical shape rather like a birdcage.

The sternum is composed of three bones: the manubrium, the body, and the xiphoid process. The xiphoid process (lower edge of the sternum) must remain mobile in breathing. In good alignment, it should point neither toward nor away from the body. The manubrium (top of the sternum) must be high to allow space for the upper ribs and upper thoracic organs.

The sternum, spine, pelvis, and ribcage must be balanced in relation to each other for the spine to support the head efficiently, releasing excess neck and shoulder tension. The head can then move freely in a high and erect alignment without the need for artificial positioning. Good alignment of these two adjoining structures helps create optimal freedom of motion for both.

Respiration moves the many joints of the ribcage in a complex manner. Generally, the upper ribs move up and down like a pump handle, whereas the lower ribs move up and down in a circular motion like a bucket handle (Norkin & Levangie 1992).

EXERCISING THE RIBCAGE AND SPINE

1. **Rib oars (supine):** Imagine the interaction between the ribs and the spine to be like a rowing team propelling its slender boat through the water. The oars move in the opposite direction of the boat as the blades push though the water and transfer their leverage to the boat. On exhalation, the oars (ribs) move downward through the water's resistance, imparting upward force to the boat (spine); on inhalation, the spine is expanded by the inflating lungs. In this way the ribs and lungs combine to create an upward push-expansion (exhalation-inhalation) against the spine (figure 13.17).

2. **Tugging the sternum:** Imagine the relationship between the ribs and the sternum to be like that between tugboats and a larger vessel. Visualize several tugboats (ribs) nudging the large vessel (the breastbone) from both sides. Watch the sternum react to the gentle pushes and shoves of the adjoining ribs until it is aligned in the same sagittal plane as the spine. Once aligned, subtle adjustments of the tugboats allow it to maintain alignment (figure 13.18).

3. **Ribs sink into spine (supine):** Imagine the ribs to be free floating, and watch as they approach the spine. Visualize each rib contacting the spine in two places: the costal articular facet of the transverse process and the costal articular facet of the body of the vertebrae. Imagine the ribs sinking into the latter facet as if it were made of clay. Begin with the twelfth rib and move up to the first. If working with a partner, lie on your side for

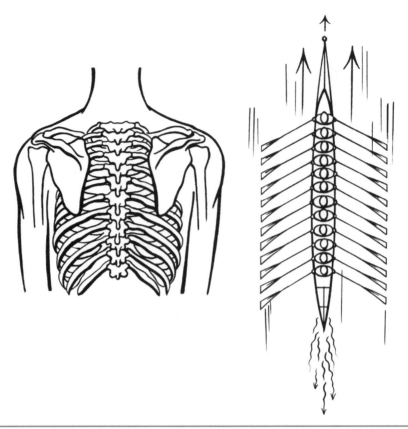

Figure 13.17   Imagine the interaction between the ribs and the spine to be like a rowing team propelling its slender boat through the water.

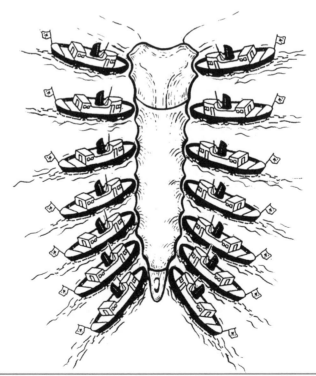

Figure 13.18   Imagine the relationship between the ribs and the sternum to be like that between tugboats and a larger vessel.

easier access to the dorsal aspect of the ribs. Have your partner slide his or her fingers along the length of the rib to its attachment with the spine. The ribs may not always be easy to discern, especially in the area between the shoulder blades.

4. **Spine attracts ribs:** Repeat the above exercise, this time imagining that the spine actively attracts the ribs. Visualize the spine's articular facet and transverse process pulling on the head of the rib like a vacuum cleaner. Adjust the spine's suction so that the ribs are held in place freely, without rigidity (figure 13.19). (Those who would like to save mental electricity may visualize magnetic attraction or simply energy rather than a vacuum cleaner.)

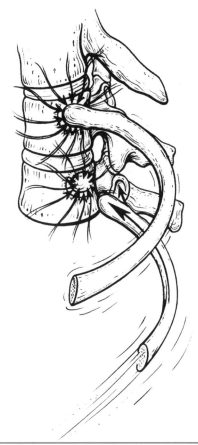

Figure 13.19   The spine's articular facet and transverse process pull on the head of the rib like a vacuum cleaner.

5. **Sternum as a cork (sitting, standing):** Imagine the sternum to be a cork floating on water. Watch the water level rise and the cork float upward. Let the sitz bones and tailbone drop downward as the cork is buoyed upward.

6. **Hanging lower sternum (standing, sitting):** Visualize the bottom of the sternum hanging down. Imagine it swinging just slightly front to back until it comes to rest perpendicularly over the pubic symphysis.

THE SACRUM

The sacrum is a three-way transfer point of force wedged between the iliac bones and the spine. Part of the pelvic girdle and the foundation of the spine, it passes weight from the fifth lumbar vertebra on a slant to the neighboring ilia. Its five fused vertebrae create a solid base for the spine. The sacroiliac joint, formed by the first through third fused sacral vertebrae and the left and right iliac bones (in adults), permits flexion and extension relative to the iliac bones. The weight of the upper body resting on the sacrum would push it into increased nutation if it were not for the strong ligaments counteracting this tendency. The sacroiliac joint forms a closed kinematic chain with the pubic symphysis, the joint between the two pubic bones. Any motion in the sacroiliac joint is reflected in the pubic symphysis, and vice versa. The sacroiliac and pubic symphysis will compensate for lack of hip mobility, differences in leg lengths, and poor postural habits, albeit in potentially detrimental ways. Abnormal pelvic tilting or twisting increases shear stresses at these joints.

EXERCISING THE SACRUM

1. **Path of weight (standing):** Visualize the transfer of weight through the body. The weight of the head transfers to the spine at the atlas, the weight of the shoulder girdle via the ribs. Then it continues down through the lumbar spine into the sacrum, dividing down into the two ilia, moving forward into the hip joints, down into the legs and feet, and finally to the ground.

2. **The sacrum as a Japanese fan (supine):** Imagine the sacrum to be a Japanese fan. As the fan opens and widens, the creases of the fan spread and flatten. As the fan spreads apart, the tail of the fan, the coccyx, also drops down (figure 13.20). (Adapted from Andre Bernard.)

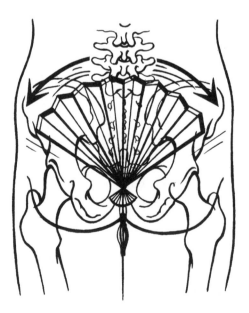

Figure 13.20   The sacrum as a Japanese fan.

3. **The sacrum as the body of an eagle (supine, standing, improvisation):**
Imagine the sacrum to be the body of an eagle and the ilia to be its wings.
Feel the strong, yet movable connections between the body of the eagle
and the wings (the joint between the ilia and the sacrum, called the iliosacral
joint). Imagine the bird slowly moving its wings. Notice how this affects
the pelvis and the entire body (figure 13.21).

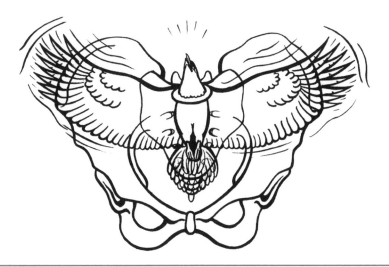

Figure 13.21   The sacrum as the body of an eagle and the ilia as its wings.

4. **Pelvic circle (standing, walking, jumping):** Visualize the closed kinematic chain
of the pelvic girdle as a circular hoop with two openings for the sacrum and the
pubic symphysis. Imagine that these openings contain elastic springs that are
able to balance the forces traveling through the circle. If the spring in the rear
expands, the one in front compresses, and vice versa. The hoop attaches to the
legs in front, creating resilient support for the spine in back (figure 13.22).

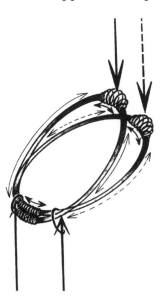

Figure 13.22   Imagine the closed kinematic chain of the pelvic girdle as a circular hoop
with two openings for the sacrum and the pubic symphysis.

THE COCCYX

The coccyx consists of four vertebral remnants attached to the lower end of the sacrum. These remnants form the very end of the spine, composing our vestigial tail. Some animals use the tail as a third leg to improve their balance; others use it to lower their center of gravity, for example, when perched on a branch. Several primate species use their tails in swinging from branch to branch. In this case, the tail has prehensile (grasping) qualities similar to those of a hand. Lions and other cats use their tails as a balancing device when running at top speed. In figure 13.23, the lioness is making a right turn (from her point of view). In a sharp turn to the right, the tail stretches and points to the right, shifting the COG toward the inside of the curve and helping the animal change direction. The tail is especially valuable during very fast and very slow movements.

Figure 13.23   Lions and other cats use their tails as a balancing device when running at top speeds.

IMAGING WITH YOUR "TAIL"

1. **Dinosaur tail (standing):** Imagine your tail extending to the floor and becoming strong, like that of a dinosaur or a kangaroo. Use this tail as a third, supporting leg. Imagine your weight balanced equally on your two actual legs and your third tail-leg (figure 13.24). (Adapted from Mabel Todd.)

2. **Trailing your tail (walking):** As you walk, imagine your tail trailing on the floor behind you.

3. **Demi-pointe in first position:** Imagine you are standing on a tripod. The balls of both feet and the tail extend downward to the floor. Connect the three points in your mind's eye to create a triangle. The long side of the

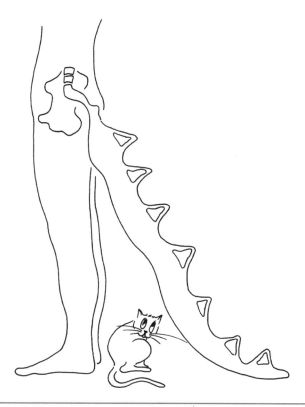

Figure 13.24   Imagine your tail extends to the floor and becomes a strong support, like that of a dinosaur or a kangaroo.

triangle connects the balls of your feet; the short sides connect the balls of your feet to the point where the imaginary tail extension touches the ground. In your imagination, put equal weight on all points of the tripod and experience their balanced support.

4. **Initiating movement from the coccyx (improvisation):** The coccyx leads you into movement, pulling your whole body with it as it reaches into space.

5. **Head-tail connection:**

   a. **Head-tail initiation (improvisation):** Alternate between initiating movement from your tail and initiating movement from the top of your head.

   b. **Head and tail unified:** Practice initiation from the tail and the head simultaneously to create unified motion of the spine. Remember that the tail forms one corner of the pelvic floor and use the unified feeling of the tail/pelvic floor/head to stand up and sit down effortlessly. Let the unified spine create powerful movement through space while your legs float effortlessly beneath you.

6. **Tail rudder (improvisation):** Imagine the sacrum to be a ship's stern and the coccyx to be the ship's rudder. The tail-rudder determines your direction in space. As you move forward, initiate a turn to the right by moving your tail to the right. Initiate a turn to the left by turning your tail to the left. Visualize the whirls and eddies created by the rudder's action. Try turning to the right as the rudder turns to the left. How does this feel (figure 13.25)?

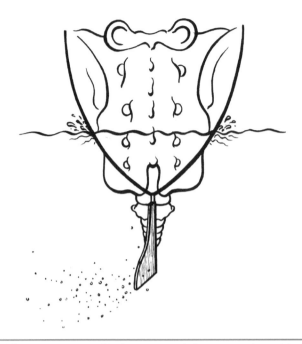

Figure 13.25   The sacrum is a ship's stern and the coccyx is a ship's rudder.

7. **Primate grasp (supine):** Visualize your tail lengthening and extending toward your feet. Imagine it reaching up and grabbing onto a strong branch so that your body now hangs from your tail. Enjoy the feeling as your entire spine slowly stretches. Swing your body back and forth as you hang from your tail (figure 13.26).

Figure 13.26   Imagine your tail reaching up and grabbing onto a strong branch so that your body now hangs from your tail.

ORGAN SUPPORT

In addition to the ribs, the spine has help from other areas in supporting the weight of the upper body both upright and in bending. The organs of the abdominal cavity provide help in the form of hydrostatic lift when they are restrained by a surrounding muscular wall. Like water-filled balloons in a tin can, if compressed from any direction, the organs generate equal, load-supporting hydrostatic pressure in all directions (Radin et al. 1992). The way you breathe influences the efficiency of upper body motion because the stomach muscles are in constant interplay with the diaphragm. Insufficient muscular tone in the abdominals and diaphragm impairs the hydrostatic system. On inhalation, the lungs more actively support the spine like air-filled balloons. On exhalation, the deflated lungs are least supportive and the stomach muscles and walls of the abdominal cavity are most active.

ABDOMINAL BALLOON

Interplay of abdominals, diaphragm, and spine (standing): Imagine your abdominal cavity to be filled with a large balloon. Visualize your diaphragm and upper torso resting on this balloon. Exhale and image the balloon shrinking to initiate a forward curling of the spine. Let your upper body be carried downward on the deflating balloon. Once you have exhaled completely, reinflate the balloon on inhalation. Watch as the increasing pressure created by the expanding balloon pushes the upper torso back up to vertical. Try this exercise at various speeds.

MUSCULATURE OF THE ABDOMEN AND BACK

The stomach muscles flex the spine and the back muscles extend it. For example, the rectus abdominis, which is attached to the pubic symphysis and the xiphoid process, contracts to shorten the distance between these two points, lifting the pubic bones, the lower front rim of the pelvis, within the closed kinematic chain of the standing position. The long erector spinae muscles at the back of the torso—the spinalis, the longissimus, and the costalis (from the center out)—lie in three strands parallel to the vertebral column. These muscles extend the spine and increase the lumbar curve within the standing closed kinematic chain system.

Below the erector muscles, several groups of short muscles lie deep within the gutter next to the spinous processes. The internal and external oblique stomach muscles rotate the ribcage on the pelvis or the pelvis under the ribcage. Essential for all spiral and side-bending movements, so important in modern dance, these muscles can be visualized as wrapping around the torso. Because they help create torque for pirouettes, balanced use of the obliques improves turning. The stomach muscles also bring the abdominal organs closer to the midline of the body, reducing the moment of inertia for rapid turning and movement initiation.

According to anatomist R.A. Dart (1950), a spiral line through the trunk of the body goes from the midline of the body, pubic symphysis, and iliac crest through the external obliques, external intercostals, ribs, and scalene musculature, to the transverse processes of the cervical vertebrae, and then through the deeper-lying sheet of the semispinalis to the cervical spinous processes and the occiput.

Thus we get a picture, or bird's-eye view, of the manner in which the single superficial sheet, formed by these two opposed diagonally-running flexor muscles in front, is continued, through the deeper-lying extensor sheet on each side of the spine behind, to suspend the pelvis from the occiput and neck vertebrae. (p. 267)

The external obliques can be visualized as continuing across the ventral (front) midline of the body through the deeper-lying internal obliques. The superficial sacrospinalis cross the dorsal (back) midline, continuing the line of force of the deep multifidus (much divided) sheet of muscles. "Thus, in a very real sense, the occiput and spines of the vertebrae suspend the body by means of two spiral sheets of muscle encircling the trunk" (p. 268). These spiral movements continue into the muscles of the extremities. Besides creating dynamic interaction between the body halves, these spiral lines enable the body to perform rapid winding and unwinding movements, contractions, and twists (figure 13.27).

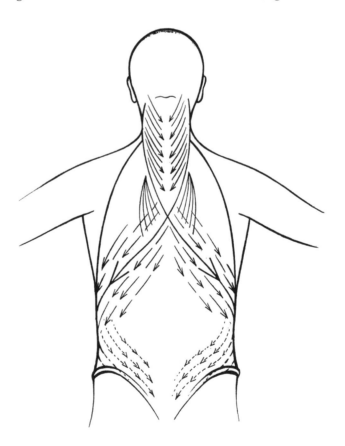

Figure 13.27 Besides creating dynamic interaction between body halves, the spiral lines enable the body to perform rapid winding and unwinding movements, contractions, and twists.

**EXERCISING
ABDOMINAL
AND BACK
MUSCLES**

1. **Centered action of abdominals (sitting, standing, supine):** Visualize four pairs of small spheres or beads on four common strings—one vertical, one horizontal, and two diagonal—all joining at the navel. As you exhale, watch the beads move toward each other and merge at the navel. As you inhale, the beads glide back to their original positions (figure 13.28).

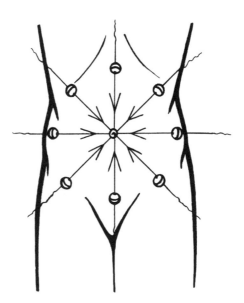

Figure 13.28   As you exhale, watch the beads move toward each other and merge at the navel. As you inhale, the beads glide back to their original positions.

2. **The pelvis suspended from the back of the neck (standing):** Imagine the front rim of the pelvis to be hanging from the back of the head on strands of muscles spiraling around to the front of the body like an apron hanging down in front, tied at the back of the neck. As the back of the head floats up, so does the front rim of the pelvis. Watch the sacrum drop as the front of the pelvis rises.

3. **The pelvis hanging from the ribcage (improvisation):** Imagine the pelvis to be a hoop hanging from the ribcage. Think of the connection between the ribs and the pelvis as being of equal strength at the front, back, and sides. When you swing the ribcage to the left, the hoop follows with a slight delay, and vice versa. The connecting strings spiral as the hoop rotates beneath the ribcage. When you rotate the ribcage, the hoop follows with a delayed reaction similar to the swirl of a long pleated skirt catching up with the twisting of the wearer's body.

4. **River down the back (supine):** Imagine a river flowing down your back, expelling all muscular tension (figure 13.29). Visualize the tension points as little rocks and pieces of wood carried out with the flow. Imagine the

murky water turning crystal clear. Watch the river flow down through the gutters between your spine and ribs to flush out all remaining tension.

5. **Stroking the cat's back (supine, sitting, standing):** Imagine your back to be covered with fluffy fur like a cat's back. Visualize the fur as ruffled and in disarray, and mentally stroke it from head to tail, untangling and smoothing it (figure 13.30a & b). (Adapted from Barbara Clark.)

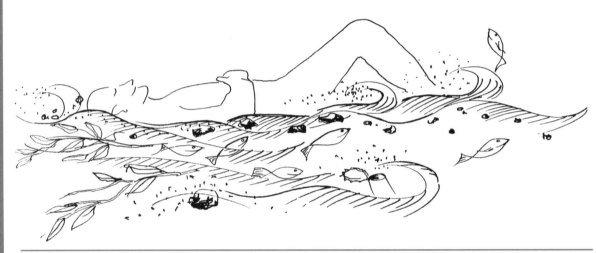

Figure 13.29　A river flows down your back, expelling all muscular tension.

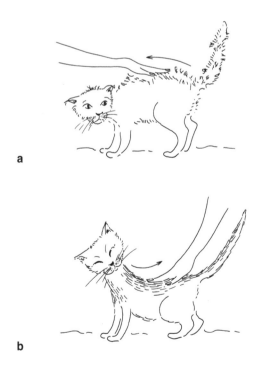

a

b

Figure 13.30　Your back is covered with fluffy fur like a cat's back.

CHAPTER

14 *The Shoulders, Arms, and Hands*

Our ancestors must have been avid pickers of fruit and berries, much of it located at or above eye level. Although our bodies are comparatively short, we can reach very high with our arms. The mobility and specialized structure of the shoulder girdle permits us to hold our arms above our heads for a fairly long time without tiring. The counterbalancing effect of the shoulder blades is especially helpful in arm elevation. Dancers need to be able to lift their arms rapidly without disturbing their centers, losing balance, or increasing tension in the shoulders, back, or torso. If it weren't for our tree-picking progenitors, we probably wouldn't have shoulders constructed to do so.

The shoulder girdle consists of two shoulder blades, or scapulae, and two collarbones, or clavicles (small forks) (figure 14.1). In German, the clavicles are called the "keybones" because they resemble S-shaped keys (figure 14.2). They are indeed key to arm movement because, at their central ends, they connect the arms to the thorax in the only truly jointed connection of the shoulder girdle.

The clavicle attaches to the manubrium of the sternum (figure 14.1). A joint disk between the manubrium and clavicle acts as a pivot to increase the mobility and stability of the sternoclavicular joint. Visualizing arm gestures originating from this point increases their fullness. If the muscles that attach to the clavicle are tense, such as the trapezius, movement will be less fluid. In Latin, the verb *sterno* means to widen or to smooth, a welcome notion for the top of the chest. Because the sternum carries the weight of the shoulder girdle and the arms, it

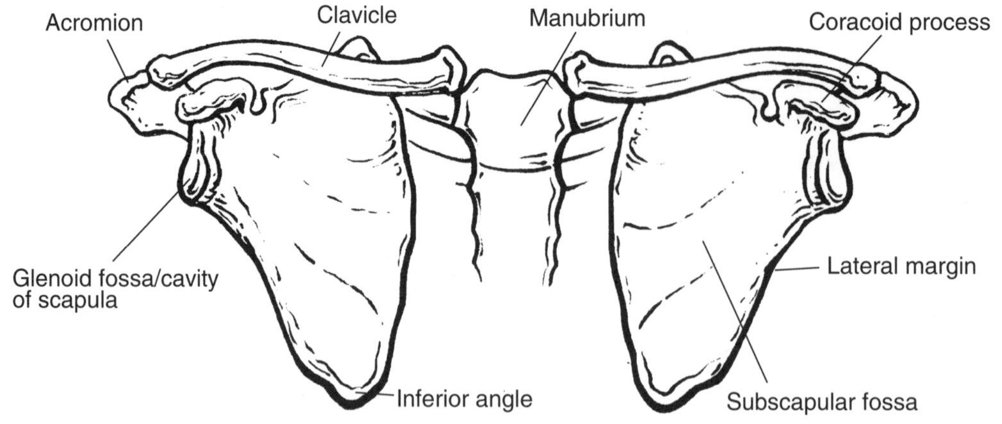

Acromion   Clavicle   Manubrium   Coracoid process

Glenoid fossa/cavity
of scapula

Lateral margin

Inferior angle   Subscapular fossa

Figure 14.1 The shoulder girdle consists of two shoulder blades, or scapulae, and two collarbones, or clavicles.

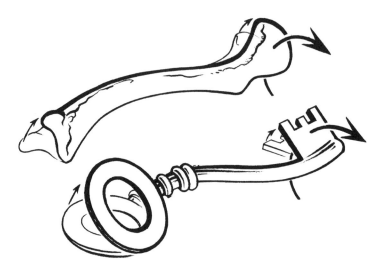

Figure 14.2 The S-shaped clavicle rotates to increase the elevation of its distal end to reduce the need for elevation where it joins with the sternum.

may be difficult to maintain width. A slouched or an arched posture impedes shoulder function, making balancing and turning difficult. The sternum transfers weight to the upper ribs, which in turn pass it on to the spine.

The shoulder blades are large triangular bones at the back of the ribcage. Parts of the shoulder blades reach to the front and sides of the body (figure 14.1). The glenoid fossa, the shallow shoulder socket, is protected by the acromion (shoulder tip), which hovers atop the shoulder joint like an overhanging cliff. Throughout the ages, fashion designers have amplified this shape with shoulder pads.

Because its socket is so small, the shoulder joint is stabilized primarily by muscles. The deltoid muscle covers this area like a cap. The spine of the scapula extends behind the acromion. The grooves above and below the spine are called fossa. Above the spine is the supraspinous fossa; below the spine is another groove called the infraspinous fossa (figure 14.3). The scapula's coracoid process (from

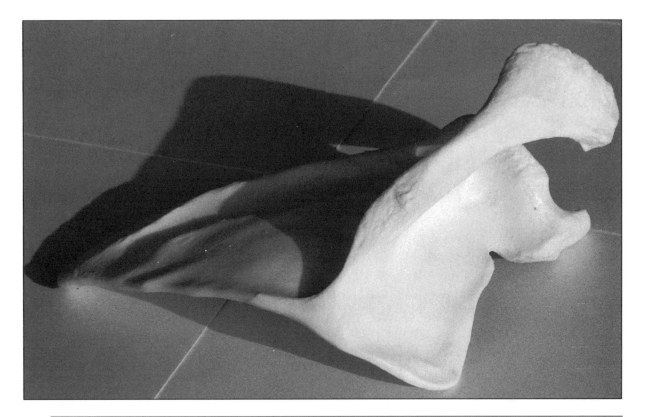

Figure 14.3   As pictured above, the acromion is behind the spine of the scapula. To the left of the spine is the infraspinous fossa; to the right of the spine is the supraspinous fossa.

the Greek word *korax*, meaning raven; *Rabenschnabelfortsatz* in German, meaning crow's beak) actually reaches the front of the body. Here the short head of the biceps, the corachobrachialis, and pectoralis minor muscles attach, the latter of which is the only shoulder muscle not connected to the arm. The inside edge of the scapula is parallel to the spine. Its lower tip, the inferior angle, points down to the pelvic floor.

The shape of the axilla (armpit) is determined by the latissimus dorsi behind and the pectoralis major muscle in front. They shape the armpit like a pyramid, with its peak at the glenohumeral joint. The inside edge of the armpit is formed by ribs, the outside wall by the arm. Shoulder tension often manifests as a tightening in the armpits.

GUIDED SHOULDER GIRDLE TOUR

1. **Touch exploration:** Walk your fingers up the outside of your upper arm. As you near the top of the arm, you will find a rounded area, which is the head of the humerus bone covered by the deltoid muscle. Just above this area, you can touch the bony process of the scapula, called the acromion. Move your fingers medially and anteriorly to find a small crevice, which is the joint between the acromion and the clavicle. If you glide your fin-

gers to the posterior part of the acromion, you will find a bony edge. As your fingers move along this edge toward the center of your back, they are traveling across the spine of the scapula. In the groove above this spine, you can feel the trapezius muscle and, depending on how tight it is, the supraspinatus, which lies beneath it. Below the spine of the scapula you can palpate the infraspinatus muscle, which you can feel in action when you externally rotate your arm.

Continue your tactile voyage along the spine of the scapula, and depending on how flexible you are, you may be able to touch the medial border of the scapula. To touch the inferior tip of the scapula, reach under your arm and place your fingers on the dorsal surface of the scapula. From here, trace your fingers vertically downward, always remaining on the bony surface, until you reach the inferior tip of the scapula. The lateral border of the scapula may be difficult to palpate as it is partially covered by the latissimus dorsi musculature.

Return to the joint between the acromion and clavicle, and from there, follow along the clavicle until you reach a large, bony prominence that marks the medial end of the clavicle. Drop your fingers over this ledge onto the bone medial to it, which is the manubrium of the sternum. Finally, glide your fingers down the sternum to its inferior tip, called the xyphoid process (figure 14.4).

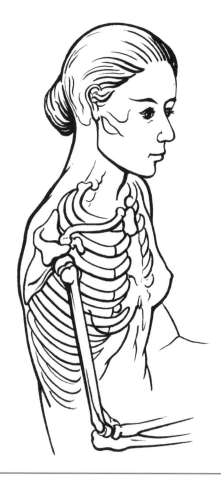

Figure 14.4   Discovering the anatomy of the shoulder girdle, the rib cage, and the arm.

2. **Coracoid spread (supine, sitting, standing):** Visualize the coracoid process and the surrounding area expanding. Touch the point just inside the shoulder joint and below the clavicle, and visualize the area spreading like cake batter in an ever-widening circle.

3. **Scapular wax (sitting, standing):** Imagine the shoulder blade to be made of beeswax. Visualize the lower shoulder blade melting downward. First, the inferior tip turns into soft drops of molten wax, and then the entire lower section melts. The drops fall down toward the sitz bones. Smell the honey-like aroma of the wax as it glides down your back.

4. **Extended acromion (supine, sitting, standing):** Visualize the distance between the tip of the shoulder and the neck increasing as the acromion elongates sideways. Imagine the acromion to be made of infinitely stretchable taffy. A partner can help you visualize this image by sliding his or her hands out and away from the neck.

5. **Clouds floating through the supraspinous fossa:** Visualize the space contained within the supraspinous fossa. Imagine this space filled with soft, fluffy clouds. Watch as the clouds move outward toward the acromion and float beneath it into the space beyond. Imagine this movement to be slow and continuous (figure 14.5). (Adapted from Glenna Batson.)

6. **Hanging arms (standing, walking):** Imagine your arms detaching from your shoulders and sliding down the sides of your body. It might be helpful to imagine your hands trailing Neanderthal-like on the floor (figure 14.6).

7. **Arms as cords (standing):** Trace the bones of your left arm with your right hand. Touch the acromion above the shoulder socket. Trace your finger

Figure 14.5 Visualize the space contained within the supraspinous fossa filled with soft, fluffy clouds.

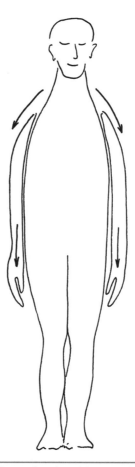

Figure 14.6 The arms detach from the shoulders and slide down the sides of the body.

along the clavicle to the sternoclavicular joint. Lift your left shoulder and feel the movement of the clavicle on the sternum. Keep a finger on the sternoclavicular joint and bend your torso sideways to the left. Visualize the arm as a heavy cord attached at the top of the sternum. As you swing your left arm front to back, imagine that you are initiating the arm swing from the clavicle. Let the arm swing higher, then decrease the swing, allowing gravity to pull on the cord. Let the arm come to a stop. Allow the manubrium to initiate the return to a vertical position as it "pulls" on your arm. Drop your right arm to your side. Stretch both arms forward and compare their lengths. Repeat the exercise on the other side. A partner can help you experience motion in the clavicle by manipulating it gently back and forth. Be careful, though, as the muscles around the clavicle may be tender (figure 14.7). (Adapted from Andre Bernard.)

8. **Deep armpits (supine, sitting, standing):** Imagine your armpits becoming deep and soft. Think of having tiny balloons in your armpits, inflating as you inhale and deflating as you exhale. Simultaneously, think of the back of your neck being soft and your jawbone heavy. Watch the balloons deflate as you exhale while making a hissing sound. Finally, imagine the balloons dropping out of your armpits on an exhalation, leaving a hollow, wide-open space behind (figure 14.8).

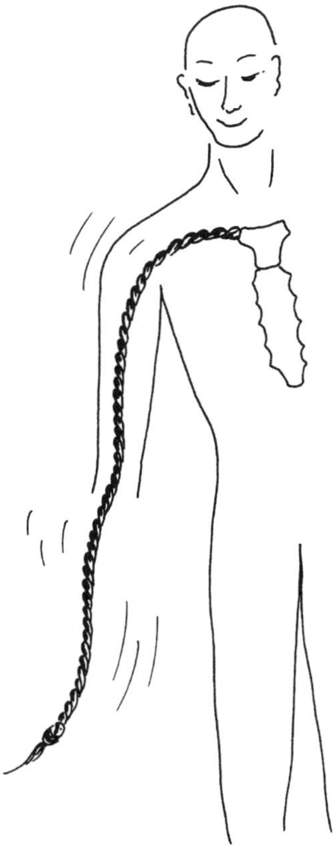

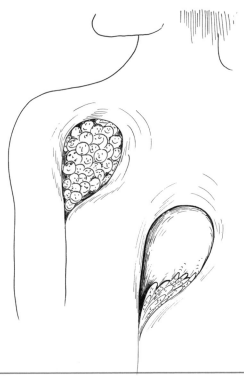

Figure 14.7   The arm as a heavy cord attached at the top of the sternum.

Figure 14.8   Think of having tiny balloons in your armpits, inflating as you inhale and deflating as you exhale.

SUSPENSION OF THE SHOULDER GIRDLE

Muscularly, the shoulder girdle is suspended from the neck and head rather like a sailing ship, wherein the spine is the mast and the shoulder girdle a cross beam suspended from it (figure 14.9). Although efficient, central suspension depends on proper alignment of the spine and poses the danger of habitual elevation of the entire girdle. If the neck and head are habitually held forward, shoulder placement suffers. Because the muscles controlling the arm and shoulder girdle extend in all directions, head placement has far-reaching consequences. For example, the latissimus (widest) dorsi muscles, familiarly known as the lats, create a connection between the top of the arms and the pelvis. Improving pelvic and spinal alignment greatly benefits the shoulder girdle.

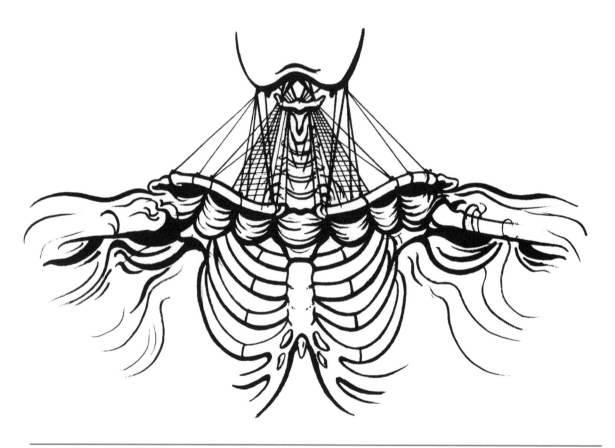

Figure 14.9 Muscularly, the shoulder girdle is suspended from the neck and head rather like a sailing ship.

SUSPENSION OF THE SHOULDER GIRDLE

1. **Turtleneck shoulder girdle (sitting, standing):** Think of the shoulder girdle as a turtleneck sweater covering your ribcage. Imagine the turtleneck being rolled down the sides of the thorax. Visualize the sweater rolling down in increments. Watch it roll down on exhalation and widen on inhalation.

Think of the sweater as being made of very wide mesh. As you inhale, imagine the mesh widening even more (figure 14.10).

2. **Dropping hoop (pirouettes):** Imagine the shoulder girdle to be a hoop draped around your ribcage. Watch the hoop dropping to the level of the ribcage. Then imagine the reverse—the thorax, neck, and head emerging from the hoop.

3. **Watershed (supine, improvisation):** Visualize a strong current of water moving up your central axis. As the water reaches the level of the shoulder girdle, it spreads sideways. The stronger the upward current, the greater the spreading of the current at the shoulder girdle (figure 14.11).

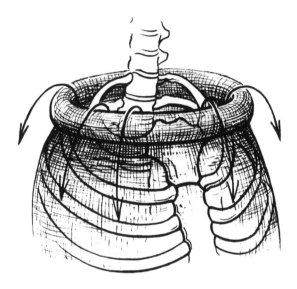

Figure 14.10 The shoulder girdle as a turtleneck sweater covering your ribcage.

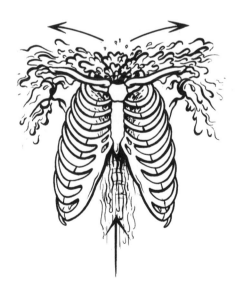

Figure 14.11 A strong current of water moving up your central axis.

THE GLENOHUMERAL JOINT

The humerus (upper arm bone) is separated from the manubrium (upper sternum) by three joints: the glenohumeral, the acromioclavicular, and the sternoclavicular. Arm movements involve all of these joints, forming a closed kinematic chain that increases shock absorption in the shoulder girdle. A blow to the arm is diverted to the scapula and clavicle and diffused before it can disturb the important functions of the heart and lungs within the ribcage. Like humans, birds and primates have long clavicles, a distinct advantage if you want to fly or hang from a tree. Long clavicles free the arms from the sides, a distinct advantage if you want to dance.

Compared to the hip socket, which covers more than half of the head of the femur, the shoulder socket is extremely shallow. Thus, the glenohumeral joint is a relatively feeble structure. Were it not for the strong muscles keeping the heads of the humerus bones in their fossa, our arms would be in constant danger of dislocating. The tradeoff for the instability is enhanced mobility—the glenohumeral joint can flex, extend, abduct, adduct, and rotate internally and externally. When the arm is abducted (lifted to the side), the head of the humerus cannot roll upward on the glenoid fossa because it will collide with the acromion. Instead, the head of the humerus glides downward over the fossa while rolling upward, actually creating a relatively fixed center of rotation for itself. The fossa can also be visualized as sliding upward in relation to the humeral head.

HUMERAL HEADS DROP

From a standing position, as you elevate your arms, visualize the humeral heads rotating and gliding downward on the glenoid fossa. Exaggerate the image by visualizing the humeral heads gliding all the way down the sides of your body to the heads of the femurs, where they come to rest as you complete the elevation of your arms.

THE SCAPULOHUMERAL RHYTHM

The scapula (shoulder blade) can glide up and down on the back side of the ribcage or thorax; it can also move toward (adduction) and away (abduction) from the spine, and it can rotate. However, the nature of scapular motions over the curved surface of the ribcage is more complex than these terms imply. It may help to visualize a surfboard (the scapula) on the crest of a rounded wave (the thorax). The surfboard can potentially dip and slide off the wave in four different ways. If the surfboard (scapula) dips and glides sideways (horizontally) down the slope of the wave (thorax), it is called abduction (figure 14.12a) or adduction (14.12b). These motions are not linear, but curved, with the surfboard (scapula) always in contact with the water (thorax). If the surfboard dips forward and glides off the wave in a superior direction, it elevates the shoulder blades (14.12c).

Once again, these are curved motions, with the surfboard (scapula) remaining in contact with the water (thorax). The reverse scapular glide in an inferior direction is called depression (14.12d).

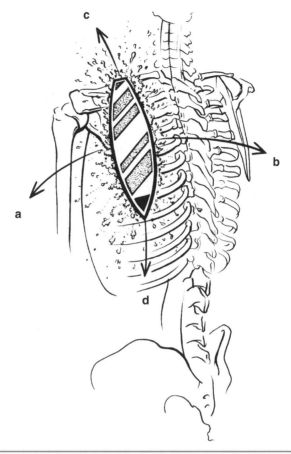

Figure 14.12   The scapula as a surfboard on the crest of a rounded wave: (a) abduction, (b) adduction, (c) elevation, and (d) depression.

When the arm is lifted above the horizontal position in elevation, the scapula rotates, changing its position considerably relative to the ribcage and thorax. The purpose of scapular rotation is to position the glenoid fossa in an upward direction. Although the scapula is moving close to the thorax, and the muscles between them serve as a gliding surface, the scapulothoracic joint is not a true joint (lacking cartilage and a joint capsule); however, it is helpful to consider it a joint because scapulothoracic motion cannot be separated from the shoulder's kinematic chain. The coordinated movement of these joints, called the scapulohumeral rhythm, is significantly greater in stability and range of arm motion than if it were only one joint. The group effort allows the shallow glenoid fossa to remain in a good position relative to the head of the humerus in elevation and permits more balanced muscle action.

As the arm is elevated, the scapula rotates first around an axis located at the base of the spine of the scapula and then around an axis located at the acromioclavicular joint. The S-shaped clavicle (see figure 14.2) rotates to increase the elevation of its distal end to reduce the need for elevation where it joins with the sternum. Imagine holding a skeleton key in your hand with its teeth pointing downward, representing the distal end of the clavicle. If you rotate the key 180 degrees, the teeth point upward. The joint at this end has therefore gained height without actually lifting the shaft of the key.

A simple way to visualize the functioning of the scapulohumeral rhythm is to think of it as a barrier at a train crossing. The barrier (arm) goes up as the heavy counterweight (scapula) arcs down and forward, saving a lot of mechanical energy (figure 14.13).

Without scapulae, we would need very thick, muscular necks to pull up our arms with sheer force. Place your hand behind your axle and lift your arm to feel the rotation of the scapula. It will glide forward under your fingers. Once the arm is elevated, the shoulder blade can also be considered a weighted ballast, a solid base for the arm, lowering the COG and making it easy to keep the arms overhead as in fifth position. Freedom in the scapulohumeral rhythm is critical for balance and pirouettes because it prevents arm gestures from disturbing the central axis. Mobility is achieved by allowing the scapula to glide over the thorax in an easy and unrestricted fashion.

EXERCISING THE SCAPULO–HUMERAL RHYTHM

1. **Train barrier (standing, sitting):** Be sure to maintain your central axis perpendicular to the floor when doing this exercise. Imagine your scapula to be the heavy counterweight of a train barrier (figure 14.13). As the barrier lifts, the heavy counterweight arcs down and forward. With the help of a partner, you can feel the connection between scapula, clavicle, and humerus. After placing his or her fingers on the spine of the scapula and thumbs on the inside border of the scapula, your partner then pushes down with the fingers and out with the thumbs to help you elevate your arms. To feel scapular restriction, have your partner reverse this action, holding the lower part of both the medial and lateral border of the scapula between thumb and fingers. To move under these circumstances, you must lift the entire shoulder girdle upward. Lifting the shoulders when elevating the arms is a common habit that can be corrected with the above exercise. Be careful, though, when touching the area around the shoulder blades, as the muscles may be tender. Complete this tactile session with an assisted arm elevation.

2. **Scapular saucers (supine):** Visualize the shoulder blades as two teacup saucers floating on water. Watch them bank and bay under the ribcage. As water flows onto the saucers from the side closer to the spine, the saucers begin to dip downward on that side. Made heavy by the water, they sink downward, away from the ribcage. Repeat this exercise two to three times (figure 14.14).

3. **Scapular sponges (supine):** Visualize the shoulder blades resting on the floor as if relaxing on the most comfortable bed imaginable. Feel a slippery sponge slide under one shoulder blade from the spinal side. As the sponge fills with water and expands, it moves the scapula down and away

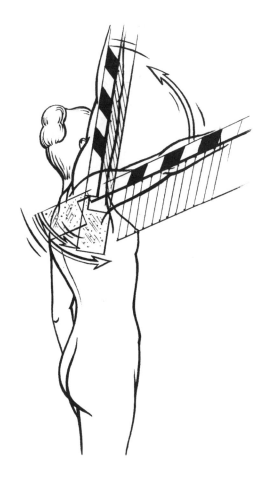

Figure 14.13   The functioning of the scapulohumeral rhythm as a barrier at a train crossing.

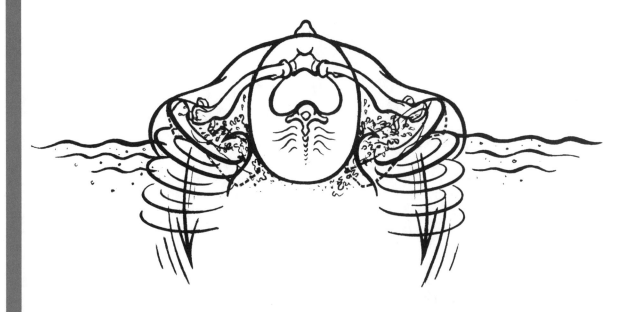

Figure 14.14   The shoulder blades as two teacup saucers floating on water, then sinking.

from the ribcage, increasing the distance between the shoulder blade and the ribcage. Repeat this exercise two to three times. (Adapted from Andre Bernard.)

4. **Shoulder girdle as cape (standing, sitting):** To free the shoulder girdle from the ribcage, visualize it as a cape lightly draped around the ribcage, open in front and attached to the top of the sternum with a sparkling diamond pin. Imagine a soothing wind blowing. As the wind sends ripples through the soft cloth, the cape (shoulder girdle) lifts, creating a space between the ribcage and the cape. As the wind dies down, the cape slowly settles against the ribcage (figure 14.15). Repeat this exercise two to three times. (Adapted from Andre Bernard.)

Figure 14.15   The shoulder girdle as a cape lightly draped around the ribcage.

5. **Clavicular rotation (sitting, standing):** Visualize the rotational action of the clavicle as you elevate your arm. The left clavicle rotates clockwise, the right clavicle counterclockwise (looking out from your perspective). Imagine the rotation creating a spiral energy flow throughout the arm and hand. Watch the countering action of the manubrium at the sternoclavicular articulation. The top of the manubrium dips forward; the bottom dips backward. Simultaneously imagine the pubic rami rotating (as if rolling up

toward you) and moving toward each other, creating an upward flow of energy to the xyphoid process (figure 14.16).

6. **Scapular fall (standing):** As you elevate your arms, picture the scapula gliding down your back to your heels. Visualize the sitz bones dropping with the scapula. For tactile emphasis, have your partner slide her or his hands down your back to your heels.

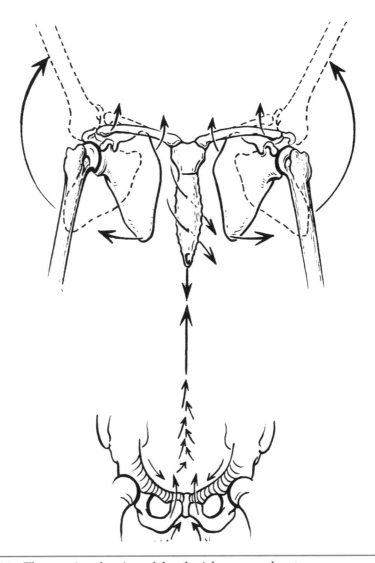

Figure 14.16   The rotational action of the clavicle as you elevate your arm.

7. **Scapulae rotating in the flow of breath (standing, sitting):** Exhale as you elevate your arms. Imagine your scapulae as pinwheels, and watch your breath float down your back and set them into rotary motion. The right scapula moves counterclockwise, the left clockwise (from your point of view). The higher you lift your arms, the more effortlessly the pinwheels spin (figure 14.17).

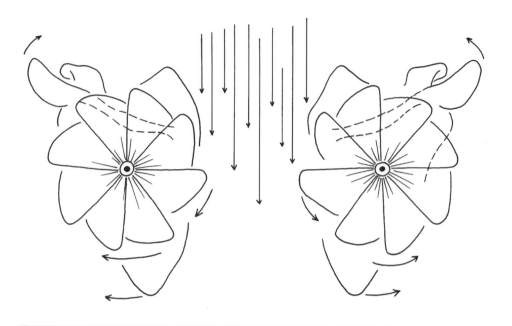

Figure 14.17 Scapulae as pinwheels.

THE ELBOW

The elbow consists of three joints: one between the humerus (upper arm bone) and the ulna (outside lower arm bone), one between the humerus and the radius (inside lower arm bone), and one between the upper ends of the radius and the ulna. The ulna is larger at the elbow, whereas the radius is larger at the wrist. The humeroulnar and humeroradial joints of the elbow allow for flexion and extension. The axis of motion for elbow flexion and extension passes through the trochlea and capitulum, the articulating surfaces of the humerus, which together look a bit like a chess pawn with its head pointing sideways. Touch the medial and lateral epicondyles of the humerus, two projections that can be easily palpated at the distal end of the humerus, and visualize the location of the axis just below these points (figure 14.18).

The ulnar articulating surface consists of a concave half circle, the trochlear notch. The articulating surface of the radius is cup-shaped. When the forearm is supinated (palm up), the long axis of the humerus and forearm form an angle (greater in women than in men) called the carrying angle. The carrying angle allows you to easily brace the humerus against the body when carrying a heavy load.

The radioulnar joint allows supination (palm up) and pronation (palm down). Proximally, the annular ligament, which attaches to the ulna, forms a ring around the head of the radius within which the head can rotate. The ulna also has a concave notch to better accommodate the radius as it turns. Simultaneously, the head of the radius spins on the capitulum of the humerus. At the distal radioulnar joint, the radius pivots around the ulna during supination and pronation.

The radioulnar joint is functionally linked to the wrist. Forces arising from the hand are transmitted first to the radius and then to the ulna. In pronation, the radius crosses the ulna; in supination, the ulna and radius lie parallel to each other. If you hold the ulna as you supinate and pronate, you will notice that it barely moves as the radius crosses over it. You can distinguish between pronation and supination by visualizing spooning soup to your mouth: You dip the spoon into the soup, flex at the elbow, and supinate the forearm to bring the food to your mouth. If you watch a toddler trying to eat soup, you will see that it is quite a complex movement. The way in which we use our arms, hands, and fingers to bring things to our mouths, and to our eyes for close examination, is uniquely human. Without supination and pronation, a port de bras would be a sorry-looking affair. The subtle and complex gestures of Indian and other Asian dance styles also require supination and pronation.

The axis of motion of radioulnar articulation can be visualized as a line passing through the heads of the radius and the ulna. In rotating the radius and ulna around this axis, you remain centered in space like a hopscotch rope swinging around the axis created by the two hands setting the rope in motion.

EXERCISING THE ELBOW

1. **Touch:** The parts of the elbow that can be easily palpated are the medial and lateral epicondyles of the humerus. What is normally considered the elbow is the olecranon of the ulnar bone (figure 14.18).

2. **Axis of lower arm (supination, pronation):** Visualize the central axis of the lower arm passing between the radius and the ulna. Pronate and supinate the radius and ulna around this central axis (figure 14.19).

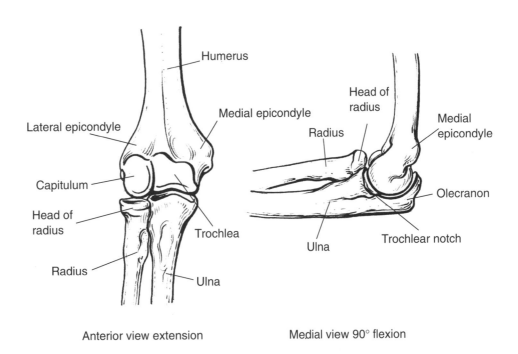

Anterior view extension

Medial view 90° flexion

Figure 14.18 The elbow consists of three joints.

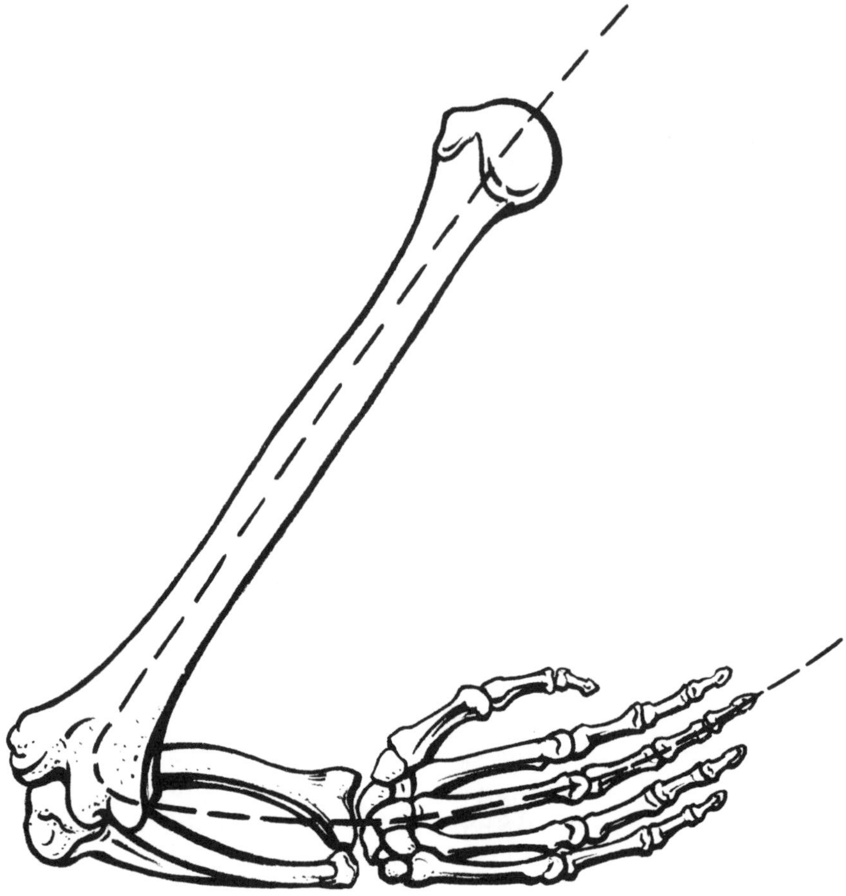

Figure 14.19 Visualize the central axis of the arm.

3. **Radioulnar counterrotation:** As you supinate and pronate, watch the radius rotate in the ulnar notch and the ulna glide in the opposite direction (figure 14.20a). To better understand this concept, compare it to the miniature merry-go-round in figure 14.20b. The child sets herself in motion in a counterclockwise direction by pulling on a center wheel in a clockwise direction. The outside observer sees the child rotating counterclockwise about a stable center wheel; the child sees the center wheel as rotating in a clockwise direction.

4. **Elbow buoy (second position port de bras):** Imagine the elbow to be a buoy floating on water. Visualize the arms floating effortlessly in space with the aid of the elbow buoys (figure 14.21).

5. **Flow of weight (fifth position overhead):** Visualize the weight of the hand resting on the lower arm, the weight of the lower arm resting on the humerus, the weight of the humerus resting on the glenoid fossa of the scapula, the weight of the shoulder blades supported by the clavicles, and the clavicles supported by the sternum.

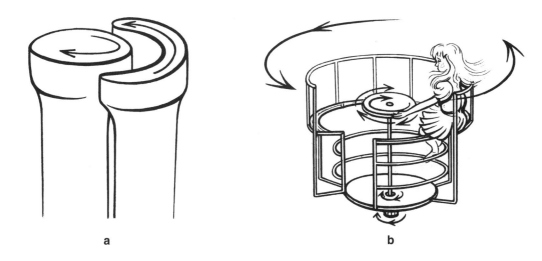

Figure 14.20   (a) As you supinate and pronate, watch the radius rotate in the ulnar notch and the ulna glide in the opposite direction. (b) To better understand this concept, compare it to the miniature merry-go-round.

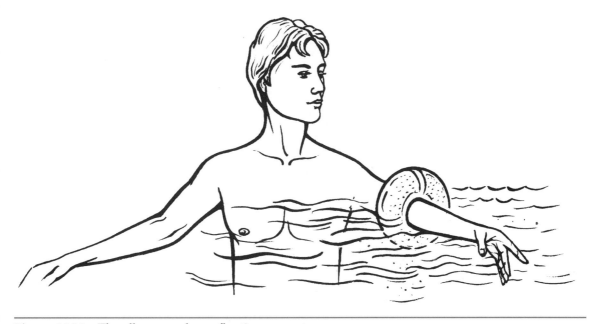

Figure 14.21   The elbow as a buoy floating on water.

THE WRIST AND HAND

From the top down, the structure of the arm increases in complexity. The upper arm consists of one bone, the lower arm of two, the proximal (upper) carpals of three bones, the distal (lower) carpals of four, and the metacarpals and the fingers of five bones. Each unit supports the next, with the purpose of maximizing the movement possibilities of the hand in space. The myriad shapes the hand can assume can hardly be categorized. Immanuel Kant said that the hand is the brain turned to the outside (Shärli 1980). In many dance styles, the hands take center stage as the communicators of plot and meaning.

The Wrist

The carpal bones of the wrist are very idiosyncratically shaped, as reflected in their names: The proximal row consists of the scaphoid (skiff form), lunate (moon), and triquetrum. With the radius and radioulnar disk, they compose the radiocarpal joint. The distal row consists of the trapezium, trapezoid (table-shaped), capitate (head), and hamate (hooked), which articulate with the proximal row to form the midcarpal joint and with the metacarpals to form the carpometacarpal joints. Although part of the proximal row, the pisiform (pea-shaped) does not form part of the radiocarpal joint (figure 14.22).

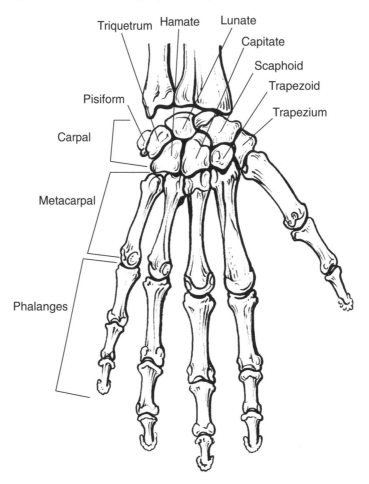

Figure 14.22   The hand and wrist.

The articular surface of the radius is concave; the surfaces of the proximal carpals are convex, like an egg, enabling the carpals to glide over the radius and radioulnar disk. The joint permits flexion, extension, adduction (ulnar deviation), and abduction (radial deviation). Touch the styloid process of the ulna and the radius to visualize the approximate axis for flexion and extension just below these two points. The proximal carpal row glides in opposition to the movement of the hand.

EXERCISING THE WRIST

1. **Flexion and extension of the wrist:** Visualize the egg-shaped convexity of the proximal carpals sitting in the concavity formed by the radius and radioulnar disk. Extend your wrist and visualize the carpal dome sliding in the opposite direction of the fingers, toward the palm (figure 14.23a). Flex your wrist and visualize the carpal convexity sliding in the opposite direction of the fingers, toward the back of the hand (figure 14.23b).

2. **Visualize the spaces between your carpal bones:** Imagine fog or mist flowing through these spaces (figure 14.24).

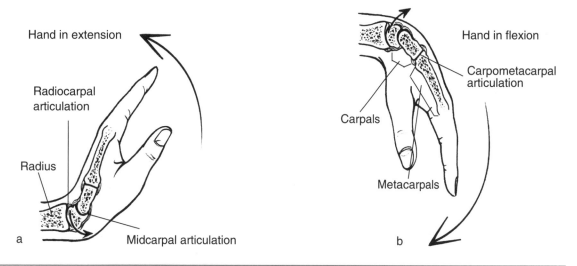

Figure 14.23   (a) Extend your hand and visualize the carpal dome sliding in the opposite direction of the fingers. (b) Flex your hand and visualize the carpal convexity sliding in the opposite direction of the fingers.

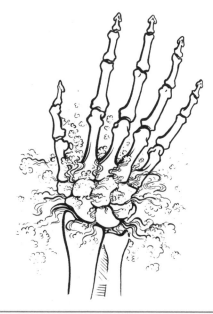

Figure 14.24   Visualize fog or mist flowing through the spaces between your carpal bones.

The Hand

The five digits of the hand consist of five metacarpal bones and 14 phalanges, two in the thumb and three in each of the other fingers. The digits articulate with the carpals at the carpometacarpal (CMC) joints. The CMC joints can flex or extend, except for the thumb CMC joint and the fifth finger CMC joint which are both saddle joints. The thumb can flex, extend, circumduct, and move in and out to touch the tip of every other finger—the thumb opposition so beloved by evolutionary scientists. The fifth finger CMC joint is somewhat less flexible than the thumb and can flex/extend and adduct/abduct. Eight intrinsic (originating in the hand) and extrinsic (originating outside of the hand) muscles control the intricate movements of the thumb. A baby's ability to grasp tiny objects (often a piece of dust an adult can hardly see) using thumb opposition is an important developmental landmark.

The CMC joints help the hand create a cup shape when holding an object. The shape of the carpals, enhanced by ligaments, creates the carpal arch, which remains even if the hand is extended. With the fingers slightly flexed, the hand serves as a miniature pouch, shovel, or watertight bowl that can carry small amounts of water to the mouth. Basically, the hand can imitate every tool made by humans. Perhaps the statement should be reversed: Humans conceive of tools that are inherent in the design of the hand.

The lumbricals, found in the hands and feet, are the only muscles of the body that attach to the tendons of other muscles on both ends—to both flexors and extensors. They flex the joints between the metacarpals and phalanges and strongly extend the joints within the phalanges, making them the muscles of choice to create the cup-shaped hands of the Graham technique. The lumbricals are also important for any pushing action initiated from the tips of the fingers or toes. Well-trained lumbricals improve a dancer's jumping ability.

EXERCISING THE HAND

1. **Arm-hand axis (port de bras, improvisation):** Visualize the axis of the hand passing through the third finger, third metacarpal, capitate (second row of carpals), lunate (first row of carpals), between radius and ulna, and through the center of the arm and into the glenoid fossa. Rotate the arm and hand around this axis. Let the axis support the entire length of the arm (see figure 14.19).

2. **Beam of light through the axis of arm and hand (port de bras, improvisation):** Visualize an arrow or a beam of light emerging from the center of the glenoid fossa and shooting out through the arm, hand, and third finger. Practice initiating arm and hand movements from the arm's central axis.

3. **Finger stretch (touch):** With the fingers of your left hand, hold the lower end of the right thumb's metacarpal (knuckle). To locate this point, slide your fingers down the thumb to a thicker area. Circle the thumb with your left hand and then slide your fingers out over the thumb. Imagine the thumb lengthening, as if it were made of clay. Repeat the following procedure with every right-hand finger: Slide the fingers of the left hand over the finger phalanges, continuing over the metacarpals on the back side of the hand until you reach the lower end of the metacarpal. Imagine that

your fingers actually begin here. Slide your fingers outward over the meta-carpal metacarpal and finger bones, giving each fingertip a little tug. Feel each finger lengthening. When you finish all the fingers, compare the sensations arising from the hand you have exercised with the left hand. Repeat for the other hand.

4. **Initiation from fingers (improvisation):** Imagine that each finger leads you into space, perhaps via a string attached to the fingertip. After you have explored individual finger strings, imagine that strings are attached to every finger simultaneously. Visualize all the finger strings in unison leading your hand and body into space.

5. **Hand sponges (improvisation):** Imagine that your hand can fill with air like a sponge fills with water. Stretch your hand and watch the air flow into your hand. Make a fist and feel the air being expelled. Imagine that you can also fill your hands with colors, scents, and sounds.

6. **Hand centering (sitting):** Grasp the second finger of your right hand with the palm of your left hand, as if trying to pull or inhale the finger into the center of your left hand. Alternate hands.

CHAPTER 15

The Head and Neck

*T*here are many advantages to having the head perched at the top of the spinal column. Ancient man could see much farther over the plain to evaluate food sources and potential dangers while they were still at a distance. Rapid surveying of the surrounding area and fast directional changes demanded a nonrigid, easily balanced structure. Watching children learning to walk, one witnesses this head-on-spine balancing act. The toddler is rather top-heavy, its head large in relation to its body as compared to an adult. The child's first steps remind us of a fledgling circus aerialist making his or her way across a tightrope (figure 15.1). This balancing act can also be witnessed at the level of pelvis-on-femur heads. The head rests on the most mobile part of the spine, its considerable weight balancing on this small base—rather like a large ball sitting precariously on a seal's nose. The seal keeps the ball on its nose through its strong muscular base and rapid, but delicate adjustments (figure 15.2).

Due to the head's high COG relative to the rest of the body, any deviations from optimal head alignment have a great impact on the entire body. The vestibular system, located in the inner ear, measures the position and acceleration of the head. The neck's receptors and reflexes indirectly measure the position of the head in comparison to the rest of the body. Thus cooperation between head and neck is essential for good alignment and movement control (Hotz & Weineck 1983). The relatively small cervical vertebrae of the neck have a shape designed to increase their stability. Cervicals three through five are slightly curved upward at their outer rims, like shallow cups. These rims are called the uncinate

Figure 15.1 Watching children learning to walk, one witnesses this head-on-spine balancing act.

Figure 15.2 The head rests on the most mobile part of the spine; its considerable weight sits on a small base.

processes. Most of us use the uncinate processes the way football players use their massive neck muscles.

Due to overzealous attempts to straighten the spine or hours spent stooped over books or a computer, many people have poor neck and head alignment. Imagine that you have to learn all over again how to balance your head on your spine (many of us do). It is much like learning how to balance a bottle on top of your head. I speak from experience, since I once danced in *Fiddler on the Roof*, where such balancing acts were required. I admit to also having experienced what it is like to witness a bottle (my own) break into a thousand pieces during a rehearsal.

THE HEAD BALANCES ON THE NECK

1. **Head as a balloon:**

    a. **Sitting, standing:** Imagine the head to be a balloon filled with helium. Remember that it is the helium that provides the lift (the space within the head), the surface of the balloon rests on the helium inside it. The neck and central axis are the string attached to the balloon that follows it as it floats upward. Imagine this string to be as soft as wool, especially in the neck area. From the balloon's vantage point, the shoulders recede rapidly, much like the earth recedes to an astronaut as he catapults into the sky (figure 15.3).

Figure 15.3   The head floating upward like a balloon filled with helium.
Adapted, by permission, from L.E. Sweigard, 1974, *Human Movement Potential* (New York: Harper and Row).

b. **Initiation:** Your new balloon-head initiates your movement in space. Use the sensory memory of letting go of an untied balloon and watching it deflate with a hissing sound as it flies off into space.

2. **Head on geyser (sitting, standing, improvisation):** Imagine your central axis to be a waterspout or a geyser. Picture your head floating effortlessly atop this gurgling column of water, which flows back to the floor in the form of your shoulders and body surface. As the geyser becomes stronger, your relaxed head is pushed upward, causing it to bob up and down. Find the place where the force of the waterspout creates the best alignment. (Also see chapter 18, figure 18.5.)

3. **Lengthening the neck (supine):** Visualize the neck lengthening and the tailbone extending in the opposite direction. The occiput (the bone at the lower back of the skull) provides a fairly easy grip (be gentle) for a partner. Lengthening should never cause the chin to point toward the ceiling. Image being pulled back and up in an arc, like a child's swing.

4. **Core support for the neck (standing, sitting, vertical leaps, pirouettes):** Imagine the neck to be the base of a long, narrow cone with its point rooted between the sitz bones, in the pelvic floor. (Instead of being a "conehead" you're a "conebody"!) Watch the axis of the cone merge with your central axis (figure 15.4).

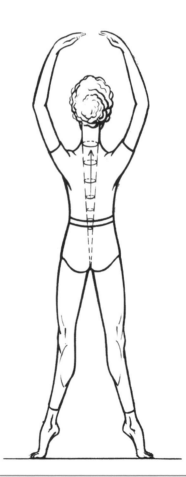

Figure 15.4   The neck as the base of a long, narrow cone with its point rooted between the sitz bones.

5. **Equal volume in neck (supine, sitting, standing, vertical leaps, pirouettes):** Visualize your cervical spine. Begin to appreciate the space between your cervical spine and the outer surfaces of your neck. Imagine that there is equal space between the bodies of the vertebrae and the front, back, and side surfaces of your neck. Imagine this space to be open and uncluttered (figure 15.5).

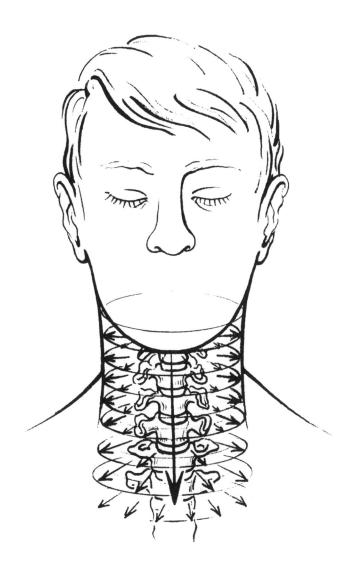

Figure 15.5 The equality of space between the cervical spine and the surfaces of your neck.

6. **Scalene tie-rods (supine, sitting, standing):** Visualize the scalene musculature extending from the uppermost ribs to the transverse processes of the second through seventh cervical vertebrae. Imagine these muscles to be tie-rods, maintaining the cervical spine in an equal, upright balance. Feel these tie-rods vibrating. Imagine this vibration eliciting the same sound on both sides of the neck (figure 15.6).

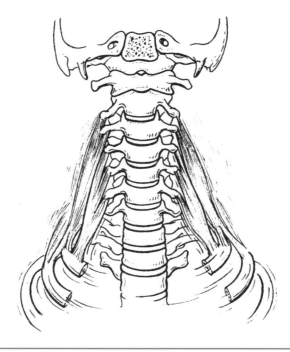

Figure 15.6 The scalene muscles as tie-rods vibrating equally on both sides of the neck.

ATLAS AND AXIS

The ring-shaped topmost vertebra, the atlas (named after the mythological Atlas who carries the earth), has no body or spinous process. The superior facets are slightly concave and articulate with the convex surfaces of the occipital condyles (see figure 9.3). The axis, the second cervical vertebra, has a dens (Latin for tooth) protruding from its front surface. The axis and atlas articulate at three points: two lateral joints between the upper facets of the axis and the lower facets of the atlas, and the atlantoodontoid, a pivot joint where the dens of the axis rotates within a ring formed by the front arch of the atlas and the transverse ligament. The axis looks rather like a human being with arms held in a circular position, ready to support the load above (figure 15.7). The dens of the axis is the slender head; the face is the posterior articular facet for the transverse ligament of the atlas; the arms are the lateral mass. The superior articular facets even look like shoulder pads, which come in handy for carrying the atlas and the head.

The pivot joint between dens and atlas enables the head to rotate quickly and economically in the horizontal plane, with little involvement of the rest of the neck. The lateral atlantooccipital joints permit flexion and extension, a nodding of the head, and a small amount of sideways flexion and rotation. The lateral atlantoaxial joint allows for flexion, extension, lateral flexion, and rotation. Half of the rotational ability of the neck resides in the atlantoaxial joint. Good head alignment minimizes the stress on the bones and muscles compared to the extremes of flexion and extension. As Jonathan Riseling, 10-year member of the Alvin Ailey Dance Company, once joked, "You can't do head rolls after you're thirty."

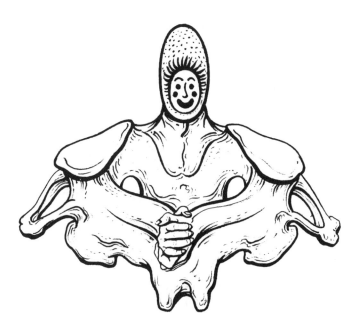

Figure 15.7   The axis.

EXERCISING THE ATLAS AND AXIS

1. **Visualizing the atlantooccipital and atlantoaxial joints:** Place the fingers on the mastoid process, the bony prominence behind the earlobes. The occipital bone is right behind this point. You may be able to feel the transverse processes of the atlas below. Be careful, as this area may be tender to the touch. Moving forward again, find the inferior section of the opening of the ear, with its adjoining cartilage. A line connecting these two points would traverse the atlantooccipital joint and the dens of the axis.

2. **Relating sitz bones and occiput:**

   a. **Aligning the occipital condyles with the sitz bones (standing, sitting):** Visualize the occipital sitz bones and the rounded inferior portion of the pelvic sitz bones. Imagine the occipital sitz bones extending downward to become aligned with the pelvic sitz bones in the same frontal plane. Visualize the central axis located between the pelvic and occipital sitz bones (see chapter 18, figure 18.2).

   b. **Relating upper and lower sitz bones (sitting):** Think of the occipital condyles as miniature sitz bones. It may be helpful to rock on the pelvic sitz bones and notice the sensations of sitting equally on these bones and transferring weight from sitz bones to the chair. Once you have established these sensations, project them up to the less accessible (through touch) occipital condyles sitting in their facets of the atlas. Visualize the shallow cups of the facets and allow the occipital sitz bones to sink into them. Now rock gently both on your pelvic and occipital sitz bones.

3. **Atlantooccipital counterrotation (sitting, standing):** Imagine balancing your occipital condyles equally on both superior articular facets of the atlas. Nod your head to the front and back and watch the occipital condyles (concave) glide in the superior facets of the atlas (convex). Now visualize the facets and condyles counterrotating. The facets of the atlas glide forward under the condyles of the occiput in flexion (forward nod). The facets of the atlas glide posteriorly under the occipital condyles in extension (nod to the rear). Reduce this rocking motion until you are just imagining the movement.

4. **The atlas as a lifesaving ring (sitting, standing, improvisation):** Imagine the atlas to be a circular lifesaving flotation ring. Visualize the head floating easily on this ring. As the water level rises, the ring floats upward, carrying the head up. Experiment with initiating side bending, rotation, and other movements from the flotation ring (see chapter 9, figure 9.3).

5. **Atlas rotates around axis:** Rotate the head to the side and visualize the atlas rotating around the dens. As you rotate, imagine the dens extending upward, creating an axis about which the entire head can revolve.

6. **Odontoid counterrotation (head rotation, pirouette):** As you rotate your head to the right, visualize the odontoid process rotating in the opposite direction (counterclockwise from above). As your head rotates to the left, visualize the odontoid rotating clockwise. In your mind's eye, picture the odontoid becoming very slippery and spinning rapidly in the opposite direction.

7. **The odontoid determines the plumb line (standing, relevé):** Visualize an axis extending upward and downward through the odontoid process being made perfectly perpendicular by the downward pull of an attached ballast. This plumb line should be identical with your central axis (see chapter 18, figure 18.3).

THE SKULL

A strong protective cover for the brain, the skull provides a safe and advantageous position for the olfactory, auditory, visual, and balancing organs. Its one large opening below the foramen magnum, an exit for the spinal cord, lies in the horizontal plane, enabling the human head to perch on top of the spine, unlike that of our gorilla cousins, who need powerful neck muscles to hold onto the head because this angle is slanted obliquely forward. At birth, the bones of the skull are widely separated by sutures (fibrous joints) to allow the slight overriding necessary for compression as this largest part of the baby's body passes through the birth canal. Located at the top of the head, the largest suture, called the anterior fontanel, is an area of softness and relative weakness.

The adult skull has a dome-shaped brain case and several flat bones: the frontal bones over the forehead, the parietals and temporals at the sides, and the occipital bone at the back. There are also several facial bones in a variety of shapes: the nasal bone and zygomatic bones, among others, and the maxilla, which forms the upper part of the jaw. The base of the skull and the containers for the sensory organs are the most ancient parts of the skull; the face, mandible, and dome are its more recent additions. The last bones of the skull to connect firmly do not do so until the age of 18. Even then, the skull retains a certain amount of flexibility due to its sutures. We benefit from thinking of the skull as a flexible, nonrigid structure. Remember, the skull's great weight and crucial role in movement initiation make its alignment critical in dance.

EXERCISING THE SKULL

1. **Touch:** Touch the forehead, called the frontal bone, and glide your fingers over the top of the head, which consists of the two parietal bones, to the back of the head, the occipital bone. The occipital bone extends under the head to areas we cannot touch and forms the back part of the base of the skull. Return to the front of the head and touch the frontal bone over your eyes. If you move your fingers down the sides of your eyes and to the rear, you will discover a ledge called the zygomatic bone. Above the zygomatic bone you will find the sphenoid bone, and if you continue along the zygomatic to the rear, you will reach the temporal bone, which extends above and behind this area. Now touch the top part of the nose, or the nasal bone; the lower part of the nose consists of cartilage. Below the nose is the maxilla, the upper jaw. The jaw itself will be explored later.

2. **Breathe into the skull (supine):** As you inhale, visualize your breath filling the skull, making it soft and malleable. Watch the skull fill and expand on inhalation and empty and relax on exhalation.

3. **Head as a ball (supine, improvisation):** Imagine the skull to be round like a ball. Explore all the surfaces of the skull in your mind's eye and see them become round. Find the center point of this ball. Practice initiating head movement from this point.

4. **Empty head (supine):** Imagine the head to be empty and spacious. Move around inside your head, clearing its interior of all obstructions. Dispel the clutter in your head as if you were doing spring cleaning.

5. **Floating skull bones (supine):** Imagine the flat bones of the skull floating on the cerebrospinal fluid (which surrounds the brain) like tectonic plates floating on the earth's mantle.

THE MANDIBLE

The mandible, or jawbone, a horseshoe-shaped bone that attaches to the temporal bones at each end, consists of the body in front, the rami on the sides, and two upward-facing projections called the mandibular condyle and the coronoid process (figure 15.8). A small disk separates the temporomandibular joint (TMJ) into a large upper and a small lower joint. The hingelike lower TMJ consists of the condyle of the mandible and the lower surface of the dividing disk. The disk freely rotates on the condyle, and vice versa. The upper TMJ is formed by the articular eminence (joint protrusion) of the temporal bone and the upper surface of the disk, allowing the disk to glide on the temporal bone. A very strong joint with a variety of movement possibilities, the TMJ can open, close, slide sideways, jut forward, and move backward. Attached at the coronoid process, the temporalis muscle, which elevates the mandible, passes beneath the zygomatic arch (figure 15.9). The TMJ is constantly in use when we speak, eat, drink, and swallow. Therefore, telltale tension patterns readily manifest in the temporalis muscle, located in front of and above the ears and seen in action during chewing.

In the back of the cheek, you can touch another powerful muscle of mastication, the masseter, which is involved in clenching the teeth. Dancers often clench their jaws during technically difficult steps, but this habit inhibits the free flow of movement and constricts the breath. Try clenching your jaw for a minute and notice that when you unclench your jaw, you instinctively take a deep breath. Releasing the jaw also helps consolidate the experience of the central axis.

Opening the mouth is a two-phased process. First, the condyle rotates on the disk, and then, to open the mouth wider, the disk slides forward and down along the articular eminence. Closing the mouth reverses these actions: First, the disk slides back and up on the articular eminence, then the condyle rotates on the disk. Thus, the opening action occurs first in the lower, then the upper TMJ. Conversely, the closing action occurs first in the upper, then the lower TMJ. Jutting of the jaw requires a forward and backward sliding of the condyle and disk. No rotation is involved, and thus the action is limited to the upper TMJ.

Sideways motion of the jaw requires a forward movement of the condyle on one side and a rotation of the condyle on the other side. If you move your jaw to the right, the right condyle rotates around a vertical axis while the left condyle moves forward. If you move your jaw to the left, the left condyle rotates around a vertical axis while the right condyle moves forward (figure 15.10).

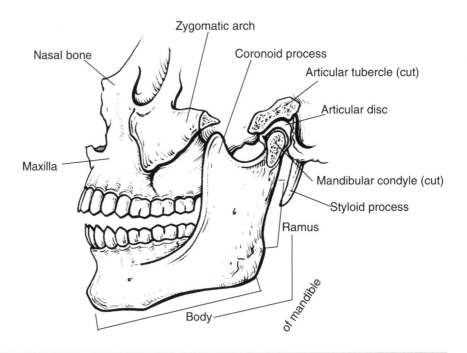

Figure 15.8 The mandible, or jawbone.

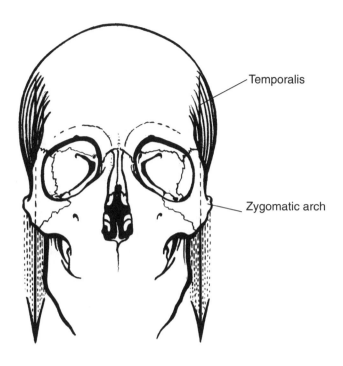

Figure 15.9   The temporalis muscle melts downward and passes under the zygomatic arch.

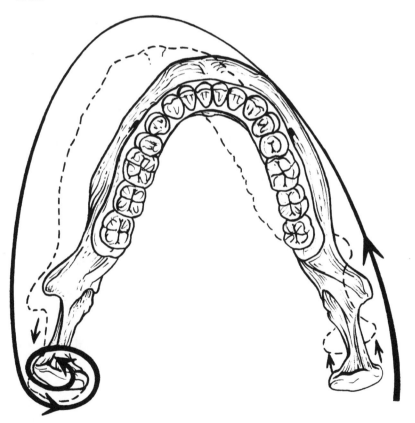

Figure 15.10   If you move your jaw to the left, the left condyle rotates around a vertical axis while the right condyle moves forward.
Adapted, by permission, from C.C. Norkin and P.K. Levangie, 1992, *Joint Structure and Function* (Philadelphia: F.A. Davis).

EXERCISING THE MANDIBLE

1. **Touch:** Let's begin at the front of the jaw, called the body of the mandible. Use both hands to follow along the sides of this body. Your fingers will glide around a corner called the angle of the mandible and will begin moving up the rami of the mandible to the joint between the skull and mandible. You can feel the activity at this joint as you open and close your jaw. Just behind this area and beyond the earlobe, you will discover a thick protrusion called the mastoid process. Just above the joint between the mandible and the skull, you will detect a bony ledge, called the zygomatic arch. The temporalis muscle passes beneath this arch. Open and close your jaw and feel the temporalis muscle in action above this arch. Move your fingers about an inch forward along the zygomatic arch and slide them downward another inch. You are now touching your mastoid muscle.

2. **Temporalis release (sitting, standing):** Visualize the temporalis muscle melting downward as it passes under the zygomatic arch. Watch it flow and hang perpendicularly down the side of the skull. See the flow of both temporalis muscles being vertically aligned with each other (figure 15.9).

3. **Masseter release (supine, sitting, standing):** Palpate the masseter muscle at the back of the cheek and imagine it softening. Move your fingers to various places on this muscle and watch these points melt. Begin to move the jaw in various directions while continuing to see the points you are touching melt away.

4. **Widening the back "arms" of the joints (supine, sitting, standing):** Visualize the mandibular rami floating sideways from each other. Visualize the space between the left and right TMJ becoming larger, widening, opening up (figure 15.11).

5. **Releasing the inner jaw space (supine, sitting, standing):** Let air flow into the mouth. Watch this air pour down the inner surface of the jaw and back out into space through the bottom of the chin (figure 15.11).

6. **Softening the floor of the mouth (supine):** Visualize the area beneath your tongue, between the rami of the mandible, becoming soft and malleable.

7. **Jaw on cloud (standing, sitting):** Imagine the mandible floating on a cloud just beneath it. Don't tighten your jaw; let the cloud support it like a cushion.

8. **Jaw drawer (sitting, standing):** Imagine your jaw to be a sliding drawer that fits very loosely on well-oiled runners. Lean your head forward and imagine the drawer sliding forward easily. Lean your head back and watch the drawer slide back just as easily. Repeat this image a few times.

9. **Disk gliding:** As you open your mouth, visualize the condyles rotating forward. Now open your mouth wider and imagine the disks sliding along the articular eminence. The motion is wavy, downward, and forward. Compare the feeling to going down a wavy slide. It may be helpful to sigh while performing this action. Finally, close your mouth and watch the disks glide back and the condyles rotate to the rear (figure 15.12).

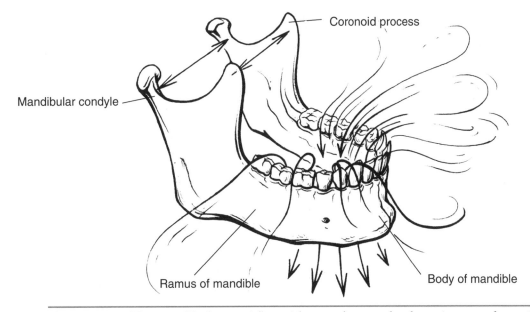

Figure 15.11   The mandibular rami float sideways from each other; air pours down the inner surface of your jaw.

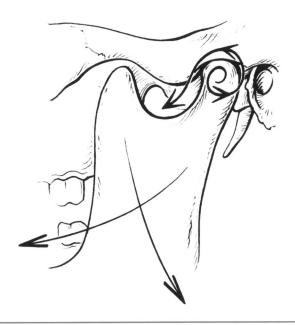

Figure 15.12   As you open your mouth, the condyles rotate forward. As you open your mouth wide the disks slide along the articular eminence.

THE HYOID AND TONGUE

The hyoid, a free-floating bone shaped like a boomerang, lies at an angle between the floor of the mouth and the front of the neck. Believed to have evolved from the second and third gill arches, the hyoid has a multitude of muscular and ligamentous attachments but no bony connections to the rest of the body. It is literally a floating way station for muscles attached to the mandible, cervical spine, sternum, and clavicles (figure 15.13). The tongue is muscularly rooted to the hyoid. Breathing is adversely influenced by tension in the tongue via the hyoid and the upper accessory breathing musculature. Tension in the tongue, bunching or sticking the tongue out of the mouth, is common. An off-center tongue influences alignment of the hyoid and neck.

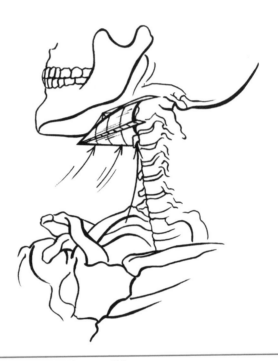

Figure 15.13   The hyoid bone as a hang glider.

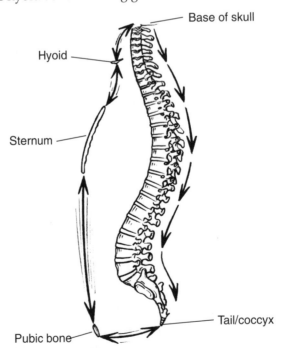

Figure 15.14   A circular chain of bony and muscular links running down the spine to the tail and back up the front of the torso.

Hyoid placement influences the alignment of the cervical spine, the head, and the shoulders. Hyoid imagery can improve forward head positions and release concomitant neck tension. To appreciate how pelvic activities can influence the neck, and vice versa, visualize a circular chain of bony and muscular links running down the spine to the tail, across the pelvic floor to the pubic symphysis, up the rectus abdominis, through the sternum to the hyoid and cervical spine and the occiput of the skull (figure 15.14).

IMAGING THE HYOID BONE

1. **Visualize the shape and location of the hyoid:** Put your fingers on the thyroid cartilage (Adam's apple), which can easily be found protruding slightly from the neck (more so in men than in women). Just above this cartilage is a small space that delineates the area just below the hyoid bone. The front and sides of the hyoid can be touched readily.

2. **The tongue sits—the hyoid hangs:** Imagine the tongue resting, sitting on a well-balanced hyoid. At the same time, think of the hyoid as suspended, hanging down from long attachments to your central axis. Compare this image to resting on the seat of a swing. You rest your weight on the seat, which is suspended from above.

3. **Hyoid hang glider (supine, sitting, standing):** Imagine the hyoid bone to be a hang glider. Visualize a strong wind current gusting up the front of the spine, lifting the hyoid. Emphasize the lifting of the wings rather than the tip of the hyoid. Watch the glider (hyoid) hanging in the air, wafting upward on gentle and consistent breezes. Watch the glider dip and bank in the air currents (figure 15.13).

4. **Tongue over clothes hanger (sitting, standing):** This image does for the tongue and neck what the Sweigardian clothes-hanger image does for the legs and back. Imagine the tongue hanging over a clothes hanger, as if it were a soft and fluffy blanket. The clothes hanger is positioned under the back center of the tongue. Imagine the tongue resting on and drooping over this hanger.

5. **Tongue centering (supine, sitting, standing):** Visualize the sagittal plane that divides the tongue into two equal halves. Think of the two halves of the tongue sliding down equally along this plane. Imagine a line of movement from the front tip of the tongue around the sides to the back. Let the rim of the tongue flow back toward this central axis (figure 15.15).

6. **Neck, mouth, and top of head release (supine, sitting, standing):** Imagine the dome-shaped top of the mouth expanding toward the top of the skull. Watch from the inside as the dome becomes larger, as if you are standing inside an expanding balloon. Imagine your whole body hanging from the top of your mouth. Let the top of the skull and the neck soften

and the tongue melt. You may also think of the tongue deflating, as if filled with air that is now escaping from the edges of your tongue (figure 15.16).

7. **Cotton tongue (supine):** Imagine the tongue becoming permeable like cotton. Let your breath float around and through your tongue.

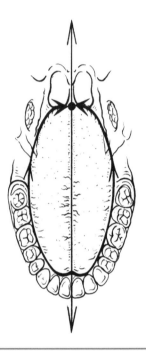

Figure 15.15   Imagine a line of movement from the front tip of the tongue around the sides to the back.

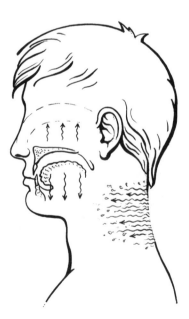

Figure 15.16   The dome-shaped top of the mouth expanding toward the top of the skull.

THE EYES

Set deep in their cone-shaped sockets, the eyes face forward and slightly outward, creating an overlap of visual fields and binocular vision. Our relatively small snout and nose area accentuates this visual field overlap. In the embryonic state, the eyes are not connected to the brain. An axon, or nerve, grows out from the back of the eye and searches for the brain. Chopra (1990) writes:

> Structurally, the retina is just a pool of nerve endings fanning out like the frayed end of a rope, the rope being the optic nerve, which gathers a million separate fibers into one bundled cord. Even though they are located deeper inside you than the nerve endings under your skin, the eye's sensory cells are also "touching" the outside world. (p. 200)

The eyes are very revealing. A baby's eyes sparkle, wide and excited. A clouded visual channel diminishes expressivity. Said to be the mirrors of the soul, the eyes are a visible part of the brain. Kükelhaus (1988) points out that developmentally the eyes are connected to the "master gland," the pituitary (in the brain). Sight directly influences the hormones of the body. Organs of reception, the eyes get filled with incoming reflected light. We usually think of looking in an active context, but the opposite notion of drinking with our eyes and allowing a visual impression to fall into the body and create a mood or an image though its transformation within us is most valuable (Kükelhaus 1978).

Tatsumi Hijikata, considered the father of Japanese Butoh dance, once said that whatever he saw, he absorbed into his body. Even his neighbor's dog lives in his body. All these things float inside him like rafts on a river, Hijikata said in a lecture at the first Butoh festival in Japan in 1985 (Haerdter & Kawai 1988). Recent studies have shown that sightless people may learn to see with their bodies—to transform tactile stimulation into a visual image, creating a "substitute" sensation. They can learn how to "see sound" via tactile stimulation patterns produced by hundreds of small points on their skin.

The eyes also aid balance through the optical righting reflexes. Try improvising or doing barre work with your eyes closed to see how much harder it is to balance without them. I often take off my glasses when dancing (and regular wearing of contact lenses irritates my eyes), so I have become rather aware of these changes in balance control. With my glasses on, everything appears sparkling clear and balancing is easier. When performing without glasses or contact lenses, I have found myself well-prepared for the impaired vision from glaring stage lights because I am used to perfect vision in dance classes. I am convinced that training balance organs other than the optical greatly improves one's overall ability to maintain balance.

IMAGING WITH THE EYES

1. **Eyes suspended:**

   a. **Central axis (standing, sitting):** Imagine that your eyes are suspended from your central axis.

b. **Suction cup (standing, sitting):** Let the eyes dangle from an imaginary suction cup. Because they are only held in their sockets by this light, airy force, they can glide freely.

2. **Eyes gliding (eye movements):** Visualize the eyes sitting in their spherical sockets. Let the sockets become very slippery so that the eyes glide effortlessly as you shift your gaze.

3. **Resting on the horizon (sitting, standing):** The horizontal plane beneath the eyes supports their weight. Imagine them resting on the horizon created by this plane.

4. **Eyes as ponds (supine):** Image the eyes as ponds of fresh, clear spring water. See the water welling up from below through the optic nerve, slowly replenishing the pond in the cavity of the eye with the clearest, purest, crystalline water. See the eyelids as lily pads floating on the pond, moving very slowly and with infinite ease, propelled by a warm summer breeze (figure 15.17). Now try imagining the area around the eyes to be a pond and the eyes as round balls floating in this pond.

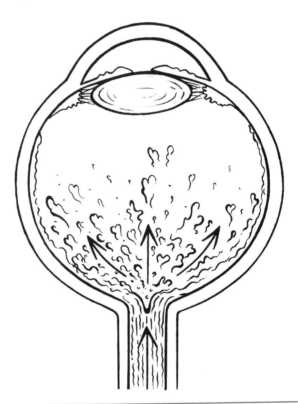

Figure 15.17   The eyes as ponds of fresh, clear spring water.

5. **Rolling eyes (improvisation):** Let the eyeballs roll gently in their sockets. Try using music that suggests a rolling motion. Bach sonatas for the flute or Scarlatti sonatas for the piano may be suitable classical selections. Let the eyes respond to the music; they are part of the total body feeling.

6. **Initiate movement from the eyes:** Now let the eyes initiate the body's motion. Experiment with letting the right, then the left, then both eyes

lead the body into space. Now imagine that you can see up, down, to the front, back, and both sides simultaneously. How does this three-dimensional vision change your movement?

7. **Light drops into eyes (improvisation):** Imagine the light coming from the scenery around you falling into your eyes without any effort on your part whatsoever. They soak up all the visual information surrounding you as you move.

8. **Whole body seeing (improvisation):** Imagine that every cell on the surface of your skin is sighted. Your sight has thousands of possibilities, thousands of angles from which to look out into space. What is it like to be the sighted cells on the soles of your feet? What is like to be the sighted cells on the top of your head?

THE NOSE AND MOUTH

What we see of the nose is largely a cartilaginous projection, not part of the skull. The actual nasal cavities, which generally are deeply buried within the skull, are separated by a partition, called the septum. A thick mucous membrane covers the inner walls of the nose to warm the incoming air and remove dust particles. The flow of air through the nasal passages creates resistance that trains the diaphragm and other breathing muscles.

The center of the baby's world, the mouth and lips, serve as a powerful built-in suction pump for mother's milk. Feeding from mother's breast is one of our first coordinated acts, involving locating the breast and nipple, reaching for it, connecting to it, correcting the whole body position, activating the suction pump, and maintaining the vacuum connection (Piaget 1993). An extremely sensitive area of the body, the lips provide our first experience of shape. A baby sucks on a wooden ring and experiences roundness, takes a wooden block into its mouth and experiences squareness. This presymbolic awareness becomes the basis for language and later imagery.

The mouth is related to the pelvic floor and anus, as they are the opposite ends of our long digestive tube. Tension in the mouth indicates tension in the pelvic floor, which inhibits the breathing process and does not allow for resilient support of the pelvic organs.

The sense of taste and the sense of smell are intimately connected. What we consider to be taste is largely a matter of adding the information gathered through smell to the findings of meagerly distributed taste receptors on the tongue. You can discover how much the sense of smell contributes to the sense of taste by holding your nose while eating—you will find that much of the taste is lost.

**IMAGING
WITH THE
NOSE AND
MOUTH**

1. **Nasal airflow (supine):** As you inhale, imagine the air flowing up the center of the nose. As you exhale, imagine the air flowing down along the sides of the nose.

2. **Soft nostrils (supine):** Imagine your nostrils to be very soft. As the air passes through them, they billow like the sides of a tent in the wind.

3. **Sucking on a straw (improvisation):** After you have been moving for a few minutes, imagine that you are sucking water up through a straw. Notice how this affects your movement.

4. **Space in lips (standing):** Visualize the space contained within your lips. Appreciate their inner volume. Notice how this affects your neck as well as your whole standing posture.

5. **Smell and alignment (standing):** If you think this exercise is humorous—it is. To discover how smell can affect your body tone and alignment, try the following experiment: Imagine the smell of cow manure, or any other smell that does not appeal to you, and notice any changes in body tone or posture. Now imagine the smell of your favorite perfume, or any other scent that appeals to you, and again notice any changes in body tone or posture.

CHAPTER 16 *Breathing*

*B*reathing is a great teacher, leading us to new experiences and telling us much about our current physical and psychological state. Any improvement in our alignment and movement patterns will improve our breathing patterns, and vice versa. We can survive without water for three days, and without food for much longer, but within minutes the brain will starve from lack of oxygen.

THE LUNGS

We absorb oxygen into the body through the inner surface of the lungs, an extremely large contact area between the air and the body surrounded by the airtight pleura. Oxygen molecules pass through the thin surface into the bloodstream where they are transported to the billions of cells contained within the body. This is where the actual breathing takes place, at the level of the cell. The "exhalation of the cells," carbon dioxide," is then transported back to the lungs where it is expelled.

Such delicate organs as the lungs needs to be well protected. The trachea and bronchi, the large passageways that guide the air to the alveoli, small bubblelike structures where the exchange of gases takes place, are fairly sturdy. Their strength reinforces the primary tunnels. The basic shape of the lungs can be visualized as a hollow, upside-down tree. The trunk is the trachea in the upper chest; the first large branches are the bronchi, subdividing further into smaller and smaller branches, which eventually reach the spherical leaves, the alveoli. The right, larger lung is divided into three lobes; the left, smaller lung is divided into two lobes (leaving additional space for the heart) (see chapter 11, figure 11.18).

If this inverted tree is distorted, the alveoli are compressed and the alignment of the upper body will suffer. Inefficient alignment hinders deep breathing. Try the following experiment: Bend over into a hunched position and try to take a few deep breaths. Your breathing will be shallow and forced, which increases tension throughout the body. On the other hand, elastic, well-aerated lungs support good alignment. The lungs need to fill the entire space allotted to them if they are to function optimally. Deep, calm, and rhythmic breathing creates balanced muscle tone which favors ease of motion and dynamic alignment.

Breathing patterns are greatly influenced by one's psychological state. You breathe differently when you hear good news than when you hear bad news. You breathe differently when you watch a romantic movie as opposed to a comedy. Our breathing patterns, as well as our alignment, are always being influenced by the people around us. When we're around a shallow breather, our breathing also tends to become shallow. If someone we're with has hunched shoulders, we tend to hunch our shoulders. Around someone whose breathing is deep and rhythmic, we gravitate toward that pattern. Breathing, alignment, and psychological factors are interdependent.

BREATHING EXERCISES

1. **Breathing with partner:** Stand opposite a friend. Focus on each other's breathing. As you exhale, descend into a plié. As you inhale, stretch your legs. Notice how long it takes for both of you to breathe in the same rhythm.

2. **Alignment:** Stand opposite a friend and repeat the above exercise. Then have your friend deliberately go into a slouched posture with shallow breathing. Notice how your friend's breathing and posture affect your own breathing and alignment.

3. **Lungs and shoulder alignment:** The lungs extend from the diaphragm, which ranges from the bottom six ribs all the way up to the space within the topmost ribs. Often we do not let the lungs own this space; when we hunch our shoulders, the upper lung becomes cramped and is pushed downward.

   Circle your right shoulder clockwise and imagine that the surrounding bones and muscles are massaging your lungs, especially the upper part. This massage allows the lungs to regain their flexibility and shape. Circle the shoulder in the opposite direction as you continue to think of this internal massage. Rest your shoulders for a moment and focus only on the lungs expanding. Imagine your breath being able to flow into this area. Think of a sponge that has been compressed and is now being released.

   Now circle your left shoulder counterclockwise and visualize the surrounding bones and muscles massaging your lungs. Imagine that this massage allows the lungs to regain their flexibility and shape. Circle the shoulder in the opposite direction as you continue to think of the internal massage. Rest your shoulders for a moment and focus on the lungs expanding. Imagine your breath flowing into this area. Again, think of a sponge that has been compressed and is now being released. Compare the sensation in your shoulders. This exercise can also be done with both shoulders simultaneously.

EFFORTLESS BREATH

Nature designed breathing to be as effortless as possible. We do not need to suck air into the lungs. If you empty a bucket of water, you hear and see the water flowing out, but you don't notice the air flowing in to fill the vacuum. The motion of the ribcage and diaphragm and the lungs' encasing pleura create a vacuum that air flows in to fill. It could be said that the lungs are suspended within the ribcage through the negative atmospheric pressure of the vacuum. On inhalation, the air freely flows into the lungs through the nose or mouth, down the trachea, and into the bronchi and alveoli. If the airtight pleura is pierced, the lungs may collapse because the vacuum is impaired.

THE DIAPHRAGM

The most important muscle for breathing is the diaphragm (figure 16.1). Dividing the body into the abdominal and thoracic cavities, the diaphragm can be visualized as a lopsided mushroom with two small stems called crura. The right side of the mushroom is higher to accommodate the liver, which is significantly larger than the stomach, situated on the left side. The diaphragm's central tendon is fused to the pericardium, the covering of the heart. The heart can be visualized as riding up and down on the diaphragm during exhalation and inhalation, receiving continuous movement therapy.

Various muscular parts of the diaphragm radiate from its central tendon. The costal part of the diaphragm attaches to the inner surface of the xiphoid process and to the lower six ribs and costal cartilage. The crural portion of the diaphragm attaches to the first, second, and third lumbar vertebrae. The crura extend downward from the diaphragm next to the psoas and the quadratus lumborum (a lower back muscle), suggesting an intimate connection between breathing and locomotion. As the psoas, together with the iliacus, is our most powerful hip flexor, restricted breathing adversely affects alignment and almost every movement.

INHALATION

As the diaphragm contracts on inhalation, its dome moves down relative to the ribs along the body's central axis. In this sense, breathing is an axial (vertical) activity. Axial movement of the diaphragm improves alignment, whereas imbalanced use of the diaphragm is detrimental to alignment. Usually, diaphragm movement needs to be more fully experienced at the sides and back of the body. The diaphragm actually moves down very little but over a very large surface,

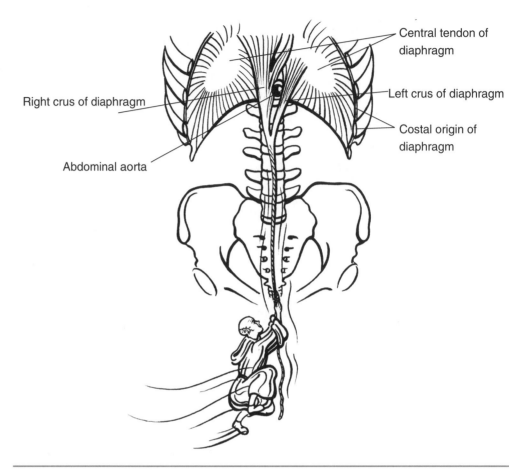

Right crus of diaphragm

Abdominal aorta

Central tendon of
diaphragm

Left crus of diaphragm

Costal origin of
diaphragm

Figure 16.1 The left and right crura of the diaphragm as imaginary cords extending all the way down to the coccyx.

creating plenty of space within the lungs. This downward motion compresses the organs, which can be visualized as water-filled balls resisting the diaphragm's descent. Because the diaphragm continues to contract for a moment without moving farther down, it helps pull the ribs out to the side and up. The crura can be visualized as muscular strings that help lower the dome of the diaphragm (figure 16.1). Expansion of the ribcage during inhalation does not take place in the same direction and at the same time throughout the ribcage. When the central tendon stops moving down, the lower ribs are pulled upward and outward along a curve, expanding the ribcage sideways like a bucket handle being lifted; the much smaller upper ribs rotate forward and lift the sternum (minimally in quiet breathing).

The diaphragm pushing down on the organs during inhalation increases intraabdominal pressure, displacing the organs downward. Since the lumbar spine blocks any path to the back, they move forward. The stomach muscles lengthen and the abdominal wall expands to afford them more room. Efficient breathing involves the abdominals and diaphragm in a constant interplay. Vehemently pulling in your stomach muscles prevents the organs from moving forward, impeding the diaphragm's downward motion. In the first phase of breathing, a certain amount of abdominal tension may augment the pull of the diaphragm on the ribs, helping them elevate. Constant gripping of the abdominals creates compensatory actions such as lifting the shoulder girdle in an effort to increase the space within the lungs. This in turn raises the COG, making the body less stable and hindering balance and turns.

The way to keep the stomach from bulging is to create efficient interaction between diaphragm, stomach muscles, and iliopsoas. Although momentarily effective, holding in the stomach muscles may weaken them in the long run by reducing (axial) movement of the (antagonistic) diaphragm. Instead, practice releasing the stomach muscles toward the spine. Unrestricted breathing creates a certain natural hollowing of the abdominal area that is greatly supported by imagery.

EXHALATION

As you exhale, the stomach muscles shorten and help push the organs back against the upward-bound diaphragm. The elastic rebound of the organs helps push up the diaphragm. The ribs drop with the pull of gravity, expelling air from the lungs. Muscle release, gravity, and elasticity combine to make exhalation the easier of the two respiratory phases. The stomach muscles actively push the organs back so that the diaphragm can easily return to its original position. As mentioned earlier, the smaller the up-and-down motion of the diaphragm, the shallower the breathing. A complete exhalation stimulates a deep inhalation. Exhaling with a sibilant hiss between the teeth and tongue encourages the stomach muscles to push in the organs and close the angle of the ribs. Hissed breath, a type of forced exhalation, lengthens expiration, teaching the abdominals complete expiration. Generally, lengthening your expiration is calming and shortening it is exciting.

IMAGING BREATH

1. **Exhaling through a straw (sitting):** Exhale through a straw. Do not take an extra-deep breath before you exhale. Do not push the air through the straw beyond your normal exhalation, and do not keep the straw clenched between your teeth as you exhale. Practice for about five minutes and notice how you feel. Repeat the exercise with an imaginary straw.

2. **Axial movement of diaphragm (supine, sitting, standing):** Imagine the diaphragm moving up on inhalation and down on exhalation. Visualize this motion in line with your central axis.

3. **Diaphragmatic elevator (supine, sitting, standing):** Imagine the diaphragm to be an elevator moving up and down in its shaft (the ribs). As you inhale, the elevator moves down; as you exhale, it moves up.

4. **Downward reach of crura (supine, sitting, standing):** Visualize the left and right crura of the diaphragm as imaginary cords extending all the way down to the coccyx. Visualize someone pulling these cords as you inhale and releasing them as you exhale (figure 16.1).

5. **Diaphragmatic parachute (sitting, standing):** Imagine the diaphragm to be a parachute. As you inhale, the center of the parachute drops downward, the sides billow, and the strings loosen (figure 16.2a). As you exhale,

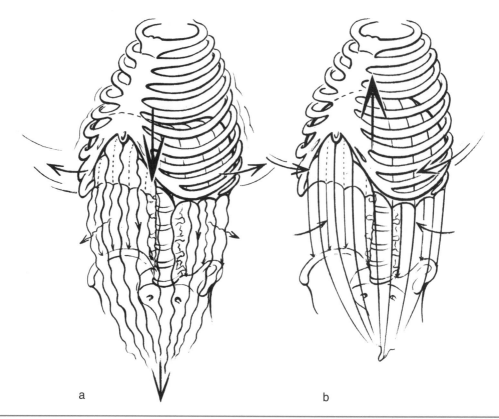

a   b

Figure 16.2   The diaphragm as a parachute.

the parachute expands its dome upward as the strings become taut and stretch down toward the pelvic floor (figure 16.2b).

6. **The ribcage as an umbrella (supine, standing):** Visualize the ribcage as an umbrella. The handle of the umbrella is in the pelvis, and the point is the top of the spine. The shaft of the umbrella is aligned with the central axis. As you inhale, the umbrella opens and widens all around—front, back, up, down, and sideways. As you exhale, the umbrella closes toward the central axis. Practice this image three to four times, accompanying an exhalation with a sibilant hiss. (Adapted from Sweigard.)

7. **Pelvic balloon (supine):** Imagine a balloon situated in the pelvis. As you inhale, the balloon expands equally in all directions. The balloon pushes against the inner borders of the pelvis, spreading the arms of the pubic bones and somewhat releasing the pressure of the two arms pushing against each other at the pubic symphysis. As you exhale, the balloon collapses toward center. The arms of the pubic bones move inward and push more solidly against each other at the pubic symphysis. Visualize the balloon from the inside as well as the outside. Be sure to visualize all sides of the balloon expanding equally. Repeat the exercise 10 to 12 times, intermittently using a sibilant "sss" on exhalation (figure 16.3).

8. **Bellybutton flower petal (supine):** Imagine the bellybutton to be a pretty flower petal. As you exhale, visualize the flower petal falling through your body to the ground. As you inhale, rest your mind or create a new flower petal. Repeat the exercise three to four times.

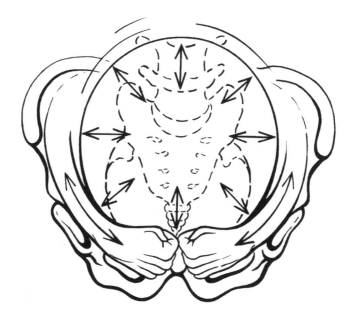

Figure 16.3 A balloon situated in the pelvis.

9. **Belly water rings (supine):** As you inhale, imagine circular waves expanding away from your bellybutton. Watch these rings expand into space throughout the length of your inhalation. Rest your mind while you exhale.

10. **Body balloon (supine):** Picture your whole body as a large inflatable balloon. As you inhale, fill your body from the center outward, expanding the balloon. In the pause before you exhale, fill your arms and legs. As you exhale, watch the air flow out of the shriveling balloon. Pause in the collapsed position before the next inhalation. (Adapted from *Zen Imagery Exercises*.)

11. **Cell-lungs (supine):** Imagine each cell of your body to be a small lung in its own right. As you inhale, imagine millions of cells inhaling, taking in oxygen. As you exhale, visualize millions of cells exhaling.

12. **Exhaling tension (supine):** As you inhale, imagine your body releasing its tension into the incoming air. All tension leaves your body with your exhalation. Let your breath discover all the areas in your body that are tense. Think of your breath as an explorer, capable of discovering hidden tension. As soon as a tense spot is detected, breath flows into the area, collects the tension, and transports it out of your body with your next exhalation.

THE SKIN

The skin, the body's protective cover, is a large, delicate sensory organ. Lungs are a comparatively recent evolutionary development, so primitive animals breathed through their skin. Humans retain some of this primitive ability to exchange gases through the surface of the skin, which is able to absorb, excrete, and respire. Surprisingly, the skin is practically waterproof.

Varying in thickness from one millimeter on the eyelids to three or more millimeters on the palms of the hands and soles of the feet, the skin has many functions. Sweat glands and sensory nerves in the skin keep the mind informed of the relationship between the body and its immediate surroundings, tactile stimulation, temperature changes, and sources of pain. The skin can even perceive sound waves (Kükelhaus 1978). If you have ever been near a large gong when it was sounded, you have experienced this. The presssure changes in the air can be felt all over the body.

IMAGING WITH THE SKIN

1. **Sensing sound through the skin (improvisation):** Imagine that you are perceiving a sound such as music with the entire surface of your body. Feel the sound reaching remote parts of the skin—the back of the neck and knees, the soles of the feet, the space between the fingers, and the heels. Then imagine the music soaking into your skin. Absorb the music with the entire surface of your body.

2. **Breathing through the skin (supine):** Imagine yourself breathing through your skin. Concentrate on specific areas. Breathe in and out through the soles of your feet . . . through your knees . . . through the back of your neck . . . through your lower back . . . through your face . . . through your shoulders. Experiment with other body parts. Notice where it seems easy to breathe and where your pores seem to be constricted.

PART

IV

Returning to Holistic Alignment

*I*n the chapter on postural models, we took a "macro" view, trying to find the overall principles and unifying theories of posture. The anatomical section focused on the "micro" aspects—on detail and subtle adjustment. The micro view creates a deeper understanding of the macro. But lest we lose sight of the spine for the vertebrae, we return for a final macro or holistic view.

Holistic alignment is dynamic in the sense that it is an expression of the whole body in motion, in a unified state of being, rather than a conglomerate of contradicting actions within the body. The way I was originally taught alignment sounded like this: "Hold this in, tighten that, push that down, lift that up!" The body seemed to be one contradiction on top of another. The question in my head was : "How can I lift *this* up when I am supposed to push *that* down?" Needless to say, this was not a very happy state of affairs. In holistic alignment, the whole body, every cell, is working toward the same goal. When your alignment is holistic, it is effortless, because you have not suppressed one of the body's needs in favor of another.

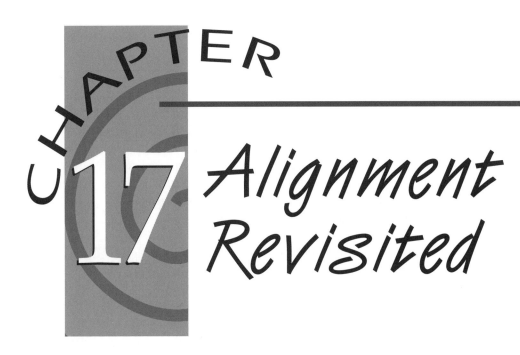

CHAPTER 17 *Alignment Revisited*

Armed with essential biomechanical and anatomical knowledge, we can return to the discussion of dynamic alignment we began in the first chapter. This will bring us to a deeper level of understanding and experience.

THE BIOMECHANICS OF ALIGNMENT

According to biomechanics, ideal posture or body alignment engenders minimal torques and stresses throughout the kinematic chain (Norkin & Levangie 1992). The ground reaction force (GRF) vector and line of gravity (LOG) create a line through the body that determines the torque in each body segment. If the LOG passes in front of the axis of a joint between two segments, the top segment will receive a forward gravitational moment. In figure 17.1, we can see a slight forward moment in the tibia because the ankle joint is behind the LOG. The femur receives a slight forward moment as well because the LOG passes just in front of the center of the knee. The LOG passes just behind the center of the hip socket, creating a backward rotational moment of the pelvis.

Anatomists disagree about the path of the LOG through the spine. In chapter 13, figure 13.1, I have depicted the LOG passing through the bodies of the lumbar and cervical vertebrae (see Kendall 1983). Other anatomists show the line passing further to the rear, behind the bodies of the lumbar and cervical vertebrae and in front of the bodies of the thoracic vertebrae. In this scenario, gravity is more likely to increase the spinal curves. The LOG is generally seen as passing through the odontoid process of the axis.

The Plumb Line

It is easy to visualize the relationship between body segments and the LOG using a plumb line of the type that builders use to ensure that a wall is being built perpendicularly to the ground. As mentioned earlier, there are differing opinions on the ideal plumb line. The following is a widely accepted version of the "correct" plumb line as viewed sagittally: The plumb line passes just in front of the outside anklebone, just in front of the midline of the knee, through the greater trochanter (round protrusion) of the femur, through the shoulder girdle, and through the earlobe (figure 17.1).

As humans are bilaterally symmetrical, it is much easier to define the ideal plumb line from the front or back. From the front, it ideally passes through the tip of the nose, the center of the sternum and the pubic symphysis, and touches the floor equidistant from both feet. Figure 17.2 shows this plumb line for a one-legged stance, where it passes through the foot of the standing leg.

Each leg can be further examined from the front. A plumb line passes through the second toe, between the malleoli (anklebones), through the center of the knee, and the center of the hip joint (see figure 11.14). In genu valgum (knock-knees), the knees are more central than the plumb line, causing compression stress on the outside and tensile stress on the inside of the knees. In genu varum (bow-legs), the knees are farther outside than the plumb line, causing tensile stress on the outside and compression stress on the inside of the knees.

Viewed from behind, the plumb line ideally passes through the center of the back of the head and the spine and touches the floor equidistant from both feet. As mentioned, sideways deviations of the spine from the plumb line are called scoliosis. Ideally, from front or back, the eyes, ears, shoulders, crests of the ilia, knees, and inner borders of the feet should be on the same level (figure 17.2). Although generally caused by postural imbalance, some deviations, especially those in the eyes and ears, are due to genetic differences. Discrepancies in the levels of the iliac crests may result from differing leg lengths or postural inequalities.

The Median Alignment

There is a certain amount of postural sway in the upright position, which means that we are never perfectly motionless when standing. The body is losing and regaining balance most of the time. An individual's alignment is truly median, the peak of a bell-shaped curve representing the sum of all his or her alignment states over time. In practical terms, this means that a dancer's alignment must be observed at different times of the day to gain a functional understanding of his or her alignment. Photographs with a plumb line in place can help evaluate posture, enabling a dancer to compare his or her own alignment self-image with the outward reality over time.

PROCESSING DYNAMIC ALIGNMENT

Knowledge of postural faults should not lead to tensing in an effort to remedy the situation immediately. Intellectual knowledge of personal postural faults is

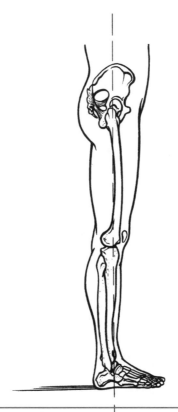

Figure 17.1   The plumb line of the leg.

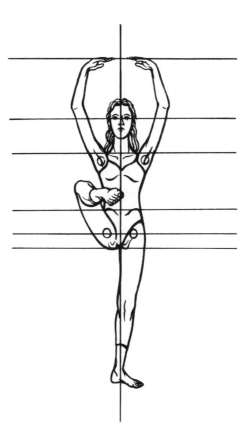

Figure 17.2   The plumb line for a one-legged stance.

only a first step, and not always a necessary one, in correcting them. Increased awareness and an experiential understanding of the problem is much more relevant. Many other factors determine good posture, such as limberness, reactivity, balance, and muscle tone. Some people are perfectly aligned when standing still but have no sense of their midlines or centers as soon as they move. Alignment sense does not necessarily correlate with overall coordination. A dancer may not be well aligned, but if his or her functional awareness of posture is superior to that of a well-aligned dancer, he or she will be more skilled at moving. If the first dancer improved his or her alignment, the improved biomechanical relationship among body segments would further improve his or her dancing. Alignment and movement are interdependent only insofar as our definition of alignment is dynamic.

Defining Ideal Posture

Sweigard (1978) defines the *upright posture* as

---

the consistent and persistent alignment of the skeletal structure in relation to the line of gravity when the subject assumes an easy standing position with the weight evenly distributed—according to his or her own judgment— on the feet, with the ankles in the sagittal plane of the femoral joints and with the arms hanging freely at the sides. (p. 173)

Andre Bernard used to define the ideal posture along these lines: "Ideal posture in the standing position can be found when you allow the parts of the structure to balance as close to the central axis as the individual structure permits" (author's notes).

The second part of the definition discusses the COG: A low COG will make the body more stable. This should be achieved without jeopardizing the biomechanical alignment principles discussed above. The body's central axis should be as long as the person's individual build allows for without the addition of any tension-producing lengthening effort.

Derived from Sweigard, this definition emphasizes the biomechanics of reducing harmful torque and the kinetic nature of the never static body segments. Energy is saved by decreasing the effort needed to balance the first-class levers throughout body (head rests on spine, vertebrae rest on top of each other, pelvis balances on femur heads).

This brings us back to the building-block model—align the major centers of mass above each other and you create ideal alignment. It is important to remember that this alone will not create good movement if the major centers of mass are above each other because they were "forced" to be there. Just as important as the mass relationships of the individual parts are their functional relationships. (How does my leg movement affect my pelvis? How does a change in my head position influence my spine?) As mentioned above, the "well-placed" dancer may not move as successfully as one who is a master at sensing and adjusting the relationships among his or her body parts. Obviously, the dancer's poor posture does not predict this skill. Ideally a dancer combines a good sense of how the centers of mass balance on top of each other with a high awareness of the functional relationships throughout the body. In the final analysis, both skills are reverse sides of the same coin.

So far, we have placed a lot of emphasis on the building-block model, but insights gained from the other postural models can also be helpful in creating a holistic definition of dynamic alignment.

- From the tensegrity model: Such balance exists between the spacers (bones) and cables (ligaments, tendons, fascia) to allow for maximum weight-supporting/moving ability while maintaining flexibility and resilience.

- From the tubular model: The individual tubular layers maintain a balanced relationship with each other, allowing for free circulation of fluids and balanced tone throughout the body.

- From the water-filled balloon cellular model: The individual balloons or cells are balanced in such a way as to permit a free exchange of nutrients and a balanced transfer of force throughout the body.

- From the atomary model: The individual circling parts of the body maintain such a distance to the center as to create the optimal functioning of the entire system.

If we consider all the models, and the fact that the body is composed of many interacting systems such as organs, fluids, and connective tissue, all of which contribute to erect posture, the definition can be expanded to encompass all its components: "In ideal posture, the sum effort of all tissues allows for minimal waste of energy in the upright standing posture and maximum use of the resources available for motion in accordance with the individual's structure."

EXERCISING DYNAMIC ALIGNMENT

1. **Relationship to center (standing, walking, leaping):** In the standing position, focus on the center of your body. Think of the relationship between the parts of your body and this center. Notice how this relationship changes as you exhale and inhale. Take a few steps and notice how the relationship changes. Jump up and down a few times and notice any changes in the relationship of the parts to the center.

2. **Breathing through layers (standing, sitting, supine):** Focus on the layers of your body. Think of your inhalation originating at your center. As you inhale, watch your breath spread radially out through the consecutive layers to the final layer, your skin. As you exhale watch your breath fall back toward your center (also see chapter 1).

Pulling Up and Ideal Alignment

This is a rather controversial subject. To maintain balance and create better standing alignment, dancers sometimes try to pull up. When pulling up, you maintain your alignment by holding body parts high and under firm control. This may cause more problems than it solves. As Mabel Todd (1972) writes, it is desirable to have a naturally high chest where "the curve of the dorsal aspect of the sternum and the curve of the ventral aspect of the spine are symmetrical in their design" (p. 166). At the same time, she points out that: "It is futile to attempt to lengthen the axis of the spine by expanding or pulling up the chest" (p. 185).

A dropped chest obviously fails to conform to dance aesthetics or alignment and disturbs organs and breathing mechanisms. In particular, dancers who started training later in life, having adopted "cool" postural habits, may not have time to go through the lengthy process of changing postural patterns to achieve a high chest. As Sweigard (1978) states: *"All voluntary contribution to a movement must be reduced to a minimum to lessen interference by established neuromuscular habits"* (p. 6, italics in original). Sweigard goes on to say: "The idea, the concept of movement, is the voluntary act and the sole voluntary component of all movement. Any further voluntary control only interferes with the process of movement and inhibits rather than promotes efficient performance" (p. 7).

When pulling up, you add plenty of voluntary control, lifting the ribs, holding the stomach, and tucking the buttocks. In dance class I have been told to "suck my stomach back and up to my spine" which would keep "the weight out of my legs and make me become lighter." I always respectfully listen to every statement, but this kind of instruction invariably caused me to become very tense and rigid (when I was supposed to become lighter). I could not breathe properly and the chance of fluid, centered movement with full spatial awareness happening under these circumstances seemed minimal.

Unless you can drop a few sandbags like a hot-air balloonist, you will not become lighter by sucking up your stomach. From the standpoint of physics, the only way to become lighter is to lose mass or to move to a planet with less gravitational pull. The intention behind "pulling up" is, of course, a very good one: You are trying to defy gravity, to improve your alignment, and be "up on your legs," and so on. New York-based ballet teacher and choreographer Zvi Gotheiner says:

Pulling up is a cultural notion, originating in the effort at the French courts to ennoble oneself with high postural carriage. There is also an instinctual aspect; you gain a certain power by looking at the world from above. Pulling up in no way benefits alignment and efficient movement. (author's notes)

In my opinion, the aim of creating strong abdominals, or a "honey bee" waist as they say in Switzerland, by artificially pulling in the abdominals is self-defeating. Holding in the stomach reduces the amount of motion available to the diaphragm. Since the abdominals oppose the action of the diaphragm and organize the organs toward the center of the body on exhalation, their activity and intrinsic training is reduced. Also, the organs receive less of a "massaging effect" since their motion within the abdominal cavity is restricted. This reduces their tone and makes the stomach "bulge out" even more. Often dancers ask me the question: "How is it possible that my stomach is sticking out when I do so many sit ups?" The answer is that there is no better training for the abdominals and the organs than deep breathing, which is not possible with your belly voluntarily compressed toward the spine. I will mention, however, that in many cases nutritional factors also play a role in such abdominal imbalances.

If your placement is good and your stomach muscles are well-conditioned, you should be able to forget about them when dancing, unless a choreographer requires their specific initiation. The stomach muscles, however, are often insufficiently conditioned. Daily exercises, including breath and sound, are required to increase the tone of the abdominals as well as the underlying organs (see chapter 11, The Pelvic Floor, and chapter 16, Breathing).

The aim is to achieve an "energized" rather than a tight feeling in the stomach area. If you join with gravity, you will be much more successful in the end. According to physics, you need to use the ground reaction force as efficiently as possible. Guide this force up through your body (primarily through the bones). Liberated from their tasks of superfluous gripping, the muscles begin to create optimal alignment and lift. The nervous system becomes more alert, the reflexes more nimble. Freeing the muscles eliminates any uncontrolled precipitation of weight down into the knees and feet. When you "feel" your weight, you gain control. Kevin Poe (personal communication, 1994), who danced the part of Mephistopheles in the musical *Cats* in New York, Zurich, and Vienna, relates:

> I was standing in the wings one day during the ballet *Raymonda*, when I noticed how completely exhausted I was from the last dance. At this point, I realized that I was not breathing correctly. As soon as I "relearned" how to breathe in movement, I did not feel exhausted anymore from dancing. Singing helped a lot in this respect. I imagine that I can sing while dancing, or at least speak. One should be free enough to sing the song of one's movement out loud. This will also greatly benefit your phrasing. If you habitually grip your stomach muscles, you cannot breathe, certainly not sing. Intentional contraction of these muscles needs to be reserved for power moves.

The lifted position also raises our center of gravity, making us less stable, necessitating even more holding and tightening to maintain position. The problem is that the way to achieve lightness is perhaps counterintuitive. To be lighter you need to appreciate your weight, to explore how the limbs lever against the ground to move the body's weight and use the ground reaction force. This requires practice because body weight and limbs are not commonly experienced as levers for movement. When you lift a sandwich weighing one-twentieth the weight of your arm, do you feel the weight of the sandwich or the weight of your arm? You feel the weight of the sandwich, although the arm is much heavier. Although feeling 15 pounds of arm every time we lift a mouthful of food would probably be an effective dieting strategy, the brain will not allow us to be overly occupied with how heavy a limb feels when moving because this unnecessary distraction would endanger our survival. As mentioned in part I of this book, we peer through a rather small peephole at incoming sensation, only getting the information we need for the immediate tasks at hand. To include differentiated experience of weight, we must widen this peephole.

CHAPTER 18 Integrating Dynamic Alignment Exercises

*T*he study of alignment includes the in-depth evaluation of the relationships among the body segments as itemized in part III. Improving one relationship improves the whole. You may also improve your alignment by consciously or unconsciously imitating people with good alignment, or through bodywork, somatic therapies, and psychological insight. However, and I cannot emphasize this enough, *for any improvement in alignment to be permanent, the changes need to become part of your body image—the new alignment pattern needs to become part of your identity, or you will always slip back into old habits.* Because our body image is based largely on how we "see" and "feel" ourselves, using imagery is a very direct way to repattern your alignment.

The following exercises focus on increasing your sense of center, facilitating a cohesive energy and biomechanical optimization in erect posture—always in a dynamic sense. The images below can be practiced individually or during a class to remind you of alignment principles. The subdivisions simply yield emphasis for each image. Visualize those that appeal to you frequently to gain maximum benefit.

ALIGNMENT IN SUPINE POSITIONS

The following exercises should be done in the constructive rest or yoga supine positions, aided by a clear horizontal sense of the floor.

THE FLOOR IS YOUR GUIDE TO VERTICALITY

Heighten your awareness of the floor beneath you. Notice which parts of the body rest on the floor and which do not. Notice differences between the right and left halves of your body. Do not force any segment onto the floor; just allow each one to rest on the supporting surface. Notice the difference in sensation in your body parts as you inhale and exhale. Notice the areas that seem a bit achy or tense. Notice those that feel good.

FLYING CARPET

Imagine that you are resting on a flying carpet. Watch the carpet slowly lift you off the ground, supporting every part of your body equally. As the carpet floats back down to the ground, see the body segments—head, torso, and pelvis— arrive at the same time.

SPHERES

One at a time, visualize the pelvis, the torso, and the head as individual spheres. Allow the three spheres to line up on top of each other. Visualize the center point of each sphere from pelvis to head. Imagine a line connecting them. Begin by connecting only two spheres at a time: Connect the center of the pelvic sphere to the center of the thoracic sphere. Then connect the center of the thoracic sphere to the center of the head sphere. Finally, connect all three spheres. Watch them float off and settle on the ground while you maintain the connection among them.

MEETING OF PLANES

Image the median frontal plane. Does it pass through the earlobes, the acromion (shoulder tip), and the greater trochanter? Which of these bony landmarks are in front of this plane, and which are behind it? Is the plane parallel to the floor? Image the median sagittal plane. Does it pass through the centers of the nose, chin, breastbone, navel, and pubic symphysis? Which of these landmarks are to the left of the plane, and which are to the right? Now image both the sagittal and frontal planes at the same time. Locate the line where the two planes meet. This is your central axis. Is your central axis parallel to the floor? Can you visualize the entire length of the axis, or are some parts easier to see than others?

ALIGNMENT IN SITTING POSITIONS

Sitting is a good place to practice alignment because you can work from a strong pelvic base, more specifically, from your pelvic floor and sitz bones, which provide a clear guideline for the structures above. Also, many alignment issues can be addressed by becoming more aware of pelvic placement.

BALANCED SITTING

1. **Balancing weight on sitz bones:** Place your weight equally on both sitz bones. Notice whether you feel the weight more on the front or back of them. Try to place your weight on the center of the sitz bones. (If you have the tendency to slouch, to tilt the top of the pelvis to the rear, you will feel as if you are hollowing your back.) Imagine the midline of the body passing through the odontoid process (dens of the second cervical vertebra) and equidistant from both sitz bones. Visualize the midline grazing the lumbar vertebrae and passing through the superior cervical vertebrae. The median sagittal plane passes through the earlobes and the acromion (figure 18.1).

2. **Regaining good sitting posture:** Starting from your head, roll your spine forward and down until your head is hanging over your legs. Now bring your head back up until you feel you have "found" good alignment. Roll down your spine once again and try an image to help you regain your upright sitting posture: Think of the pelvic floor dropping down through the chair toward the floor as you bring your head back up. How does this method "compare" to the original way of coming up? Now try again, only push the pelvic floor down to bring you up. Practice visualizing the pelvic floor dropping/pushing down on an exhalation or an inhalation to bring you back up.

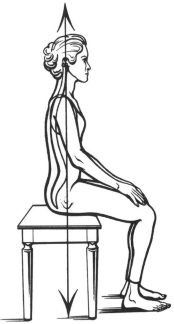

Figure 18.1 Sitting alignment.

STANDING AND WALKING ALIGNMENT

Compared to body size, human beings' COG is relatively high, making standing a challenge. Walking is easier because the continuous momentum of moving forward has a certain stabilizing effect. Except for the first exercise below which should only be done while standing, I recommend doing the exercises first while standing and then while walking.

NOTICING REFLEXES

Stand with your eyes closed and become aware of your whole body. You may notice continuous tiny adjustments in your posture taking place automatically. These are your reflexes operating at a subconscious level keeping you from falling over.

BUILDING BLOCKS

See yourself as a stack of colorful, wooden building blocks. Restack the blocks from the bottom up and adjust them into perfect alignment on top of each other.

SPHERES ON A STRING

Picture yourself as a series of spheres on a string: The string is your central axis, the spheres your body segments. An imaginary force is pulling both ends of the string in opposite directions, aligning the spheres on top of each other. See and hear them (as they touch) in perfect alignment, with their centers of gravity directly above each other (see figure 2.4a and b).

MEETING OF PLANES

In this position the median frontal plane is perpendicular to instead of parallel to the floor. Does it pass through the earlobes, the acromion, and the greater trochanter? Which of these bony landmarks are in front of this plane, and which are behind it? Image the median sagittal plane perpendicular to the floor. Does it pass through the centers of the nose, chin, breastbone, navel, and pubic symphysis? Now image both the sagittal and frontal planes at the same time. Find the point where the two planes meet. This is your central axis. Is your central axis parallel to the floor? Can you visualize the entire length of the axis, or are some parts easier to see than others?

MAGICAL PLANES

Visualize the median sagittal plane passing through the nose, the center of the chin, the sternum, and the pubic symphysis. Visualize several parallel horizontal planes passing through the body, as though the plates of a magician have sliced painlessly through it. One is touching the bottom of the sitz bones, one passes through the center of the hip sockets, one grazes the superior crests of the hips, and one passes through the left and right acromion. The eyeballs rest on another one, and the arms, which are held overhead, as in figure 17.3, touch still another one. (Figure 17.3 shows a modern dancer. Even without perfect balletic turnout, the above instructions hold true.)

IMAGING YOUR CENTRAL AXIS

1. **Sitz bones and condyles melt:** Imagine the convexities of the occipital condyles (projections at the bottom of the back of the head) and the sitz bones lengthening downward until they are aligned in the same frontal plane. Visualize the central axis located between the sitz bones and the occipital condyles (figure 18.2).

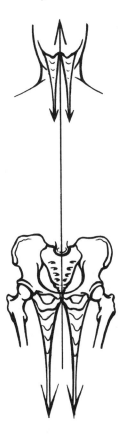

Figure 18.2 Convexities of the occipital condyles and the sitz bones lengthening downward.

2. **The odontoid determines the plumb line (first position, heels on floor, and first position relevé):** Visualize an axis through the odontoid process extending upward and downward and made perfectly perpendicular by the downward pull of a ballast. The ballast is aligned in the same frontal plane as the talus (figure 18.3).

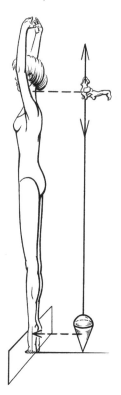

Figure 18.3 An axis through the odontoid process extends upward and downward, made perfectly perpendicular by the downward pull of a ballast.

RELEASING EXCESS TENSION

Obviously, one of our main goals is to create alignment that is dynamic and as effortless as possible—ready to meet any challenge. Tension is not a good state of readiness because it exhausts the muscles and other tissues of our body. If your muscles are tense they are overly contracted. Needless to say, when we move we need to contract our muscles, which is less feasible if they are already contracted. Therefore, tension defeats our purpose of readiness and ease.

RELEASING AROUND A POLE

Visualize your central axis as a round pole. Surrounding this axis is your body, which is composed of layers of soft cloth draped over the top. Watch the cloth fall toward the central axis.

VISUALIZE YOUR CENTRAL AXIS

Like clouds surrounding a mountain peak, your body surrounds your central axis. As you move, the fluffy layers of clouds move with you. Experiment with the image in movement. Start with sitting, then walking and running (figure 18.4).

Figure 18.4   Imagine your body consisting of soft clouds that hover around your central axis.

HANGING FROM A STRING

Imagine your body hanging easily from a string attached to the top of your head and dangling into perfect alignment. Experiment with this image in movement—start sitting, then walk and run. Allow the string to initiate your motion. Don't focus on the fact that the string is pulling you upward, but concentrate on the feeling of suspension. (Of course, the string pulls you upward, or you could not hang from it, but direct your attention to the fact that you are hanging from it.) (Adapted from Stephanie Skura.)

EXPERIENCING CENTRIFUGAL FORCE

Imagine that your body is attached to the center of the earth via your LOG and that the centrifugal force created by the earth's rotation extends your axis, making it point away from the core, perpendicular to the earth's surface. You can visualize this image more easily by comparing it to swinging an object around on a string held in your hand; in this case, you are the object and the earth is your hand. If you swing the object quickly enough, the string becomes taut.

HANGING UPRIGHT

As you stand, think of yourself hanging from the ceiling. Your shoes are glued to the ceiling and you are hanging from them (you can't fall out of them, of course). You are now falling upward. In this position, gravity (coming from above your head) pulls you into perfect alignment.

INTENSIFYING THE EXPERIENCE OF THE CENTRAL AXIS

1. **Head on geyser:** Imagine your central axis to be a waterspout or geyser. Your head floats effortlessly on top of this column. Visualize your shoulders and the surface of your body as the water falling back down to the ground. Allow your head to bob on top of the column of water. As the geyser becomes stronger, your head is buoyed upward; as it weakens, your head bobs back and forth. Let the power of the water increase the height of your head (figure 18.5).

2. **Ice cream pop:** Imagine your body to be an ice cream pop. As the ice cream (shoulders) melts, the stick (central axis) emerges (figure 18.6).

3. **Flowing water:** Stand with your feet on a small wedge of wood so that the front of your feet is higher than your heels, or lean against a wall with your hands. This position will stretch the back of your calves. Maintain this position for a minute while visualizing water flowing down your back, carrying all tension down over your heels and into the ground. Get off the incline and stand upright. You may immediately notice a floating, lifted feeling. (To simulate the flowing of the water, a partner can brush his or her hands down your back and the back of your legs.)

4. **Tiny bubbles:** Imagine the central axis to consist of a stream of tiny bubbles like those found in champagne or mineral water. The bubbles surge upward between the sitz bones, through the thorax and neck, and out the top

Figure 18.5   Imagine your central axis to be a waterspout or geyser. Your head floats effortlessly on top of this column.

Figure 18.6   Melting like an ice cream pop.

of the head. They come from an inexhaustible source located between your feet. Hear the crackle and pop of the bubbles; feel them gliding up the front of the spine (perhaps tickling it on their way). You may imagine the bubbles to have a color—red, as in raspberry syrup, or green, as in peppermint syrup. How do the different colors affect you?

5. **Volcano erupts (standing, improvisation):** Visualize a volcano shooting its fiery missiles into the air up along your central axis.

6. **Spiraling plant (standing, improvisation):** Visualize a plant spiraling up around a wooden shaft. The shaft is your central axis. Watch as the plant grows ever taller, its leaves reaching up toward the sky.

LEG ALIGNMENT

1. **Creating equal footprints:** Imagine yourself standing on sand. Look at the impressions your feet are making to see if they are equal in shape and depth. If not, imagine a smooth patch of sand and create equal footprints.

2. **Melting greater trochanter:** Visualize the leg axes. Imagine the outside of your legs melting downward. Specifically, imagine the greater trochanter melting down the sides of your legs (figure 18.7).

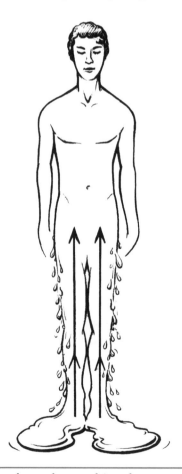

Figure 18.7 The outside of your legs melting downward.

3. **Waterspouts:** Visualize water shooting up through both legs, as if fire hoses are located under your feet. The waterspouts are perpendicular to the floor and shoot straight up into the acetabula (hip sockets) (figure 18.8). These water columns can support the weight of the pelvis. The returning water flows back down the outside of the legs. Have your partner place his or her hands around your ankle as both of you visualize the force of water shooting up through the area being touched. Repeat the procedure several times with your partner's hands around your lower leg, your knee, the middle of your thigh, and finally, over your hip socket. To complete the exercise, your partner should glide his or her hands down the sides of your legs, then glide one hand out over the toes and the other down over the heel.

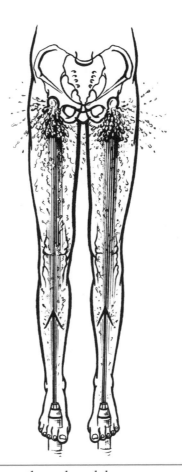

Figure 18.8   Water shooting up through each leg.

OTHER DANCERS AND YOUR ALIGNMENT

If you are standing at the barre with a beautifully aligned dancer in front of you, performing every exercise exquisitely, this sight will certainly inspire your nervous system to improve your own alignment as well. Our brains are sponges that absorb the visual impressions placed in front of them. In this sense, you are constantly surrounded by imagery. After watching a good dance performance, you will invariably dance better the next day. This does not mean you should shun bad dancers. A lot can be learned from dancers who seem inferior; understanding other dancers' problems can give you insight into your own. In dance class, imagine that you are surrounded by incredible, superbly aligned dancers, no matter what the skill level of the other dancers relative to you. Notice how this affects your dancing.

CONTINUING IMAGING

Although we are all born natural imagers, many of our imaging skills may dissipate in adolescence and adulthood, when exposing one's fantasy life becomes an aberration outside of psychotherapy or personal development workshops. The inner eye often becomes dark and shrouded as the immense influx of visual information from every direction saturates our senses. Television, movies, and billboards offer captivating prefabricated visions. Turning on the inner screen is hard work and seems rather unexciting by comparison. I hope that this book has helped you find the wealth of beauty and information available through that inner screen.

Bibliography

Achterberg, J. 1985. *Imagery in healing.* Boston: Shambhala Publications.

Alexander, G. 1976. *Eutonie.* Munich, Germany: Kösel Verlag.

Alfassa, M. 1982a. *A diary for all times.* Pondicherry, India: All India Press.
— . 1982b. *The great adventure.* Pondicherry, India: All India Press.

Barba, E., and N. Savarese. 1991. *A dictionary of theatre anthropology.* London: Routledge.

Bäumlein-Schurter, M. 1966. *Übungen zur Konzentration.* (*Exercises for concentration*). Zurich: Origo-Verlag.

Chiao, R.Y., P.G. Kwiat, and A.M. Steinberg. 1993. Faster than light? *Scientific American,* 269: 38-46.

Chopra, D., MD. 1990. *Magical mind, magical body.* Chicago: Nightingale-Conant Corporation.

— . 1990. *Quantum healing.* New York: Bantam.

Clark, B. 1975. *Body proportion needs depth--front to back.* Champaign, IL: Author.
— . 1968. *How to live in your axis--your vertical line.* New York: Author.
— . 1963. *Let's enjoy sitting-standing-walking.* Port Washington: Author.

Cohen, B. 1993a. *Sensing, feeling, and action: The experiential anatomy of body-mind centering.* Northampton, MA: Contact Editions.

— . 1993b. *Dynamic rotation of foreleg* (course manual, p. 5-6). Amherst, MA: Author.

Cohen, B., and M. Mills. 1979. *Developmental movement therapy* (class manual). Amherst, MA: Authors.

Dardik, I., and D. Waitley. 1984. *Quantum fitness.* New York: Pocket Books.

Dart, R.A. 1950. Voluntary musculature in the human body: The double spiral arrangement. *The British Journal of Physical Medicine,* 13(12): 265-68.

Dossey, L., MD. 1985. *Recovering the soul.* New York: Bantam.

Dowd, I. 1990. *Taking root to fly.* Northampton, MA: Contact Editions.

Durkheim, K. F. G. 1992. *Hara, the vital center of man.* London: Allen & Unwin. (Original German edition)

Epstein, G., MD. 1989. *Healing visualizations.* New York: Bantam Books.

Feldenkrais, M. 1972. *Awareness through movement.* New York: Harper Collins.

Flanagan, O. 1991. *The science of mind.* Cambridge, MA: MIT Press.

Franklin, E. 1996. *Dance Imagery for Technique and Performance.* Champaign, IL: Human Kinetics.

Fuchs, M. 1984. *Funktionelle Entspannung. (Functional relaxation)*. Stuttgart: Hyppokrates-Verlag.

Gelman, D., et al. 1992. Is the mind an illusion? *Newsweek,* 116 (April 29): 46.

Gottlieb, D. 1988. GABAergic neurons. *Scientific American,* 258(2): 38-45.

Haerdter, M., and S. Kawai. (Eds.). 1988. *Butoh*. Berlin: Alexander Verlag.

Hawkins, A., 1991. *Moving from within*. Pennington, NJ: A Capella Books.

Hotz, A., and J. Weineck. 1983. *Optimales Bewegungslernen. (Optimal kinesiology)*. Erlangen, Germany: Perimed.

Jacobsen, E. 1929. Electrical measurements of neuromuscular states during mental activities: Imagination of movement involving skeletal muscle. *American Journal of Physiology*, 91: 597-608.

Juhan, D. 1987. *Job's body*. Barrytown, NY: Station Hill Press.

Kavner, R.S. 1985. *Your child's vision: A parent's guide to seeing, growing and developing*. New York: Simon & Schuster.

Keleman, C.S. 1985. *Emotional anatomy*. Berkeley, CA: Center Press.

Kendall, F.P. 1983. *Muscle testing and function*. Baltimore: Williams & Wilkins.

Kingmann, L. 1953. *Peter's long walk*. New York: Doubleday.

Klein-Vogelbach, S. 1990. *Funktionelle Bewegungslehre. (Functional kinetics)*. Berlin: Springer.

Kosnick, H. 1971. *Busoni: Gestaltung durch Gestalt. (Shaping through form)*. Regensburg, Germany: Bosse Verlag.

—. 1927. *Lebensteigerung. (Life-enhancement)*. Munich: Delphin Verlag.

Krauss, R. 1950. *I can fly*. (Little Golden Book Series). New York: Simon & Schuster.

Kükelhaus, H. 1988. *Unmenschliche Architektur. (Inhuman architecture)*. Cologne, Germany: Gaia Verlag.

—. 1984. *Urzahl und Gebärde. (Primal number and gesture)*. Zug, Switzerland: Klett und Balmer. (Original edition, Frankfurt am Main, Germany: Alfred Metzner, 1934)
—. 1978. *Hören und Sehen in Tätigkeit. (Hearing and seeing in action)*. Zug, Switzerland: Klett und Balmer.

Lips, J.E., PhD. 1956. *The origin of things*. New York: Fawcett.

Masunaga, S. 1991. *Zen imagery exercises*. Tokyo: Japan Publications.

Matt, P. 1993. *A kinesthetic legacy: The life and works of Barbara Clark*. Tempe, AZ: CMT Press.

Maxwell, M. 1984. *Human evolution*. Sidney: Croom Helm.

Mees, L.F.C. 1981. Das menschliche skelett. *(Form and metamorphose)*. Stuttgart: Urachhaus.

Merlau-Ponty, M. 1962. *Phenomenology of perception*. London: Routledge.

Miller, J. 1982. *The body in question*. New York: Random House.

Naville, S. 1992. Class notes, Institute for Psychomotor Therapy, Department of Special Education, Postgraduate Studies, Zurich, Switzerland.

Norkin, C.C., and P.K. Levangie. 1992. *Joint structure and function*. Philadelphia: Davis.

Ohashi, W. 1991. *Reading the body*. New York: Penguin Books.

Olsen, A. and C. McHose. 1991. *Body stories: A guide to experiential anatomy*. Barrytown, NY: Station Hill Press.

Overby, L.Y. 1990. The use of imagery by dance teachers: Development and implementation of two research instruments. *Journal of Physical Education, Recreation and Dance,* 61 (February): 24-27.

Piaget, J. 1993. *Der zeitfaktor in der kindlichen entwicklung,* Aus Probleme der Entwicklungspsychologie. (The time factor in child development: A problem in developmental psychology). Europäische Verlagsanstalt, 16.

Pierce, A., and R. Pierce. 1989. *Expressive movement: Posture & action in daily life, sports, & the performing arts.* New York: Plenum Press.

Radin, E.L., R.M. Rose, J.D. Blaha, and A.S. Litsky. 1992. *Practical biomechanics for the orthopedic surgeon.* New York: Churchill Livingstone.

Rolf, I.P. 1989. *Rolfing.* Rochester, VT: Healing Arts Press.

——. 1977. *Rolfing: The integration of human structures.* Santa Monica, CA: Dennis Landman.

Rolland, J. 1984. *Inside motion: An ideokinetic basis for movement education.* Northampton, MA: Contact Editions

Rossi, E. 1986. *The psychobiology of mind-body healing: New concepts of therapeutic hypnosis.* New York: Norton.

Samuels, M., MD., and N. Samuels. 1975. *Seeing with the mind's eye.* New York: Random House.

Schrader, C. 1993. *Geo.* Hamburg: Gruner und Jahr.

Schultz, I.H. 1982. *Das Autogene Training.* Stuttgart: Georg Thieme Verlag.

Schwarz, S. 1988. *Wie Pawlow auf den Hund kam. Die 15 klassischen Experimente der Psychologie.* (How Pavlov got the idea of the dog: 15 classic experiments in psychology).

Selver, C., and C. Brooks. 1981. Sensory awareness. In G. Kogan, Ph.D. (Ed.), *Your body works* (pp. 122-123). Berkeley, CA: And/Or Press.

Shärli, O. 1980. Leib, Bewegung und Bau (Body, movement and structure) (p. 5). *Resonanzen.*

Sherrington, C. 1964. *Man on his nature.* New York: Mentor Books.

Skura, S. 1990. Interview with Joan Skinner. *Contact Quarterly,* 15(3).

Smith, F. 1984. *The path of least resistance.* Salem, MA: DMA.

Suzuki, S. 1970. *Zen mind, beginner's mind.* New York: C. John Weatherhill.

Sweigard, L. 1978. *Human movement potential: Its ideokinetic facilitation.* New York: Dodd, Mead.

——. 1961. The dancer and his posture. *Annual of Contemporary Dance.* (Reprinted from *Impulse.*)

Todd, M. 1977. *Early writings: 1920-1934.* New York: Dance Horizons.

——. 1972. *The thinking body.* 1937. Reprint, New York: Dance Horizons.

——. 1953. *The hidden you.* New York: Dance Horizons.

Topf, N. 1994. John Rolland remembered. *Contact Quarterly,* 19(2): 13-17.

Verin, L. 1980. The teaching of Moshe Feldenkrais. In G. Kogan, PhD. (Ed.), *Your body works* (pp. 83-86). Berkeley, CA: And/Or Press.

Vitruv. 1993. De architectura (E. Franklin, Trans.). *Tages Anzeiger Magazin,* (December 18) no. 50: 39 (Original work published 33-14 B.C.)

Vojta, V. 1992. *Das Vojta-Prinzip. (Vojta-principle).* Berlin: C. Springer Verlag.

Weed, Donald, L.D.C. 1990. *What you think is what you get.* Langnau am Albis, Switzerland: 1445 Publications.

Werner. H. (Ed.). 1965. *The body percept.* New York: Random House.

White, R. 1989. Visual thinking in the Ice Age. *Scientific American,* 26(1): 74.

Index

About the Author

*E*ric Franklin has more than 20 years' experience as a dancer and choreographer. In addition to earning a BFA from New York University's Tisch School of the Arts and a BS from the University of Zurich, he has studied and trained with some of the top movement imagery specialists around the world and has used this training as a professional dancer in New York.

Franklin has shared imaging techniques in his teaching since 1986. He is founder and director of the Institute for Movement Imagery Education in Lucerne, Switzerland, and professor of postgraduate studies at the Institute for Psychomotor Therapy in Zurich, Switzerland. He is a guest professor at the University of Vienna (Musikhochschule) and has been on the faculty of the American Dance Festival since 1991. Franklin teaches at universities, dance centers, and dance festivals in the United States and throughout Europe.

Franklin is coauthor of the bestselling book *Breakdance,* which received a New York City Public Library Prize in 1984, and author of *100 Ideen für Beweglichkeit* and *Dance Imagery for Technique and Performance* (both books about imagery in dance and movement). He is a member of the International Association of Dance Medicine and Science.

Franklin lives near Zurich, Switzerland, with his wife, Gabriela, and their two children. He may be contacted in writing at Mühlestrasse 27, CH 8623, Wetzikon, Switzerland.